M000307054

- postnal
care

Push Back the Dark

Push Back the Dark

Companioning Adult Survivors
of Childhood Sexual Abuse

Elizabeth M. Altmaier, PhD
foreword by Mary S. Hulst

CASCADE *Books* • Eugene, Oregon

PUSH BACK THE DARK
Companioning Adult Survivors of Childhood Sexual Abuse

Copyright © 2017 Elizabeth M. Altmaier. All rights reserved. Except for brief quotations in critical publications or reviews, no part of this book may be reproduced in any manner without prior written permission from the publisher. Write: Permissions, Wipf and Stock Publishers, 199 W. 8th Ave., Suite 3, Eugene, OR 97401.

Cascade Books
An Imprint of Wipf and Stock Publishers
199 W. 8th Ave., Suite 3
Eugene, OR 97401

www.wipfandstock.com

PAPERBACK ISBN: 978-1-4982-0209-1
HARDCOVER ISBN: 978-1-4982-8479-0
EBOOK ISBN: 978-1-4982-0210-7

Cataloguing-in-Publication data:

Altmaier, Elizabeth M. |

Push back the dark : companioning adult survivors of childhood sexual abuse / Elizabeth M. Altmaier.

Eugene, OR: Cascade Books, 2017 | Includes bibliographical references and index.

Identifiers: ISBN 978-1-4982-0209-1 (paperback) | ISBN 978-1-4982-8479-0 (hardcover) | ISBN 978-1-4982-0210-7 (ebook)

Subjects: LCSH: Adult child sexual abuse victims, Counseling of. | Survivors psychology. | Sexual abuse therapy.

Classification: RC569.5 A28 A32 2017 (print) | RC569 (ebook)

Manufactured in the U.S.A.   January 2017

ESV: Scripture quotations marked (ESV) are from The Holy Bible, English Standard Version® (ESV®), copyright © 2001 by Crossway, a publishing ministry of Good News Publishers. Used by permission. All rights reserved. The "ESV" and "English Standard Version" are registered trademarks of Crossway. Use of either trademark requires the permission of Crossway.

KJ21: Scripture quotations taken from the 21st Century King James Version®, copyright © 1994. Used by permission of Deuel Enterprises, Inc., Gary, SD 57237. All rights reserved.

MSG: Scripture taken from The Message. Copyright © 1993, 1994, 1995, 1996, 2000, 2001, 2002. Used by permission of NavPress Publishing Group.

NIV: Scripture quotations marked (NIV) are taken from the Holy Bible, New International Version®, NIV®. Copyright © 1973, 1978, 1984, 2011 by Biblica, Inc.™ Used by permission of Zondervan. All rights reserved worldwide. www.zondervan.com The "NIV" and "New International Version" are trademarks registered in the United States Patent and Trademark Office by Biblica, Inc.™

NKJV: Scripture taken from the New King James Version®. Copyright © 1982 by Thomas Nelson. Used by permission. All rights reserved.

NLT: Scripture quotations marked (NLT) are taken from the Holy Bible, New Living Translation, copyright © 1996, 2004, 2007 by Tyndale House Foundation. Used by permission of Tyndale House Publishers, Inc., Carol Stream, Illinois 60188. All rights reserved.

This book is dedicated to those survivors of childhood sexual abuse who on their own journeys to healing had been ahead of me, who were next to me, and who are following behind. Never give up, because God will never give up on you.

"The steadfast love of the Lord never ceases; his mercies never come to an end; they are new every morning; great is your faithfulness."
(Lam 3:22–23 ESV)

"For now we see through a glass, darkly, but then face to face. Now I know in part; but then shall I know, even as also I am known."
(1 Cor 13:12 KJ21)

Table of Contents

Foreword

THERE ARE FEW THINGS more wrenching for a pastor to hear than "I need to tell you something that no one else knows. I was sexually abused." Even the most seasoned professional plunges into heartache for this dear person who has now entrusted us with her or his deepest wound.

As Elizabeth Altmaier describes so well, what happens next is crucial in restoring the victim to full health, particularly spiritual health. How the pastor responds is seen by the person as a marker for how the church will receive them, how their future will unfold as a follower of Jesus, and most importantly, how the relationship with God will be rebuilt and renewed or completely abandoned.

Most victims of sexual abuse are very young at the time of first contact, too young to understand all that is happening but aware enough to know that it is something that terrifies them deeply. This terror remains, despite the perpetrator's assurances that "it's just fine" or "this is how you show Daddy that you love him." Sometimes, the perpetrator is cruel even after the act: "If you tell anyone about this, I'll hurt you." Because the victims are often young, vulnerable, and confused, the terror of being abused is locked away deep in their psyches. For some, the pain reveals itself later in rebellious behavior, often sexual in nature. Others seek to be the "good girl" or "good boy," believing that if they meet everyone's expectations the abuse will stop or perhaps they can undo the damage the abuse has caused. For many, the full realization of what happened to them does not come into full consciousness until much later.

And this is where the pastor often comes in. While we clergy are occasionally asked to intervene in an active abuse situation, it is much more likely that we will be engaging with adults who were abused as children. Because the abuse may have happened years before, we can be perplexed as to why it is now surfacing in such a painful way in the life of a parishioner. Why is this previously competent adult suddenly unable to work? Why is this extrovert unable to go to church? How can a person enjoy a satisfying marriage for several years and then become unable to enjoy any level of physical intimacy?

One temptation for clergy in these situations is to quickly pass the person off to a trained psychologist and leave it at that. While that is a good and necessary first step, we need to remember that our parishioner has trusted us with this part of the story because they need our help. As Altmaier states, the effect of sexual abuse on a Christian has significant ramifications on his or her life of faith. To send our parishioner elsewhere when they have come to us to explore these issues in the context of faith is simply unacceptable.

So what do we do? We listen. We believe them. We let them ask the hardest questions, and we aren't hasty with our answers. We commit to walking with them through this valley of the shadow of death as long as it takes. Because it is a valley of shadows. Family relationships may be revealed as false. God may seem cruel. Spouses may appear unsupportive. Their own minds and memories may seem out to get them. This is a scary, shadowy valley.

Elizabeth Altmaier has walked this valley. She has experienced clergy who were enormously helpful and others who added to her pain. As someone who is walking through the valley and is now coming into the light, she uses her experience, training, intellect, and faith to help clergy navigate these challenging paths with grace and truth.

Studies have revealed that 20 percent of adult females and 5–10 percent of adult males recall childhood sexual abuse (Crimes against Children Research Center). If your congregation has 150 adult members, over thirty of them have experienced sexual trauma as children. How do you preach so that these members will know that you are a safe person? How do you incorporate times of lament in worship? How do you pray in public worship settings for those who have been abused? The temptation is to keep this quiet and to respond to people as they come to us, one on one. But keeping sexual abuse quiet is part of the trauma. Speaking about it in a worship setting will be transformational for the people in your congregation who thought that they were all alone. Having their pain spoken of in worship will allow them to see church, God, and you as partners in their healing, traveling companions as they walk through the valley.

This is not easy work. But it is vital. Read this book. Read it with other clergy. Take it to heart. Incorporate it into your preaching and your prayers. Ask God to show you how to pastor the many abuse victims in your church.

Of course, some of us who are clergy are victims ourselves. We need this book, too. It's a reminder that despite the shadows we have walked through, God is light and in God there is no darkness at all. As we learn how to help others in their healing, God will continue to heal us as well.

May Emmanuel, God with Us, bless your ministry to victims of abuse and allow you to walk with them from the shadows of victimhood into the light of a full and beautiful life.

Rev. Dr. Mary S. Hulst

Acknowledgements

BOOKS DO NOT MERELY spring into being from the generative mind of the author; rather, they are birthed through a painful process that is centered on the author who is fortuitously sustained by a team of companions.

Thank you first to my therapist. She has been my wise guide and counselor for many years. The arc of my journey to healing is witness to her steady presence in my life. One day, she said brightly, "Why don't you write a book?" and I thought, "That's an interesting idea!" And here we are.

Adult survivors of childhood sexual abuse have many physical problems that stem from the abuse. I made a deliberate decision early in my treatment to change to healthcare providers who were Christian women with whom I could be truthful and transparent. They loved and supported me in return, and I am so thankful for them.

Randy, Rusty, and the guys at Hope House: you simply accepted me without question, and you served as role models for strength and hope. You were true companions for me. Thank you.

Thank you to Kathleen Mulhern of Patheos Press: she encouraged me when my publication path was murky at best. I deeply appreciate her assistance.

Thank you to my editorial team at Wipf and Stock: their guidance, feedback, and expertise contributed greatly to the book. I also wish to thank my Shaly Moyal, my "second reader," for her honest and sound feedback. Mollie Burke and Anna Hoffman, who were my first readers, also assisted with the vignettes and the glossary, respectively. Patricia Martin was my proofreader and copy editor; her conscientiousness is deeply appreciated. Over the years of my journey, my students—knowing or perhaps sensing my troubled mind and heart—have been caring and compassionate; I am so indebted to them.

Acknowledgements

I am deeply grateful to Ted Kaul, my doctoral advisor, who challenged and supported me in equal measure. Without his having been my advisor during my graduate studies, I would not be the psychologist that I am today. Likewise, I have benefited from persons who maintained that support and challenge throughout my professional life.

In today's world, books and websites go together. My website designers, Cat and Cheryl (Lakeside Creative Resources), pushed me to think about communicating with my readers in new ways: both my book and my website are the better for their efforts. Thank you also to Justin Salem Meyer who graciously provided the stunning images for my website.

Christian writers who have already published works on abuse and trauma gave me courage and provided reassuring role models of speaking difficult truths to a skeptical audience.

My children and grandchildren have been a steady and inspiring presence in my life: they provide love in abundance and reveal a God in action in their lives.

Finally, I thank my husband. When he took me *for better or for worse*, he had absolutely no idea of how bad the *worse* could be. But he kept his promise. Thank you, Michael.

To the Reader

THE PURPOSE OF THIS book is to generate motivated and educated companions who will sustain adults on a journey to healing after childhood sexual abuse. Although its focus is on companionship as a church ministry, the book is not limited to that context. Each reader will find such helpful content as

- the reasons that childhood sexual abuse is so damaging into adulthood,

- misunderstandings about and stereotypes of childhood sexual abuse,

- the characteristics of environments that create a climate that is open to ministry to victims versus those environments that foster a climate that silences and shames victims, and

- the redemptive experience of creating personal meaning after its destruction during trauma.

What is meant by *companioning*? A companion has many privileges, with one privilege being that he or she travels alongside another person. This is in fact the most common view of what a *companion* is—one who "goes alongside" for some duration, which can range from brief to a long time.

Another view is that the companion is intended to *complement* the traveler. That is, the companion is seen as having qualities—such as personality traits or a given set of skills—that assist the traveler who has need of those qualities. A beautiful analogy is one that is nautical: a *companion* is the raised frame with windows on the quarterdeck that allows light to shine onto the decks below.

The companion is needed for what type of journey in this book? The journey focus is that of healing and recovery from childhood sexual abuse.

A common tragedy in our culture, childhood sexual abuse can also occur in contexts that are defined as *Christian* such as youth groups, church camps, and families. What in fact compounds the tragedy of such occurrences is that insufficient information and misleading stereotypes about childhood sexual abuse have often resulted in wrongful choices by pastors, ministry staff, youth workers, and church leaders with regard to victims and offenders.

Reading and hearing about childhood sexual abuse both frightens and compels Christians. Unfortunate reactions to widespread media coverage are often fear-based responses, such as an overly rapid implementation of a child protection policy by church leaders. The conclusion is that *we have taken care of it*. Yet, an accurate understanding of the tragedy of childhood sexual abuse requires the digesting of extensive mental health scholarship and contemplation of difficult and emotionally challenging content. Such information builds into a compelling call to respond lovingly and scripturally to adult victims of childhood sexual abuse.

Wait, what if you do not call yourself a Christian? If instead, you are reading this book to better understand a Christian client whom you are helping or because you are interested in learning about the topic, you may wonder, "Is the author going to be too preachy for me?" Certainly not. Instead, I will present content in a Christian perspective that is not characteristic of secular academic writing for mental health professionals and that will enhance your multicultural knowledge, skills, and attitudes for clients with a strong faith history and/or commitment.

1. *What is childhood sexual abuse? What are its consequences for adult life? How does childhood sexual abuse within a Christian context especially damage the adult victim's faith life?* Childhood sexual abuse will be considered in chapters 1 and 2. Then, misunderstandings and deliberately wrongful responses that can be particularly characteristic of faith communities will be examined in chapters 3 and 4. (The aftereffects of childhood abuse on the adult's circles of family, friends, and colleagues are considered in chapter 7.)

2. *What is forgiveness? What can help the victim forgive the offender? In contrast, what damages the victim and prevents true forgiveness?* Forgiveness as the first step in the process of reconstructing meaning after trauma is considered in chapter 5.

3. *Why is the reconstruction of meaning so important after trauma?* The process of *meaning making*—how a person, whose core beliefs have been shattered, reconstructs personal meaning and creates new directions—is described in chapter 6.

4. *How can companions and others who wish to help—particularly those in teaching, counseling, or ministering positions—be better informed?* The characteristics of effective companions are expanded on in chapter 7. Resources for those wish to help and for victims are detailed in chapters 8 and 9, respectively.

It is important that the book chapters be read in sequence. Understanding why childhood sexual abuse is damaging from the perspective of developmental psychology, for example, allows the reader to gain a better realization of why certain responses wound and why other responses help the victim. Each chapter presents information, a toolkit for companions, and a case vignette of a person who needs help. Information in this book comes from the disciplines of psychology and from related mental health fields such as psychiatry and counseling; the book is meant to provide—in language that is understandable to the educated lay reader—knowledge that has been established by scholarship over many years.

A note about the use of terms: within the conversation about childhood sexual abuse, there is a debate about whether the term *victim* or *survivor* should be used. Mental health professionals prefer the term *survivor* because it implies an empowerment for surviving the trauma. A key observation is that the term *victim* can suggest passivity and an inability to fight back, whereas the term *survivor* hints at resourcefulness and taking action in the face of obstacles.[1]

However, there is another side, and that is the one that I chose: the term *victim* means that the recipient of child sexual abuse is *actually a victim*—attacked, brutalized, and then often further mistreated by not receiving justice after the attack.[2] Because there is *doubt* in the church, there must be *acceptance* that persons who experienced childhood sexual abuse had not been at fault, had not been able to defend themselves, and are actually *victims*. Thus, I use the term *victim* primarily throughout this book.

Who am I and why am I writing this book? I am a Christian, a psychologist, and a victim of childhood sexual abuse. My career in psychological

1. Akhila, "Why Words Matter," para. 2.
2. Ibid., para. 5.

research has been directed by the difficulties that I had faced in my own life: stress, trauma, coping, forgiveness, and meaning making. God has given me the remarkable and miraculous gift of recovery and a deep passion for helping others who may not have had the resources to which I had access. I believe that the church, *broadly writ*, has failed in the task of reaching adult victims. I equally believe that companions—with accurate information and clear instruction—can go alongside victims on challenging journeys to wholeness and a new life. The goal of this book is to make that *companioning* be fruitful—bringing glory and honor to God.

1

Little Girl Dead

Chapter Objectives

1. Learn correct information about childhood sexual abuse, and stop believing wrong and misleading stereotypes.
2. Understand how sexual abuse during childhood damages every aspect of adult development, including spiritual development.
3. Gain sympathy for the background of what might appear to be willful, wrong actions—or *lifestyle choices*—among adult victims.
4. Learn how to actively listen to victims' stories.
5. Learn journey skills that you can assist victims to acquire.

I AM A CHILD in your congregation. I am the youngest child in my family and the only girl. When I am in grade school, I am "just the cutest thing." My long hair is in pigtails or a ponytail, my dresses are adorable, and I have a bubbly personality. I have memorized more Bible verses than any other child my age, and I wear with pride my Sunday school attendance award each week. I go to a Christian camp each summer. As I get older, I volunteer in the church nursery. I announce that I want to be a teacher when I am a grown-up, just as my mother had been before she married.

I am a teenager in your congregation. It is rumored that I drink, use drugs, have sex, and run with the fast crowd at school. The high school boys in the church's teen group are alternately attracted to and repelled by me, and they exchange glances and smirk in my presence. My behavior shames my parents, and you can't decide whether you should say anything to them or not. My parents, however, carry on as if nothing is wrong, so you decide against making things more difficult. They are still somewhat in control of me, you think, because I am in Sunday school and attend church each week. Perhaps it's just a phase, you tell yourself. You are relieved when you hear that I will attend a prestigious Christian college where you are sure that I will get my life back on track.

I am a student at a prestigious Christian college. Because my attendance at daily chapel is enforced, I listen to hundreds of sermons over a four-year period, participate in numerous Bible studies, and even come forward to testify during a revival. Other behaviors contradict this appearance: in conflict with the college's code of behavior, my hidden life revolves around substance abuse and illicit relationships. I am adept at living under the radar of behavioral expectations. Unexpectedly, I find comfort and a sense of belonging in my psychology major and my professors, and I begin to embrace a dedicated student role. Yet the darkness of my life continues.

I am an adult in your congregation. I attend regularly, and my financial contributions are above expectations. I am successful in my career and well known in the community. I greet you warmly every Sunday, and I regularly volunteer for church needs; but you are disturbed to realize that you can't decide whether you like me or not, partly because I don't fit the mold of women with whom you are comfortable. For one thing, I visibly relate more easily to men than to women. I look people directly in the eye, and I talk about sports and local politics. For another, I don't go to any women's Bible study group, and I am not a member of the group of women in your congregation whom you trust.

I am that little girl with the storybook upbringing, and I am a victim of childhood sexual abuse. The abuse began when I was a preschool child and continued into my elementary school years. That out-of-control teenager started drinking, using drugs, and having sexual relationships as a twelve-year-old. My teen years were desperate—dark with confusion, depression, and anger. That prestigious Christian college that I attended? My parents forced me to go there, but my behavior continued unabated. In fact, it was in that Christian environment that I learned how to live on two levels. As an adult, my life continued on two parallel tracks: the *outer* woman was adjusted, competent, and high functioning and was able to combine her career with marriage and two children. The *inner* woman used substances excessively; had an array of psychiatric disorders including eating disorders, depression, compulsions, and panic episodes; and dealt with life through hypervigilance, workaholism, and obsessions about control.

I began this chapter with a brief introduction to me and to what I looked like to others. I did this because the aftereffects of childhood sexual abuse are misunderstood and often mislabeled.

- Had you known me as a successful professional, you might have perceived me as being a *perfectionist*, which I was.

- When I was a teenager, however, you would have encouraged your child to avoid me because I was *sinful*, which I was.

- Your confusion about my inability to have normal friendships with you in college was understandable: I had *no boundaries*.

- My own students suffered while they were trying to please me because I had become an *unpleasable person*—the supervisor who could not be satisfied.

This chapter explains why childhood sexual abuse causes such a range of difficulties in life for many years after the abuse. The italicized writings are taken from a journal that I began keeping after I started treatment.

The Trauma of Childhood Sexual Abuse

Dread sits on my chest like a grey stone.

The light in the door slits open

And Death walks in

And I am frozen in place and time.

And that child is entombed in her aloneness.

How can I find her?

The scientific study of childhood sexual abuse as a specific category of trauma began in the late 1970s. In 1980, the American Psychiatric Association[1] published a revised diagnostic guide with new categories of mental health problems such as post-traumatic stress disorder (PTSD). These

---

1. American Psychiatric Association, *DSM-III*; see also American Psychiatric Association, *History*.

3

categories of psychiatric disorders had been prompted, because professionals were treating Vietnam veterans who had returned from combat with pervasive and disabling mental health problems. None of the then-current mental health labels accurately captured these symptoms; mental health professionals thus began to describe veterans who had symptoms such as uncontrollable intrusive thoughts and pictures and enduring high levels of physiological arousal as being survivors of *trauma*. Previously, *trauma* had been limited to physical wounds. By using the term *trauma* in a psychosocial context, people were recognizing that trauma could by psychological as well as physical.

During the 1980s, public attention to other psychological traumas—domestic violence and childhood abuse—increased. Rape crisis centers began reporting on the use of their services by adults who described having been sexually abused as children. Memoirs that were written by child victims, now adults, were published.[2] Professional attention to trauma also increased, and mental health professionals[3] concluded that persons who experienced ongoing abuse in the context of their family (i.e., physical or sexual abuse) or during extremely stressful situations, such as captivity and hostage taking, had unique problems and needed as-yet-unknown treatment solutions.

All the attention that professionals and the public gave to these disorders resulted in differences of opinion on the most appropriate diagnosis of and treatment for adults who reported trauma symptoms that dated back to childhood. Media attention focused on adults who asserted that they were being falsely accused of child abuse, often by their adult children. Some professionals alleged that these memories of childhood abuse were false and that they were created by unscrupulous therapists who had implanted memories in their patients. *False memories* was a topic of vigorous public debate that was not limited to the United States: over a dozen organizations worldwide[4] issued reports on this topic during the 1990s.

In 2002, the tenor of public discourse with regard to sexual abuse dramatically changed with a yearlong series of reports in the *Boston Globe*[5]:

2. For example, Armstrong, *Kiss Daddy Goodnight*.

3. J. Herman, *Trauma and Recovery*; J. L. Herman, "Complex PTSD."

4. For example, American Medical Association (AMA Council on Scientific Affairs, "Report on Memories"); Royal College of Psychiatrists in the UK (Brandon et al., "Recovered Memories"); and The Royal Australian and New Zealand College of Psychiatrists (RANZCP, "Guidelines").

5. *Boston Globe*, "Archive of Coverage." See especially 2002. Note that this is part

these reports revealed that the incidence of priests who abuse children was more prevalent than what had been previously acknowledged. More troubling was the perception that these concerns had been seriously mishandled by the priests' supervisors within the Catholic Church. The liability, both moral and financial, for these acts led to increased legal and public scrutiny. For example, the Catholic Church established panels to review all policies and practices that were related to oversight of priests and their interactions with children.[6]

During the early 2000s, widely publicized cases of child kidnapping and murder[7] led to the development of communication systems that were designed to involve the public in locating abducted children (e.g., Amber alerts) and legislation that was intended to honor child victims of sexual predators and protect other children in the future (e.g., Megan's Law). Also during this decade, state and federal governments joined with private foundations to establish centers and networks to prevent and treat childhood trauma. For example, the federal government established the National Child Traumatic Stress Network[8] as a location for resources that deal with a range of childhood traumas such as domestic violence, childhood abuse, neglect, and school violence.

Currently, conversations about childhood sexual abuse occur at a previously unforeseen level in the public square. In contrast to these widespread discussions, the evangelical church for the most part has remained silent. Recent courageous actions from well-known pastors who shared childhood trauma histories and from other victims who have united in online communities are creating a climate of opportunity. In that climate, honest conversation should begin to occur—in a parallel fashion to how revelations by victims and their supporters opened up dialogue in our larger society.

In the remainder of this chapter, stereotypes about the definition, prevalence, and consequences of childhood sexual abuse are considered.

---

of the original series website. The current website can be accessed via http://www.bostonglobe.com/metro/spotlight; additional coverage by the *Boston Globe* can be found at http://www.cruxnow.com/tag/sexual-abuse.

6. Merz, "History," 6–22. See also United States Conference of Catholic Bishops, "Board"; "Protection."

7. Many were highlighted in the *America's Most Wanted* television show, hosted by John Walsh who himself was the father of a murdered child.

8. www.nctsn.org.

Also, assumptions or beliefs about childhood sexual abuse that more specifically operate within the church will be described.

Victim or Survivor

Before I continue with the next section, I will reiterate what I wrote earlier.[9]

Within the conversation about childhood sexual abuse, there is a debate about whether the term *victim* or *survivor* should be used. Mental health professionals prefer the term *survivor* because it implies an empowerment for surviving the trauma. A key observation is that the term *victim* can suggest passivity and an inability to fight back, whereas the term *survivor* hints at resourcefulness and taking action in the face of obstacles.[10]

However, there is another side, and that is the one that I chose: the term *victim* means that the recipient of child sexual abuse is *actually a victim*—attacked, brutalized, and then often further mistreated by not receiving justice after the attack.[11] Because there is *doubt* in the church, there must be *acceptance* that persons who experienced childhood sexual abuse had not been at fault, had not been able to defend themselves, and are actually *victims*. Thus, I use the term *victim* primarily throughout this book.

An Accurate Portrayal of Childhood Sexual Abuse

Your fingers are there and they are feeling and groping

And prying me open

And I want to stay closed to you but I can't

And I drift away, and I am gone

But my body is dead and it's yours.

The first misunderstanding or stereotype of childhood sexual abuse is that the assailant is a stranger who traps the child in an off-guard moment or at an isolated location.[12] In actuality, while such events occur, they are a minority. The presumption that the abuser is a stranger to the child is

---

9. This discussion is excerpted from the *To the Reader* section.
10. Akhila, "Why Words Matter," para. 2.
11. Ibid., para. 5.
12. For example, see Snyder, "Characteristics," 6.

contradicted by data[13] that indicate about 90 percent of sexually abused children know their abuser: family and extended family members are half of this group and acquaintances of the child make up the other half. Strangers actually are the smallest group of offenders, about 10 percent.

However, the stereotype of *stranger danger* is maintained despite situations that are tragically familiar from the evening new: an adult who volunteers as a youth athletic team coach or as a leader of a local chapter of a national organization is charged with sexual exploitation of a minor. A protective shield that parents hold to protect themselves from fear is the belief that childhood sexual abuse cannot be done by someone whom the child knows or loves. However, this is wrong. While it is helpful to train children not to be victimized by strangers, the implication is that only strangers can do these acts. However, it is better to focus on the acts themselves and the ways that the child can communicate any abuse to a trusted adult.

It is a tragic misunderstanding of childhood sexual abuse—and the second stereotype—to believe that only genital penetration is abuse. A variety of acts constitutes childhood sexual abuse—acts that are sometimes disturbingly ambiguous in nature: a child is held or caressed for an adult's sexual gratification. During a bath, a child is fondled. While watching a child, an adult masturbates. A child poses innocently for sexually suggestive or explicit photographs. An adult forces a child to watch or to make pornographic movies.

Even though none involved vaginal or anal penetration ("rape"), each of these examples represents sexual abuse because the intent of the act is the *gratification of adult desires without consent.*

One distinction is that of *gratifying adult desires*. The desires may be sexual in nature; a person with a sexual preference for children by definition is a *pedophile*. Yet an adult can have normal nonsexual desires—such as closeness, control, or sensuality—that may be expressed in a sexual way.[14] Therefore, this gratification can either be of sexual desires or of nonsexual desires that have become sexualized in their occurrence in some sexual activity.

The other distinction is *without consent*. Because of age, the dependent relationship with an adult, and the emotional attachment to this relationship, a child cannot consent to such an activity. The child also is unable to

---

13. US Department of Justice, "Facts." See also US Department of Health and Human Services, "Child Abuse."

14. Allender, *Wounded Heart*; Courtois, *Healing*.

give consent because of a power imbalance: an abuser is older, larger, and more powerful than a child; and may have more authority, a higher position in the relationship, or more experience. In addition, developmental immaturity can prevent the child from understanding the true nature of the actions. This discussion applies all the more vigorously when the *child* is a teenager and the abuser claims that consent had occurred.

Sexual abuse can also occur as psychological boundaries are violated. For example, a child is set up within a family as a surrogate spouse and is involved in conversations and situations only appropriate within an adult relationship. The sexual overtones of that relationship and the resulting power differentiation in the family are deeply confusing to a child.

A third stereotype is that childhood sexual abuse occurs only in families that are obviously and outwardly troubled, a so-called chaotic family. An alcoholic father, who beats his wife and rapes his daughter; who is unemployed; and whose family is dependent on the community's legal and social welfare systems is a scenario that matches our stereotypes.

In contrast to that stereotype is the fact that families in which childhood sexual abuse occurs appear normal and even successful from the outside. The parents have a long-term marriage, the family is financially stable, and both the husband and wife are involved in the community and often in a church. The stereotype that reduced education, lower socioeconomic status, or a particular ethnic background is a reliable indicator of childhood sexual abuse has been refuted.[15]

A fourth misunderstanding of childhood sexual abuse is that it is an unusual event or even rare. Statistics about incidence and prevalence of childhood sexual abuse show this stereotype to be false. These statistics derive from the following sources:

1. rates for a single year that are reported by official agencies, such as child welfare agencies;

2. rates for a single year that are reported by children themselves through survey research; and

3. lifetime—or full childhood—rates that are reported though survey data from adults.

---

15. US Department of Justice, Center for Sex Offender Management, "Section 3." See US Department of Health and Human Services, "Child Abuse."

The first two sources are *incidence* data—the number of new cases at a given duration; whereas the last source is *prevalence* data—the total number of cases in a population. The following statistics come from these data sources.

According to law enforcement and social service agency reports[16], 1.5 children per 1,000 are abused within a single year. To put this number into context, the incidence rate of child sexual abuse is equivalent to the rate of onset of diabetes among 18- to 44-year-olds or, to use another example, the same as the number of cases in which job injury and illness require time away from work. In other words, the occurrence of childhood sexual abuse is the same as that of life events that we consider relatively frequent.

Reports that are directly obtained from children and teenagers[17] reveal a higher incidence rate, which ranges from more than 4 to 32 per 1,000 children. Finally, survey data of adults indicate that a higher number of adults report that they had experienced sexual abuse as children. According to Briere and Elliott,[18] 20 percent of adults reported sexual abuse during childhood; 30 percent were women and 13 percent men. The Centers for Disease Control's survey on adverse childhood experiences[19] that were reported by adults revealed that 12 percent of adults had experienced childhood sexual abuse; 17 percent were women and 7 percent men.

Each of these data sources contains limitations. Child welfare systems use a process that is initiated by reported maltreatment that includes an investigation by a trained professional. The evidence must conform to a certain legal standard which is not met in all reported cases. Rates from self-report depend on the definition of sexual abuse that is used in the survey. For example, the National Incidence Studies of Missing, Abducted, Runaway, and Thrownaway Children[20] established that approximately 285,000 children[21] had been sexually assaulted; this number, however, did not include acts that were sexual in nature but were without physical contact or force.

---

16. Hammond et al., "Law Enforcement.

17. Douglas and Finkelhor, "Fact Sheet," 2–4. See US Department of Health and Human Services, "Child Abuse."

18. Briere and Elliott, "Prevalence and Psychological Sequelae."

19. Centers for Disease Control and Prevention, "ACE Study."

20. Finkelhor et al., "Children." For the first study, see Finkelhor, et al., "First Report."

21. Ibid., 2.

Our stereotypes about childhood sexual abuse—that it is rare, that it is only genital penetration by a stranger, and that it is limited to groups who are racially or socioeconomically different from that of the majority population—must be corrected by accurate data and information.

A quarter of women experience childhood sexual abuse. Although at lower rates than women, men are also victimized as children; however, statistics suggest they are more likely to be physically rather than sexually abused. Childhood sexual abuse is almost always perpetrated not by a stranger but by a family member or by someone known to and trusted by the child. Although girls are more likely to be sexually abused by a family member, boys are more likely to be sexually abused by trusted males who are outside the family. The majority of childhood sexual abuse victims are girls, and the majority of abusers are men.

Additionally, religious affiliation by the family is not a protective factor against child abuse within the family. In fact, childhood sexual abuse occurs as frequently among *religious* families—as defined as those who believe in the literalism of the Bible, attend services frequently, and endorse a separation from society based on moral values—as among nonreligious families.[22] Other studies[23] of sexually abused children indicate that victims who had been raised in an evangelical/fundamentalist Protestant home were more likely to experience their abuse from a family member than were victims who had not been raised in a religious family.

Another stereotype that has wrongly persisted is that sexual abuse does not happen within church organizations. In contrast, Harvey[24] noted that churches are a "natural target for predators," because there are "large numbers of children, a shortage of willing workers, and a culture of trust that assumes no Christian could be suspect of such exploitation." Within this group of victims are children abused by pastors, youth leaders, Christian camp counselors, and other church staff.

Uniquely Christian myths about childhood sexual abuse—that lay responsibility for the abuse on the victim—may have prevented appropriate consideration of this issue.[25] One myth that children are *provocative* victims is a deeply perverted message that places responsibility for the abuse on the victim rather than on the perpetrator. Knowledge of children's

22. Elliott, "Impact of Christian"; Gil, "In Thy Father's."
23. Stout-Miller et al., "Religiosity."
24. Harvey, "Cleaning Up," para. 5.
25. Cook, "Ultimate Deception"; T. Samples, "Myths."

developmental abilities contradicts any statement that the child had been *seductive* or *asking for it*. Another myth that the victim could have stopped the abuse when it happened denies the reality of children's dependence in their relationships with adults—a reality that is especially true when the relationship is one from which there is no escape, such as a family. A third myth is that childhood sexual abuse is a matter of church discipline with the assertion that it is wrong to involve outsiders such as legal authorities. As a consequence, the myth allows the perpetrator's actions, which is likely against the law.[26]

Whether children are abused within their home, by a family friend, within a church-sponsored youth organization or team, by pastors, or by youth workers, the experience is the same: the sexual abuse is from someone who is trusted by children to keep them safe, cared for, and loved.

How childhood sexual abuse results in significant long-term negative consequences in mental, emotional, and physical health is explained in the next section. These consequences are deepened in children whose abuse comes from a person whom the child understands to be a Christian.[27]

Tragic Compounding Consequences

Death has a river.

All boats go there.

Some boats have dead bodies.

Some boats have live bodies.

Some boats have children. They are the sad boats.

Tears carry those boats down the river.

Death stands and he smiles

He loves children and he waits for them in particular.

Buy me a boat on death's river.

The process of healthy development in infancy and childhood provides insight into understanding the consequences of childhood sexual abuse. Children are not just smaller versions of adults; rather, they are uniquely emerging beings who are faced with essential tasks in physical,

26. The legal aspects will be discussed in a later chapter.

27. This topic is considered in the next chapter.

cognitive, and emotional development that are the necessary foundation for later abilities as adults. Parents are familiar with such milestones as when infants sleep through the night, begin cooing, or play peek-a-boo. When parents see the child taking a first step or waving goodbye, they are reassured of the healthy physical growth of their child.

Psychological Developmental Milestones and Attachment

There are parallel psychological developmental milestones as well. These are clearly explained by Erikson.[28] In infancy, children develop *trust*—the first milestone. Children's understanding of the world is formed by their interactions with parents. Children who feel warmth and experience consistency in having their physical and emotional needs met develop trust in others and a sense of their own worth. However, children who are neglected or mistreated or whose needs are not met in an ongoing way cannot form that trusting relationship. If this happens, the entire foundation of development is harmed.

A second milestone is *autonomy*. Children who are given freedom to explore within boundaries that protect them develop abilities to set appropriate limits for themselves and to express and meet their needs. Parents are familiar with the difficulties of raising young children who want to do more than they are allowed to and who want their own way. Although this is a difficult stage, autonomy is achieved when parents allow exploration—within appropriate limits—and negotiate the expression of needs paired with the appropriate meeting of needs.

Initiative is the third milestone. At this stage, trust combines with autonomy to give children the power to master new challenges and to set and reach goals. *Initiative* can be seen when a child is determined to go down the playground slide alone and happily achieves that success. During this milestone, *emotional regulation* begins to occur.[29] *Emotional regulation* is the term for the process that occurs as children understand their own emotions, obtain emotional nourishment from others, and successfully deal with negative emotions such as disappointment and anger.

The work of John Bowlby[30] on *attachment* was the beginning of our understanding that children's attachment to a caregiver is more than just

28. Erikson, *Identity*.

29. Heller and LaPierre, *Healing Developmental Trauma*.

30. Bowlby, *A Secure Base*.

the development of trust in the particular parent. In fact, attachment is crucial in the construction of the means or pathways by which *all* interpersonal relationships are formed during childhood into adulthood. Infants are hardwired for relationships with caregivers, most notably mothers—relationships that are essential for development. Children who are met with warmth and loving responses from parents have pathways that encourage interactions with others: these pathways help children see themselves as *good* and to also see others as people who can be trusted to return the interaction. A child who says "hi" brightly to strangers from the seat of the grocery cart is demonstrating this ability.

However, when a child's needs are not met with consistency or when the child is rejected by the caregiver, those developing pathways cause the child to see him- or herself as *bad* and to see other children and adults as being untrustworthy. The long-term outcomes of these negative childhood experiences are adults who desperately want and need intimate human interactions, but who cannot form or maintain them.[31]

Developmental Roadblocks

This developmental context[32] also helps us understand three critical roadblocks to normal development that are caused by childhood sexual abuse. These are shame, profound fear, and human relationships.

Perhaps the first and most tragic roadblock to normal development is *shame*. Rather than a sense of self-worth, the child feels deep shame within a relationship.[33] This shame can manifest itself in self-blame, belief that the abuse is deserved, and coping mechanisms that create and feed more destructive behaviors.

- *Self-blame.* Children who are abused cannot understand why the abuse is happening. They blame themselves—a misbelief that is often reinforced by an abuser who shifts guilt and blame to the child.

- *Belief that abuse is deserved.* It is developmentally impossible for the child to conclude that a parent or other trusted adult is bad. Rather, it is only possible for children to believe that *they* themselves are bad and therefore must deserve the treatment that they are receiving.

31. Fonagy and Target, "Rooting of the Mind."
32. See Franklin and Fong, eds., *Church Leader's Counseling.*
33. Tracy, *Mending the Soul.*

13

- *Coping mechanisms and destructive behavior.* Children and older survivors of childhood sexual abuse may cope in such ways that bring blame and disapproval onto themselves. Examples are acting out among children, self-mutilation among adolescents, and promiscuity among adolescents and adults. These actions and their accompanying blame and disapproval lead to more shame and self-loathing, which in turn drive more destructive behavior.

Because all humans experience shame, it is essential to make a clear distinction between normal shame and the shame that develops after abuse, that is, between healthy and unhealthy shame. Normal or *healthy shame* is the painful recognition of a personal failure. Healthy shame leads to the conviction of *guilt*, which is the recognition of a shortcoming that leads to confession and repentance. The Apostle Paul wrote of the process in this way:

> Even if I caused you sorrow by my letter, I do not regret it. Though I did regret it—I see that my letter hurt you, but only for a little while—yet now I am happy, not because you were made sorry, but because your sorrow led you to repentance. For you became sorrowful as God intended and so were not harmed in any way by us. Godly sorrow brings repentance that leads to salvation and leaves no regret, but worldly sorrow brings death (2 Cor 7:8–10 NIV).

Then there is the unhealthy shame that can develop after abuse and that is different from knowing that wrong has been done. *Unhealthy shame*[34] is the feeling at the core that the *self* is and will always be wrong. Unhealthy shame results in an enduring sense of deep inferiority that may be permanent. A person with this pervasive insecurity who seeks validation from others will never find it. The reason is that when this person compares him- or herself to others, other people will always appear perfect and the *self* appears bad. Adults with this shame are often unable to accept criticism and in turn may react to criticism by blaming others. This type of shame can also prevent children, adolescents, and adults from fully accepting God's love and salvation.[35]

The second roadblock to positive development that is caused by childhood sexual abuse is *profound fear*. It is important to distinguish between fear that is normal and that which is profound. It is of course normal for

---

34. Smedes, *Shame and Grace.*

35. Cloud, *Changes that Heal.* This will be further discussed in the next chapter.

fear to accompany or follow a *harm*: this is the logical way that we learn to avoid that harm in the future.

There are many manifestations of fear in those children whose harm is ongoing, is caused by a trusted person, and cannot be avoided. A child may show extensive self-protective behaviors, which might include hiding, sleeping in a closet, or running away. Compulsive or ritualized behaviors such as skin-picking or hair-pulling are often present. Physical health problems and medical symptoms (for example, migraines, fatigue, or nausea) can signal the conversion of the fear to physical disorders.[36]

Another way that abused children deal with their fear is with emotional numbness. One form that this numbness can take is *alexithymia*—a condition in which a person may experience no emotions. In societies that place major emphasis on emotions, it can be confusing or difficult for people with alexithymia to know whether someone who is talking about feelings is actually experiencing them. In contrast, people in general are able to tell what another person is feeling by picking up the nonverbal cues that are associated with a certain emotion. That is, a person who is sad might sit slumped in a chair, look down or away, talk very quietly, or shed tears; whereas a person who is angry might get up from a chair, glare, speak very loudly, use short direct sentences, or physically bristle in response to some slight.

Another emotional problem that can arise may be that the victim of abuse might have difficulty in identifying feelings or in distinguishing between feelings and physical sensations. Adults whose emotions had not been accepted during childhood *turn off* those emotions.[37] That is, rather than knowing oneself to be angry, the adult may turn that anger around and blame or criticize someone else instead. Alternatively, the anger could be turned against the self and the adult may feel deeply depressed as a result.

An extreme form of numbing is *dissociation*, that is, the person *detaches* from the experience itself. When dissociation[38] is present, abuse survivors may describe themselves as being present but not in their body, perhaps even hovering over themselves.

36. Kendall-Tackett et al., "Impact of Sexual Abuse."

37. Active learning is a tool that involves helping the person who is speaking to know and to accept emotions that are being experienced. See the discussion in the toolkit section of this chapter.

38. The relation of dissociation to memory is discussed more fully in a later chapter.

Finally, the third roadblock to normal development that is caused by childhood sexual abuse occurs in human relationships. Abused children have great difficulty trusting others and are afraid of intimacy with another person. Sometimes attempts by abused children to seek relationships with other children are characterized by *neediness* and extreme dependence. At times, older abused children may attempt to be valued for what they *do* because they are not valued for who they *are*. They may thus work at finding out what adults deem to be desirable actions, which they then perform. These *super children* appear to be excessively mature for their age, because adult approval of their actions is their only source of validation.

Adult Survivors of Abuse

Abused children cannot have a *normal* childhood during which they accomplish developmental milestones. Instead, the pathways between childhood sexual abuse and adult survivor damage are those of trauma, betrayal, stigma, and powerlessness. Often the adult victim who suffers from extremes of anxiety, depression, and self-hatred will use substances— alcohol, prescription and nonprescription medications, and street drugs— to deaden these emotions. A chronic sense of worthlessness may lead to self-mutilation or *cutting*, suicidal ideation, para-suicidal behaviors such as extreme risk-taking or suicide gestures, and suicidal attempts. Nightmares, insomnia, and night terrors frequently occur. The victim also experiences the aftermath of the abuse in the brain itself: cognitive function is slowed, learning difficulties may be apparent, and memory is injured.

There are also long-term consequences for physical health. Adults survivors of sexual abuse were found to have more gastrointestinal, gynecological, and cardiopulmonary problems; pain; and obesity than non-abused adults had.[39]

Physicians have tried to understand how trauma during childhood can result in adult health problems. One suggestion[40] is that abuse during childhood disrupts the correct maturation of neuroendocrine and sympathetic nervous systems; this in turn leads to more adult diseases that are influenced by those systems such as cardiovascular diseases. This suggestion is supported by a recent study[41] of almost 7,000 adults which found that

39. Irish et al., "Long-Term Physical Health."

40. Shonkoff et al., "Neuroscience, Molecular Biology."

41. McCrory et al., "Lasting Legacy" In this study from 2015, data from four types of

childhood sexual abuse was positively associated with the highest number of doctor-diagnosed diseases, which included lung disease and ulcers.

In a long-term study[42] that included over 900 adults at age thirty who had been sexually abused during childhood, the long-term effects[43] of childhood sexual abuse were clearly demonstrated across life domains. Outcomes included mental and physical health problems and socioeconomic effects.

- Mental health problems were extensive: victims were more depressed and anxious, had more suicidal thoughts and intents, and described lower life satisfaction.

- Physical health problems were also significant: for example, victims had more hospital and doctor visits than did nonvictims.

- Finally, socioeconomic domains were affected: for example, victims more often left school without finishing and were dependent on welfare.

Wrapping Up

What is the damage[44] that is caused by childhood sexual abuse? Abuse is a *bodily* sin that attacks the boundary of the child's body and results in body-related problems. Childhood sexual abuse is a *relational* sin: within the child-caregiver relationship that is meant by God to create a positive pattern for all interpersonal relationships, the child experiences such wounding that any future relationship is damaged. Abuse is a *social* sin, because it occurs in the social context of a family, church, team, or school and creates secrecy that allows it and related sins to continue. Last, abuse is a *sexual* sin: it denies the sacredness of a being that was made in God's image and prevents the victim from developing healthy sexuality. For these reasons, the

childhood adversity—growing up poor, substance abuse in the family, childhood physical abuse, and childhood sexual abuse—were considered.

42. Fergusson et al., "Childhood Sexual Abuse."

43. To study long-term effects of a particular topic (say, sexual abuse), the researchers use statistical methods that remove from consideration those factors that are not involved but that might influence the outcome (that is, *confounds*). In this particular study, eliminated confounds were family income, parental violence and criminal history, and childhood physical abuse.

44. Fortune, *Unmentionable Sin*. See also Fortune, *Sin Revisited*.

Christian community should be among those leading the way to helping adult survivors on their journey to healing, wholeness, and spiritual health.

Toolkit

The tools in the toolkit for the companion are *active listening*. The journey tool the companion can offer to the victim is *emotional recognition*.

Active Listening

We usually believe that we are *good listeners*. In fact, many of us pride ourselves on receiving such a compliment. The reality is that most people are *ineffective* listeners. Too often people are busy forming a response rather than hearing what the speaker is saying; perhaps they are distracted; or they could be disagreeing with the speaker before the speaker has even finished speaking.

Active listening is a skill that can be practiced and learned. Here are the specific parts:

- *Focus.* An active listener is focused on the speaker. The active listener has the physical posture of focus: body leaning toward the speaker, faced directly toward the speaker, a quiet body (not fidgeting), and a comfortable open posture. The active listener has a mental attitude of focus. The listener's mind is emptied of unrelated thoughts, concerns, and worries and is filled with the speaker's words and nonverbal communication.

    Contrast that focus with harmful listening, which we have all undoubtedly experienced. The listener is looking away, at a phone, or at the floor; the listener has his or her arms crossed across the chest and fidgets in the chair or leans back. Those physical signals are communicating that "I am not really listening to you."

- *Validation.* An active listener validates the speaker. Validation does not mean agreement; rather, it means that the listener is present, attentive, and understanding the speaker. Examples of specific validating responses are as follows:
    a. *Minimal encouragers.* Minimal encouragers are cues that help the speaker to keep going—"uh huh," head nods, and the like.

Other minimal encouragers are short phrases such as "tell me more" or "how were you feeling?"

b. *Mirroring*. To help the speaker continue, repeating a few words of what was just said. This is mirroring. For example, in response to a speaker who tells a listener of her distress after she had been criticized, the speaker ends by saying "and that really upset me, that he would say that to me in front of other people." Mirroring would be repeating back that "you were upset Grant did this to you in public."

c. *Paraphrasing*. When the listener paraphrases, the speaker's words are put into a different perspective and fed back to the speaker. If the listener were to use *paraphrase* in the previous example, she might say, "It felt like Grant was making you an example of what not to say."

d. *Open-ended questions*. Questions that are open-ended cannot be answered by a simple *yes* or *no*; rather, they require more talking by the speaker. They can also open up new conversational directions as well.

e. *Labeling the feeling*. Although this type of response may be helpful, it should be used with great caution. It is difficult to understand how a speaker is feeling. Furthermore, if the listener uses the wrong feeling term, the speaker may not wish to correct the listener. A better way to *label* a feeling is to use metaphoric language for the feeling, such as you felt like you were in a box, you came to the end of the road, a wave of anger swept you away, or you were in a dark hole. If you want to be sure that you understand the feeling as a speaker, put your label within a tentative question: "I want to be sure I am hearing you correctly: it seems to me that you felt angry, because your contribution had been deliberately overlooked. *Is that right?*"

Contrast these validating responses with two nonvalidating responses that speakers often receive.

a. *The "fix it" response*. Examples are "you should tell Grant that he was wrong"; "you shouldn't have felt angry because he was just trying to help you—try accepting instead"; and "maybe it's time to join a different group." These responses are not helpful for two crucial reasons. First, because the listener never completely understands all the parts of the speaker's experience, any "fix it" response is most likely wrong. Second, the response tells the speaker that he or she can't come up with a solution and instead must rely on advice from others.

b. *Response from the listener's feelings.* Rather than coming from the speaker's feelings, this nonvalidating response actually comes from the *listener's* feelings. For example, the listener becomes anxious when the speaker is anxious, or angry, or depressed; and the listener begins to feel ineffective. The subtle pull then is to get the speaker to be less emotional; thus, the listener says that "you shouldn't let them get you upset" or that "you need to ask God to help you be less angry." The message that is conveyed is that "I can't comfortably hear your feeling of anger/sadness/distress."

- *Supportive statements.* Whether they actually take the form of statements or questions, *supportive statements* convey an accurate understanding of the speaker without the listener trying to manage the speaker's problem; they communicate the listener's confidence that the speaker will be able to get through the difficulty; and they open the door to the speaker becoming more mindful of what he or she really needs in the conversation. Some examples are "That was dreadful—you were so shamed and humiliated. I am sorry"; "I am positive that your being able to talk about this problem will help you to figure out the best solution"; "What would be most helpful for you right now?" and "What can we do together today that will help?"

Emotional Recognition

The first task for the victim is to gain a better understanding of his or her feelings. From this chapter, we learned that feelings can be buried, misunderstood, or hidden. Thus, the adult survivor needs to learn how he or she is feeling. In a scene from *Runaway Bride*, a popular movie from 1999, Ike confronts Maggie over how disconnected she is from herself by pointing out to her that she doesn't even know how she likes her eggs cooked. While this may be humorous in the movie, the parallel for victims is that they honestly do not know how they are feeling. So the first journey skill is *emotional recognition.*

In order to recognize emotion, the victim needs to be *in the present*. That goal may be hard to achieve at first, because both the past and the future tug on the victim. To be in the present means to *stop* (discontinue responses such as ruminating, blaming, or worrying); *breathe*; and *check*. This process will need to be repeated by the survivor innumerable times, because *being fully present in the present* contains so many challenges. Active listening works because it brings the speaker back into the present, into current feelings, and into current experience.

The second task of emotional recognition is to slow down emotional reaction. *Emotional reaction* is the fast, immediate replay of the same as before. In order to reduce emotional reaction, the victim first needs to breathe, to calm down, and to focus just as the listener needs to focus. A listener can help by giving examples while they are talking: "I noticed that you are breathing really quickly. Let's take a minute. Both of us will be quiet, and breathe slowly and calmly."

The third task of recognition occurs while the speaker is focused on the present. In the present, the speaker can begin to find clues to feelings. These include body sensations such as churning stomach, dizziness, sweaty palms, or tense shoulder muscles. Other clues are thoughts or conversations with oneself: if I tell myself that "I can't believe that I am so stupid," I am probably feeling disgusted and shamed. Other clues are "big picture" beliefs, such as "I am a complete failure" or "God will never love me." Those high level worldviews lead to depression and hopelessness.

Summary

While the listener is focused on the speaker, the speaker begins to slow down, to become better acquainted with parts of him- or herself that were not previously known. This process is what the term *empathy* means—an accurate understanding of another person and an appreciation of their circumstances. Empathy is a gift that is offered by the speaker to the listener, and the listener receives that gift with gratitude. Think of the last time that you felt yourself listened to and completely supported by a close friend; you may have even been tearful in thinking back over that moment. That is the goal of these tools in the toolkit.

Case: Kaden

You are a thirteen-year-old boy in the summer before your first year of high school. You have always been talented in sports; this summer you are excited about your baseball season—your favorite sport. Your church youth pastor used to be a college baseball player at a Christian college. At youth group, he asks you about how your season is going, what position you play, and after a long discussion, what time your practices are. You enthusiastically tell him; it's fun to have someone so interested in you and your baseball prospects. When he originally starts coming to practice, you enjoy having him there to watch you, help you with your hitting, and give you tips for the game. When you're batting, he notices that your stance is off at times and offers to take you to the batting cages to work on it. You are very serious about playing baseball long term, especially in college, and you are hoping for a scholarship. Not only is your pastor helping you with your skills, but also he said that he knows people at the college that he attended and can help your prospects there. You are grateful to him for his help and excited about the opportunities that he could help you to get.

After a while, however, team members start teasing you and asking you whether your youth pastor is your *boyfriend*. None of them goes to your church; they make fun of you because this man comes to your practice every day and you talk to him afterward for extended periods of time. The next time that you see him, he offers to drive you to his college campus so that you can meet his coach and tour the campus grounds. You're grateful; but when he says it, you can feel your face get hot and discomfort swirls in your stomach. You also feel stuck and pulled to do the "right thing," although you're not sure in this case what the *right thing* is. You don't want to hurt your coach's feelings by not going with him; but at the same time, you want to fit in with your peers and not feel like an outsider. You end up feeling very nervous about being alone with him; when the day comes when you are supposed to go, you make up a reason why you cannot go. He reschedules with you, and you again come up with an excuse about why you can't make it.

You're confused, and you don't know who to turn to for support. The youth pastor just seems to be very enthusiastic about your baseball; but especially with your teammates teasing you about him, you start to wonder about his motives. Is he interested in you? Is he trying to get alone time with you—is that why he wants to take you to the college campus? You never thought so before, but now you are concerned that maybe that is what he wants. Your uncertainty about his motives causes you to feel less and less confident about your own way of handling the situation. You're not gay, but you start to feel worried that other people will think that you are gay because you spend so much time with him. To prove to your friends that you are not gay, you start becoming much more aggressive with girls in your class and bragging to your teammates about sexual activities with girls. You want to prove to everyone that you are "normal" and that there is nothing wrong with you.

1. How do you think Kaden's sense of self, including emotions, is being affected by this? What factors, in addition to the youth pastor's attention, are affecting his experience?

2. If Kaden confided in you about this problem but said that he didn't want your help—just your advice, what would that advice be?

3. Would you approach the youth pastor, and if so, how?

4. Other than talking with another person, what actions might be important to consider?

2

God, Who is Gone

Chapter Objectives

1. Understand the additional damaging consequences of childhood sexual abuse when committed by a person or in a context the child knows to be Christian.

2. Learn the skills involved in establishing a working alliance with victims.

3. Learn the *journey skill* of hope in connection that you can help survivors to acquire.

> He has planted eternity in the human heart, but even so, people cannot see the whole scope of God's work from beginning to end. (Eccl 3:11b NLT)

> For now we see through a glass, darkly, but then face to face. Now I know in part, but then I shall know, even as also I am known. (1 Cor 12:13 KJ21)

In my Starbucks moment with God

I will ask Why.

And I'd like to know if everyone else involved

Will ask Why or

Will be asked why.

OUR SMALL GROUP STUDIED the book of Revelation one year. It was the first time many of us had explored this book, and our Bible study guide produced many enthusiastic conversations. One insight that I gained was that my lifelong perception of *judgment*—my crawling across endless marble floors to the base of a towering throne where God wreathed in smoke and incense thunders at me, "You have been *so very wicked*"—may not be correct. My new image, perhaps not completely theological, is that God and I are having coffee at Starbucks. This is judgment day; and along with the Israelites of the Old Testament, I am eagerly anticipating it—no longer dreading it. Jesus has paid for my sins, and I am fully accepted by God. Now God and I can review my life over my skinny latte.

When events occur that contradict basic worldviews, such as *life is fair* and *people get what they deserve*, humans ask deep questions. When tragedies strike and the nature of these tragedies conveys to some people that God is vengeful, rather than loving, Christians hear "How can a loving God allow this to happen?" Even among the most dedicated Christians, singular events such as the loss of a child or the diagnosis of a fatal illness lead to faith challenges and accompanying distress.[1] Traumas cause us to ask how this could happen, why me, and especially "where was God when this was happening?"

Christians who experience these doubts often engage in religious and spiritual activities to restore meaning and hope. Christians pray and use ministry from others to shape their understanding of events from a position that threatens faith to one that promotes continued reliance on a loving, personal God. This process is grounded in the conviction that when our faith is challenged, we can restore our faith by reclaiming the truths of God's love, care, and sovereignty.

For Christians who have known Christian truths since childhood, the reclaiming process can occur when they talk with other Christians, share concerns in a Bible study or small group, or read Christian writers who address specific contexts. However, for Christians who are new to their faith or for whom these truths were not so tightly held, that reclaiming process might be more difficult. These persons will need to read deeply, listen to many others, and search for answers in the Bible, and they must be willing to acknowledge their own struggles in belief. Yet, the reclaiming process is not available to adult survivors of childhood sexual abuse because the foundation for it had not been established during childhood.

1. Barkin et al., *Beyond Tears*; Mabry, *Tender Scar*.

This chapter considers *spiritual damages,* which occur in addition to the consequences that were discussed in the previous chapter. These spiritual damages occur when the child is abused within an explicitly Christian context—such as within the family or the church—or by a person whom the child understands to be a Christian authority (such a pastor or youth leader). The chapter will have a discussion on how our concept of God is formed in a normal childhood and warped by the experience of childhood sexual abuse. The chapter concludes by revisiting the notion of trauma and by extending the trauma to the adult's loss of self in relation to God.

Like Acid Corrodes Metal, Spiritual Damages Corrode the Victim's Faith

I am crushed by my fear

And my breathing stops

And my lips form the word "no"

But there is no force to the form

And my no is unsaid.

But I can hear it echoing in the silence of my mind.

Victims Abandon Their Faith

The first and most obvious spiritual damage that is done by childhood sexual abuse is that adult survivors leave their faith and/or their faith community. Leaving may mean that they depart from the church that was associated with their childhood while they maintain a loose connection to some church, continue to pursue a personal life of faith without any church affiliation, or reject a life of faith altogether.

One of the first scholars[2] to study this issue documented that of adults who experienced incest during a religious upbringing, over 50 percent no longer identified with any faith. A team of researchers[3] compared victims of sexual abuse to victims of childhood physical abuse and emotional abuse: only sexual abuse was associated with reduced religious behaviors

2. Russell, *Secret Trauma.*

3. Lawson et al., "Long-term Impact."

(i.e., church attendance, Bible reading) and greater spiritual injury (i.e., anger, despair, meaninglessness) in adulthood. Among women who had been sexually abused as a child by a father figure, 60 percent had rejected a formalized practice of religion—27 percent because of the incest and 33 percent for other related reasons.

An in-depth examination[4] of religious and spiritual consequences was conducted among women who had been sexually abused as children but who were still affiliated with a Christian church. These adult victims were compared to Christian women who were in treatment for other mental health concerns (to have a clinical comparison) and to a group of same-age Christian women (to have a normal comparison). Women who had been sexually abused as children reported lower levels of faith-related attitudes and behaviors than did the other two groups of women. Examples of the attitudes and behaviors that were measured were confidence in knowing God's direction for one's own life, acceptance of God's grace, and participation in activities such as Bible study and church attendance. Experiencing Christian fellowship[5]—an aspect of religious life that previously had not been studied—was also lower for the sexually abused group.

In the church today, it is a frequent lament[6] that young people leave the church as adults. It is important to note, however, that in this chapter the data on adults who had been sexually abused as children reflect an earlier era when continued church attendance from childhood through adulthood was the norm. Because the norm was so strong then, it was a radical departure for these adults to leave the church. Moreover, these results also show a negative effect of childhood sexual abuse on adults who do stay affiliated with a church. Because these participants reported less interest in all aspects of church activities, it is likely that the association is tenuous and thus more liable to be broken by life events such as illness, work schedule changes, and other factors.

---

4. Hall, "Spiritual Effects."

5. This component of fellowship was defined as being able to connect in a special way with other Christians for worship and for other activities such as service (e.g., ministry), education (e.g., Bible study), and emotional support (e.g., MOPS groups, recreational activities).

6. See Solas, "Reasons Our Kids Leave."

Difficulties in Relationships with other Christians

The second spiritual damage that is caused by childhood sexual abuse is a struggle to maintain healthy and satisfying relationships with other Christians. Abuse victims continue to view God as punitive, harsh, and distant.[7] They see themselves as deeply undeserving of God's love—different from other Christians, whom victims believe do deserve this love.

Sometimes, in an attempt to fight against this overwhelming inadequacy, victims will pursue perfection in their visible religious life: they show extremes of service, zealousness, and lifestyle, so that they will be affirmed by other Christians. For the observer, it may be difficult to differentiate their motivation from the genuine intentions of exercising spiritual gifts of mercy and service that are present in the hearts of Christians who are passionate in their faith lives. One difference for the victims is that the affirmation that is received from others never fully removes the inadequacy because it is deeply rooted and not easily changed.[8]

Why then are interpersonal relationships so difficult? This aspect of faith damage is important to understand, because companioning underlies the healing journey that is described in this book. When we open up to another person about our own failures or fears, for all of us there is normal apprehension: what will the other person think about me? If I think badly of myself for having certain thoughts/feelings/experiences, surely that other person will reject me.

For a victim of childhood sexual abuse, those fears are dramatically heightened. *Being open* to another is a terrifying challenge because there is deep shame, lack of healing, and even a lack of understanding of the self.

An Immature Faith Weakens When Challenged

The third spiritual damage that is caused by childhood sexual abuse is that faith does not mature. Christians learn to respond to dead ends, failures, and problems by knowing God as having qualities of love, protection, and comfort that can sustain a person through difficult times. Responding affirmatively to life's challenges matures our faith in God and deepens our trust in his plans for us.

7. Kane et al., "Perceptions."
8. Tracy, *Mending the Soul.*

However, adults who had experienced childhood sexual abuse continue to perceive God as being either distant and impersonal or as actively judging and punitive. Because of how they see God, they use withdrawal and avoidance as ways of dealing with difficulties.[9] Thus, adult victims are easily disturbed by life challenges and suffer significant disappointment and frustration; these life challenges actually result in weakened rather than stronger faith.

So, what happens when faith is weak, and why is it difficult to strengthen? When abuse occurs in childhood, the development of faith is blocked in the same way as psychological development is blocked. Barriers to normal development after abuse are fear and lack of trust, despair and hopelessness, and anger. These barriers prevent the adult from faith development in several ways. Adult victims

- cannot get rid of their feelings of unworthiness and the accompanying experience of shame;

- have difficulty seeing their place in a faith community and feel isolated from others; and

- cannot see a future, and they are not able to have faith and trust in a plan for their lives from God.

The best metaphor for this faith damage is *corrosion*. Picture a metal container such as a pail into which battery acid is poured on various occasions. True, the pail can hold the acid for a while, but not forever. Eventually the acid will eat away the metal container that surrounds it.

So, too, will the *acid* of past experience and current emotional problems *eat away* at a life. Knowing God intimately, having a steadily maturing faith, and enjoying healthy and satisfying relationships with others—all these critical components of Christian life are significantly damaged by childhood sexual abuse. but not impossible

Betrayal Trauma

When a child is dependent on a certain person or institution and when that person or institution participates in sexual abuse or fails to protect the child from being sexually abused, betrayal trauma occurs.[10] In addition to

9. Rizzuto, *Birth of God*.
10. Freyd and Birrell, *Blind to Betrayal*.

violating the victim, *betrayal trauma* is abuse that violates the *culture* in which it occurs.

We all live within cultures—our families, our churches, our communities. These cultures are webs of interconnected networks. An example is that of a college or university alumni organization. The alumni feel a sense of pride in events that occur long after their graduation because of their attachment to the culture of that institution.

Thus, betrayal by a person within a shared culture is then all the more damaging because people depend on social and cultural connections. The closer and more necessary the cultural connection is to the victim, the deeper the damage will be to the victim.

How does betrayal trauma affect a person? Results of betrayal trauma have been shown to be increased dissociation,[11] amnesia (forgetting an experience), and shame.

In a study[12] with college students who reported a range of traumas, students who experienced moderate and high levels[13] of betrayal trauma in childhood reported less fear of strangers and more numbing and unawareness within close relationships. This finding explains why so many victims experience multiple occasions of abuse from the same person or from different people; and it answers the accusation of why the victim *chose* to keep being involved in an abusive relationship, kept working with an abusive youth leader, or continued visiting the abusive pastor.

In betrayal trauma, the relationship of the victim to the offender is central, because the abuse occurred at the hands of someone whom the child trusted within the context of that relationship. Thus, the abuse is not only an assault on the child but also an assault on the relationship. In the case of a child who is sexually abused by an adult in an explicit faith culture, the ensuing *institutional faith betrayal* irreparably damages the child's developing sense of self and developing sense of God. When a perpetrator represents an institution such as a local church, these feelings transfer to the institution itself.

11. *Dissociation* is detachment from feelings (or at its greatest level, detachment from conscious experience).

12. Bernstein et al., "Hypervigilance."

13. A moderate level of betrayal trauma would be physical abuse by someone who was known by the victim, whereas high level would be sexual abuse by someone who is very close to the victim.

The Greatest Faith Loss: A Lost God

God, where did you go?

Were you watching?

What were you thinking?

The four-year-old wants to know

And the fifty-five-year-old wants to know too.

And if they are in heaven with me

It had better be a big place.

Big enough so that they aren't there for me.

In the previous chapter, childhood sexual abuse was placed in the context of the normally developing child in order to better understand the consequences of abuse on development. A similar context of normal spiritual development helps to illuminate the central loss of faith after childhood sexual abuse—the loss of a God who personally and intimately loves us.

How do we come to know God? This process—considered by adults regarding their own faith lives—seems straightforward: we listen to instruction in church or from teachers, we read our Bibles, we pray, and so on. Perhaps we study theological material, in which the nature of God is painted with his characteristics—omniscience, omnipotence, omnipresence, immutability, holiness, righteousness, sovereignty, love, mercy, and a triune nature. We might read a book in the Bible and come to meet God as the biblical participants did. When we do this as adults, we have mental *structures* for concepts such as God's power, his plan for our lives, his mercy for our sins; and his overwhelming love for us; and we are able to understand these concepts and build on them in our minds.

Yet children begin learning concepts and categories that are *directly* perceived—seen, tasted, felt—such as *dog* or *blue*. Children then progress to actions that they can perform and can watch others perform, such as *give Mommy the ball* and playing peek-a-boo. The development of concepts and categories among children occurs in tandem with the children's development of language and their understanding that language is *representational*: the word *ball* is like or can stand for the ball itself.

So how do we explain God to a child? We as Christian adults know that we are created in the image of God. Several verses of the Bible speak to our innate knowledge of him. For example, his creation testifies to us of his existence:

> The heavens declare the glory of God; the skies proclaim the work of his hands. Day after day they pour forth speech; night after night they reveal knowledge. They have no speech, they use no words; no sound is heard from them. Yet their voice goes out into all the earth; their words to the ends of the world. (Ps 19:1–4 NIV)

Another example is that his qualities are said to be clearly understood by all:

> What may be known about God is plain to them, because God has made it plain to them. For since the creation of the world, God's invisible qualities—his eternal power and divine nature—have been clearly seen, being understood from what has been made, so that people are without excuse. (Rom 1:19–21 NIV)

However, because God cannot be directly perceived, the child builds the concepts of *how* God is perceived and his character and nature based on experiences with caregivers. God is a special—in fact, unique—object, because his concepts are built on children's *relationships* with mothers and fathers.[14] Fathers and mothers are given the responsibility of creating and nurturing their children's concepts of God until the children achieve the necessary developmental maturity to form their own. In fact, one of the primary responsibilities of parenting is this goal: "A father is called to be a trustworthy, and life generating surrogate for God until the child develops the capacity to see his or her heavenly Father as the only perfectly trustworthy Source of life."[15]

Recall the concept of *attachment* from the previous chapter. When the normal process of attachment is violated, there are several results.

- One result is the fear of being dependent on others—being truly frightened about having to depend on someone when previous reliance on a person resulted in abuse.

- There is great anxiety over being abandoned: Previous supposed caregivers abandoned the victim, why won't others?

- There is a conflict, a push-pull of wanting relationships but feeling threatened by becoming too close to another person.

14. Wolf, *Treating the Self*.
15. Allender, *Wounded Heart*, 53. See also Allender, "Dealing," para. 9.

God is distorted by those concerns and feelings. Bishop[16] writes how a normal but less-than-perfect father shapes and defines—and distorts—how we view God. Thus, the child creates views of God that match childhood experiences such as having a father who wasn't around, or one who expected and accepted only perfection, or one who was *always right*. The concept of God is distorted even more by childhood sexual abuse.[17] Experience of abuse forms the distorted view of God as either wrathful and avenging or as distant and uncaring. Only these two notions of God can exist next to the shamed, unworthy, and "cowering before God" characteristic of an adult who has experienced childhood sexual abuse.[18]

Childhood Sexual Abuse Damages Truth

The biblical story of Tamar (2 Sam 13:1–31), who experienced both sexual abuse and betrayal within a family, piercingly illustrates what happens when truth is silenced to cover up sexual abuse. Tamar is David's daughter (2 Sam 3:3); Absalom and Amnon are her brothers. Amnon is "in love" with Tamar, but his love is incestuous lust. His advisor, Jonadab, asks him one day about his despondence, and Amnon explains that he desires "his brother's sister." Jonadab then devises a strategy for Amnon to be alone with Tamar, the strategy of pretending to be ill. David orders Tamar to go to Amnon's house to care for him during his supposed illness. When she does, Amnon brings her into his bedroom and rapes her. After the rape, Amnon orders his personal servant to remove her from the house. Although David was informed of the rape, he did not confront Amnon. Absalom instructed Tamar to remain quiet; two years later, he avenged Tamar's violation by murdering Amnon. Tamar remained "desolate in her brother Absalom's house."

In the story of Tamar, truth is attacked at every opportunity. After the rape, they treated her with contempt, silenced her, and ultimately shamed her. Her father David does not appear to have done anything to restore her honor or to further protect her; in fact, it is clear that she continued to live at her brother's house rather than her father's. These characteristics describe any system in which the truth is hidden and falsehood is promoted—actions of silence, covering up, and denial.

16. Bishop, *God Distorted*.
17. Ganje-Fling and McCarthy, "Spiritual Development."
18. Tracy, *Mending the Soul*.

Christians, in contrast to contemporary society, maintain a certain view of *truth*.[19] God is the ultimate truth and the source and ground of all truth. All truth is God's truth, and he has revealed it to humankind through the person of Jesus and through general and special revelation. Truth is objective, knowable, universal, and absolute. Finally, truth negates or denies untruth, whether asserted by a person or an organization or society.

How do children know what *truth* is? This interesting question has unfortunately been studied primarily within a forensic context, which is whether or not children are reliable witnesses in a courtroom setting. In general, to be a reliable witness, the person must know the difference between the truth and a lie, understand a duty to tell the truth, and be motivated to perform that duty.[20] Consequently, how children think about truth and lies is important to understand if they provide testimony in a courtroom setting.

Scholars[21] suggest that children form judgments of truth based only on *factuality*, the degree to which a statement conforms to the evidence concerning it. This finding is true of children up to ages ten to twelve. At that point, judgment of truth incorporates an additional component, which is the child's assessment of the beliefs of the speaker—an acceptance that the speaker believes what he or she says to be truth.

In contrast, when adults judge the truth,[22] they rely on three features of the situation. Most important is the opinion of the speaker's belief in the truth of the statement. Second is their opinion of the *intent* of the speaker to tell the truth versus to deceive. In direct contrast to children, adults rely least on the objective factuality of the statement.

When a child is raised in a Christian environment, parents typically emphasize the importance of *telling the truth* versus *telling a lie*. However, for a child who is sexually abused, the meaning of the words *truth* and *lie* are dramatically affected. The entire foundation of abused children's understanding of truth versus lie is undone by the contradiction of one with the other in personal experience. Children judge truth based on *factuality*—the degree to which the evidence corresponds to the statement. In a family, a church, or a relationship in which the child experiences abuse but is told that he or she is loved and cared for, the child cannot develop an

19. See Samples, *World of Difference*.
20. Goodman, "Child Witness."
21. Strichartz and Burton, "Lies and Truth."
22. Coleman and Kay, "Prototype Semantics."

accurate sense of Truth. Yet, Truth cannot be understood as *truth*, because the necessary developmental task of knowing truth cannot be completed when truth and experience are radically discrepant.

Little Girl with No Voice

We return now to the concept that childhood sexual abuse is considered a *trauma*. A *trauma* is the survival of a death experience—an event that carries with it horror, extreme personal danger, and vulnerability. The use of the word *survivor* is meant to carry this meaning: while a trauma survivor has survived a death experience, he or she has not completed it and thus continues to deal with it. The trauma survivor re-experiences the trauma through vivid sensations, images, flashbacks, nightmares, and the like. Yet re-experiencing the trauma does not *solve* the problem of the trauma's effects on the body and the mind.

It is a tragic consequence that a person's attempts to cope with the trauma damage the person's identity. This is especially true because mechanisms that are dissociative in nature are often used. *Dissociation* is the act of splitting certain experiences out of consciousness. This coping method is common with combat veterans who may have no memory of certain horrific aspects of war because they have separated those memories from their accessible memories. Henry Cloud[23] explains how children use dissociation to split off a part of the self and maintain it separate from the regular identity. As a psychologist, I believe God created the mind with this ability in order to protect persons during unbearable trauma. Its results, however, are that memory is affected—either lost entirely or kept in fragments rather than whole.

During childhood sexual abuse, therefore, the developmental process of a whole self is damaged.[24] All persons form their healthy sense of self within relationships, which are initially formed through parent and familial relationships and later shaped by social relationships with other children and adults. As this chapter and the previous one have explored, interpersonal relationships are difficult for victims. The victim's relationship with God is also terribly damaged, and truths that the survivor hears about God and life are difficult to believe because they contradict personally experienced evidence.

23. Cloud, *Changes that Heal.*
24. See Davies and Frawley, *Treating the Adult.*

Sometimes this disjunction takes the form of a split person: I, myself, experienced this splitting. There was the *outward me*, who believed what I knew of God and who interacted with people whom I loved and trusted. Yet no one knew the *inside me*, who was in the shadow of my fear, shame, and anger. I wasn't sure that God knew the inside me, but I suspected that he did. That was the most frightening aspect of all, and consequently, it was the greatest awakening in my journey. God knew and loved *both* versions of *me*, and he wanted me to allow him to join the two into one renewed and redeemed version of *me*. That wholeness was achieved toward the end of my healing journey—a realization that I was complete in God, including my past abuse and my own actions, all of it redeemed by his love.

Wrapping Up

With words that reflect this tragedy in contrast with the joy that comes at the end of a healing journey, Mary DeMuth[25] writes movingly of her own journey:

> Have you ever felt like sexual abuse is your exile? That it's set you in a place you'd rather not be? A place not of your choosing? A mindset that haunts you? God spoke to the Israelites in their exile, encouraging those exiles to change their thinking or they would miss the great things He planned to do. If we stay locked in the isolation of our minds, always rehashing the old story, preferring the place of exile, we will not be able to perceive or see the cool things God will do. I am proof that God hews rivers in dry river-beds, pathways through thorny thickets. He does the impossible. I'm living a life of impossible joy right now because of the new things God has done. Had I coddled my thoughts of unworthiness and believed them forever, I would not have seen God's great deliverance in the now.

Toolkit

The tools in the toolkit for the companion are establishing an *alliance*. The journey tool that the companion can offer to the victim is *hope in connection*.

---

25. DeMuth, *Not Marked*, 160–1.

Alliance

In a companioning relationship, the companion is ready and willing to come alongside the survivor on a journey, yet not completely knowing where that journey will end or when the companion's role will end. However, the companion is joining with the *other* to go forward. In the initial stages of the journey, the companion must develop an alliance with the victim—a very difficult task for the victim given the damaged relationships in his or her past. Here are specific ways to develop an alliance.

- *Providing hope to the victim.* Hope gives the victim an immediate space that is positive and that provides safety and affirmation. The companion alone does not provide that hope; in Christian companioning, the companion assists the victim to find that hope in God. Hope is the possibility that God is available, loving, and trustworthy rather than distant and rejecting. The companion can be the physical embodiment of those attributes to the victim and can also provide ways for the victim to experience God's loving presence.

  As an example, a companion can provide hope by using selected Scripture readings to give the victim a new sense of hope. There are many resources that can be used to select such readings. Still, it is a very easy mistake to simply read Scripture and say to a victim: "See, there it is in the Bible!" Rather, a companion might ask the victim to read the verse. The companion then might gently inquire whether the verse feels *true* to the victim and accept the victim's initial inability to genuinely hold the truth of Scripture. That may be a prayer request for the victim—that he or she be given assurance of the truth of one verse that initially feels unavailable.

- *Focus on the victim.* The togetherness that they are experiencing is for the victim. The companion will certainly talk about him- or herself, drawing on past experiences, hopes for the future, and the like. Yet these conversations are in service to the greater understanding and spiritual growth of the victim. If the focus turns to the companion, then companioning is lost. The victim will feel rejected and may even say that "I was right not to trust this person. My life is so damaged and my past is so terrible that no one can bear to really listen to me." Instead, if the companion shares a story about his or her own life, link it to the victim, such as, "When I told you about my sister, it was because she made me feel so inadequate. I wondered if that feeling happened for you in your relationship to your own sister."

- *Allow the victim to discover his or her own insights, next steps, and solutions.* When you are *companioning,* you are coming alongside someone else who is directing the movement along the path. During part of the journey, victims feel discouraged, confused, and distressed. When that occurs, it is very tempting for us to present the solution. Refrain from doing this. Instead, remember that God is with both you and the victim. When you are gentle and patient, you show that you understand and accept that confusion, contradiction, discouragement, and hope are all mixed together.

- *Learn to allow silence.* So many of us see silence as something to be filled immediately. When a person is thinking or working, he or she will look that way—likely not directly at you but away, up, or down. Don't interrupt the work of thought and consideration.

These tools allow a companion to establish an alliance with the survivor. An *alliance* is a particular, special type of relationship that is distinct from a friendship or a partnership.

An alliance stands in contrast to a *friendship,* which is two or more people who are mutually bonded over one or more of several types of goals that vary from work to play. Friendships are bi-directional: friends expect that other friends will alternate roles of giving and receiving.

An alliance also stands in contrast to a *partnership,* which is two or more people who have made an explicit commitment to work together to achieve a certain goal. Even if the people who are working together are not friends, partnerships can be effective because their purpose is the achievement of a goal.

Hope in Connection

The journey skill for the victim is hope in connection. Hope is a powerful tool, one which victims do not have. Victims must first make the connection that there can be *hope in relation to another person.* Yet hope is not an easy achievement for a person who has been abused. Leehan[26] discusses the

26. Leehan, *Defiant Hope.*

38

importance of hope for spiritual healing. Moreover, Brueggemann[27] makes the critical observation that hope belongs *especially* to persons who have not experienced the regularity of blessings in their lives: hope "emerges among those who publicly articulate and process their grief over their suffering."[28]

If the survivor is beginning a companioning relationship with you, then he or she has already taken a big step toward recovery. That step should be celebrated and reinforced. Even that first feeble step of *hope in connection* is a big move toward recovery. However, that hope is fragile. Don't overwhelm the victim with reinforcement. In particular, the use of physical touch needs to be very carefully considered. In general, touching a person who has been abused is something that should always be initiated by the victim. If he or she reaches out and touches you on your arm or hand, this is a wonderful step. Don't make the mistake then of pulling him or her into a hug.

After this first step, the second skill for the victim is to begin to *connect in hope with God*. Because God has been seen as distant, avenging, or angry, the task will seem daunting. Still, the victim must learn for himself or herself who God truly is. It is helpful to begin to *meet God anew* by reading the Bible in a very different translation. I found *The Message* to be a new language, and I have read it twice from cover to cover. Another helpful task is to write a journal. If the victim can begin a journal, thoughts and insights will be visible and more available. I journaled as I read *The Message*. On the first page of my journal, I wrote "Who is God and what is he like?" I found surprises every day and wrote them down. The contemporary language of *The Message* allowed me to revisit themes without the previous sense of dread and fear.

The third skill that the victim will need is to *connect hope to a new self*. The companion can help this process by questioning and leading the victim to think deeper and more positively about him- or herself. "What do you think are your top three personal strengths?" "In what situations do you feel positive, capable, and strong?" Watch the survivor for when he or she begins to *brighten up* in conversation. Begin talking about personal strengths when the victim is beginning to talk about them. You can also use a list of character or personal strengths to discuss. Many are available online from both Christian and secular sources. Research[29] has shown cer-

27. Brueggemann, *Hope*.
28. Ibid., 84 (original italicized).
29. See University of Pennsylvania, "Authentic Happiness."

tain qualities are most associated with happiness: gratitude, curiosity and interest in the world, hope, the capacity to love and be loved, and energy and enthusiasm.

Hope will be maintained when the victim can better regulate his or her emotions. Victims will begin quickly to feel overwhelmed with an array of emotions when they think over and talk about past abuse and current problems. Familiar and distressing feelings of anger, sadness, grief, loneliness, shame, and hopelessness will surface. Note that feelings such as these can be used as navigation points in the journey. There are many resources that will help the victim.

Briefly, *emotional regulation* consists of four steps. These steps will be repeated many times. When the steps need to be repeated, it should not be considered a failure or setback. As with learning any new skill, many repetitions will be required for success.

- *Step 1: Being safe from dangerous situations and protected against being revictimized.* If the victim is not in a safe situation—as would be the case if he or she were still under the control of the perpetrator, then companioning is not the correct vehicle for caring. Other steps such as notifying authorities or involving mental health professionals must be taken.

- *Step 2: Physiological control.* With regard to physical presence, the victim is partially separated from his or her own body. Thus focus on the body is important. This focus can occur through slow deep breathing. Then use observation to locate physical difficulties. Is the victim's throat tight? Is the victim feeling as though he or she is being suffocated? Breathing *through* those moments is important. Being calm and counting to ten can create more relaxation and less muscular tension.

- *Step 3: Thinking rationally.* What are the thoughts that are swirling around? Can they be teased apart so that they can be individually considered? When one thought can be isolated, it can be rationally evaluated. For example, a victim might say, "I should have told someone." The thought can then be looked at from the knowledge that the companion has to offer. Using knowledge about how children develop, the companion can say, "That makes sense to the part of you that is now an adult, but children can't stand up to something that they can't really understand and are powerless to prevent."

- *Step 4: Using emotion to go deeper.* This last step is deeply challenging for both the companion and the victim. We are all uncomfortable with emotions that are deeply felt. Sometimes it is helpful to change the emotion to a picture. What does that anger look like? If depression, is it a hole in the ground? How big? How deep? What is in it? If it were becoming a movie, what would happen next? Note that this step can only be taken when the companion and the victim are connected and when the victim feels supported by both the companion and by God. It will also be a step that is done by the victim in Bible study, during reading, and in writing a journal.

Red Flags

The journey and the companioning skills are meant to allow a companion to come alongside and assist the victim during his or her journey. Sometimes that journey is one of being stuck, caught, or jammed—that is a normal part of travel. We don't always go forward in a straight line. Still, there are signs that the victim needs more help than the companion can provide. Each chapter after this will describe the most relevant *red flags*, that is, signs the companion needs to assist the victim to seek a higher level of skilled help.

The red flag that is most relevant to this chapter pertains to the emotional experience of the victim. It is normal for the victim to have distressing emotions, which are hard to hold and at times overwhelming. However, if the regulation skills in this chapter do not allow the victim to be able to regulate, the following might occur:

- The victim might report being unable to sleep due to invasive thoughts and images.
- The victim might be unable to go to work due to depression.
- There might be a drawing back from regular activities—"I just don't feel like doing that anymore."

The victim should see his or her physician or healthcare provider if the victim reports physical dysfunction, headaches, fatigue, or gastrointestinal distress. The red flag here is *impairment*: the victim cannot function in the life activities that would be normal for him or her.

For this reason, the companion should have access to referral resources—a range of care providers including mental healthcare providers. Because some providers may have wait lists, a more immediate resource may be a local community mental health center or crisis center. In case of an emergency, the emergency room of a local hospital may be needed. It is not a sign of failure to need more resources. Instead, it is a sign that problems are being faced and more resources are being brought to help. The companion should be an encouragement to seek and use these additional resources.

Summary

The victim and the companion are together on a journey to rediscover the victim's connection to others and to God. There can be no more important goal for the victim and no more rewarding work for the companion.

Case: Taylor

You are a twelve-year-old girl who is being homeschooled by your conservative Christian parents—a choice that is highly respected among your congregation. You spend most of your time in the home with your mom, dad, and siblings—two older brothers who are fourteen and sixteen and a baby sister who is only four. Your mom does most of the teaching, but your dad sometimes comes in to do special lessons to give your mom a break. He talks a lot about the roles of women and men in God's teachings. Your mom repeats your dad's teachings that a woman's role is to submit to the men in her life and to make sure that the teachings are well kept. You have been taught this your whole life and are beginning to feel more capable and comfortable in that role.

Recently, your dad has begun to take you aside for special lessons. He asks you to touch him in ways that make you uncomfortable. When you hesitate or protest, he reminds you that God teaches us to respect our elders and that you are a young woman who should serve God and man. You don't like these lessons, but you trust your dad and know that he is just trying to teach you how to behave correctly. Afterward, you have a heavy pit in your stomach and you wash your hands so hard that your skin is raw. As time goes on and knowing that you cannot refuse your father, you learn to unfocus your eyes and to let things become a blur—you imagine yourself playing outside or picking up the kittens in the barn. Sometimes you just try as hard as you can to think about nothing and to wait for him to say, "That's a good girl." Then you know your lesson is over.

When you walk through the house after these sessions with your dad, your mom sometimes will ask you how it was. The first few times that it happened, you expected her to see your face and to ask you whether you're alright. You even fantasized that she would yell, that she would cast your father out, and that she then would scoop you up and protect you.

Doesn't she know? Why isn't she asking? After a while, you simply tell her that it was fine. You've become angry with her because she doesn't seem to notice that you are changing, notice your discomfort; or worse, that she does notice, but doesn't care to intervene.

You've become a stranger in your own house. You're nervous about spending time with your brothers, who are nearly grown men themselves. You aren't sure whether they expect the same from you as your father does or whether or not all men do. You avoid family activities and have missed out on fun activities with your friends because you're afraid to be alone in a car with your brothers long enough for them to drive you into town. You've retreated into yourself; you're going through the motions of your day without enthusiasm or interest.

Worst of all, you feel distanced from God. At times, he is your savior and you allow yourself to hope that he will deliver you from these experiences. Other times, you hate him, curse him, and even demote him to fiction and fantasy. You don't know how or what to believe, and you now resent all your teaching. You know that you can't be the kind of woman that you're supposed to be, but you don't know how to be anything else either.

1. What are the most concerning parts about this case?

2. Does the context of Taylor's case in a Christian home affect how you understand her experiences? How so?

3. How do you think Taylor sees herself as a *young woman*? How do you think this has been changed by her father's abuse?

4. How are you reacting to Taylor's family members?

5. What steps could be taken by the church to help Taylor? Identify at least one step, and discuss the actions that are needed to implement that step.

3

At First I Thought–Then I Realized

Chapter Objectives

1. Learn common reasons that reports of sexual abuse are not believed.
2. Understand correct information that refutes common reasons for disbelief.
3. Learn correct information about supposed *false memories*.
4. Learn policies and procedures on prevention and reporting abuse for churches and other faith organizations.

Telling

Telling is odd and awkward

But it feels good too.

To use the words robs them of their power

At least during the act of the telling—and depending on the receiver's reaction.

But after the telling

And the tears

The words sneak back inside me.

AT THE END OF the evening, Mark[1] paused at the top of the stairs and looked down to the landing, where Elaine was already putting on her boots. Having moved away five years ago, he and Elaine were back in town for a visit. He looked troubled, and I knew that he was thinking how best to express his and Elaine's deep concern and compassion. So, what had happened?

When Mark and Elaine contacted us a few weeks earlier and suggested having dinner with us during their brief trip to our area, I knew that we would tell them our news.

Mark and Elaine had been members of our Bible study group. This was a group that had been made up of four couples that had been somewhat randomly put together merely because we were all free that same evening. Our backgrounds were dissimilar. First, there were the life stage differences: two couples with children, one engaged couple, and one recently married couple. We held different jobs or had no job at all. We also did not share theological backgrounds. Some of us had experienced a Bible study group, and the rest had never been involved in a small group. Even so, as we shared personal information and prayed together for God's guidance, we came to trust and care for each other.

So, how could we explain to Mark and Elaine that we left our church— that we had in fact left church altogether, not just changed our membership? When they asked us at dinner how things were going at our church, we were honest. We told them about my situation and described the long process of my healing. We described our small group's stunned but courageous response after I revealed my abuse history.

I made an appointment to meet with our pastor after I had begun to accept my abuse history and started counseling. I had a strong need to confide in him and to have a pastoral response in addition to counseling. I didn't go into detail, but I was honest about my childhood and my current difficulties.

Still my husband and I continued to attend services and volunteer at our church. We led our small group Bible study and continued small group leader training. Yet both of us were starting to struggle. I was challenged by flashbacks, nightmares, and other symptoms. I longed to have my pastor ask me how I was doing. During coffee time after the worship service, I would stand near him hoping that he might come over to me. He never did.

---

1. All names and places have been changed.

My husband was having an equally difficult time. My husband's feelings of betrayal were especially strong due to my abuser's standing as a *devoted Christian*—a particular stumbling block for my husband. Finally, my husband stopped going to church.

I continued attending church alone. One Sunday I broke down. I approached another pastor and asked him to help my husband. I was in tears as I recounted the conversation that I had had with the other pastor almost two years before. The second pastor took out a business card, handed it to me to give to my husband, and said: "Here's my card. Have him call me."

After we told Mark and Elaine the events, our feelings tumbled out. Was I so unworthy that I didn't deserve any contact from my pastor? Couldn't the pastor have called my husband rather than expected my husband to contact him? We both felt abandoned by our pastors. We told Mark and Elaine that we had scheduled an appointment with our pastors nine months afterward. The pastors still hadn't contacted either of us, and we had begun to understand and label their response as wrong.

Here is a portion of the letter I wrote to the pastors that I read to Mark and Elaine:

> Although you both abandoned me, God did not. Our small group, when Michael and I finally told them, although deeply shocked, responded with support and encouragement. I have Christian friends who frequently ask how I am doing, offer their support, and pray for me. Our children have responded with maturity that far exceeds their years. Both have been baptized in the past year, both have joined churches, and both are deeply committed to their faith in ways they were not at the beginning of this process. I have also been blessed by God's presence in our marriage. I do not believe I can adequately convey the strains this situation puts on a marriage. However, during this entire process, you have not been walking alongside me, and thus you were not a part of my healing.
>
> Michael and I are resigning from Community Church. We cannot continue being "pastored" by people who, for whatever reason, have chosen not to pastor us. Therefore, I am not telling you of my feelings today to restore a working relationship with you. But I am deeply concerned for the man or woman who next tells you of childhood sexual abuse. I do not want him or her to be treated as I was, for that person may not have the resources I do. So I ask as sincerely as possible that you reconsider how you interact with persons who seek out your pastoral care. I am sure there are

issues that make you uncomfortable, but the person seeking your help wants spiritual comfort and advice and not expert therapy.

You have said more than once in the pulpit that you believe pastors will be held to a higher standard by God. I agree with you. I ask that you prayerfully consider how you are meeting that standard.

So how had Mark reacted at the end of the evening, after he paused at the top of the stairs? Mark looked at me said, "Christians are the only army that shoots its wounded."

In society today, our American soldiers and their experience in combat are a topic of national discourse. The homelessness rate and increased suicidality among returning veterans both tell us that these soldiers' physical and emotional needs are not being met. As a country, we have responded with compassion, focus, and determination.

The church has wounded soldiers, too. These persons are wounded from present experiences such as divorce or job loss or from experiences in their past such as a parent's death during their childhood. Still, many are wounded from childhood sexual abuse: it is this group that most challenges the church.

I want to believe that a Christian church is the least likely place for childhood sexual abuse to occur and the most likely place in which healing can take place. As a survivor, I want God's healing promoted within the church to all adults and adolescents who have experienced childhood sexual abuse. I desire that all *servants of Jesus* in ministry are sensitive and open to those wounded by childhood sexual abuse. This is a calling that the church has failed to meet.

My experience telling my own pastors and my talking with other survivors about their conversations with Christians has helped me to understand that hearing of a report of childhood sexual abuse prompts several immediate responses. Those responses may be legitimate concerns, questions that are worth asking, or reasonable doubts in the face of such a report.

- Sometimes the report comes from someone like me, who to my pastor undoubtedly appeared to be a successful and well-adjusted adult.

- Sometimes the report raises questions of timing: why am I *now* hearing about something that happened twenty or thirty years ago?

- Then there are the times that the report raises real concerns about a necessary response—particularly if the alleged abuser is a church member whose reputation is unsullied.

First Responses of Hearers

In this chapter, the *first responses* of hearers are explored. Both actual and implied sources of doubt that the hearer has in response to the reporter of the abuse are answered by information that includes scholarly data.

"I Would Have Known about It, Had It Been Happening in My Church."

Public discussions of childhood sexual abuse—and even abuse of children within Christian contexts—is not recent. However, church leaders continue to demonstrate a distressing lack of knowledge of childhood sexual abuse. In addition, they continue to express confidence that such a tragedy could not be happening in their own church/ministry for a variety of reasons that range from *they know everyone who works with them* to their belief that it is utterly impossible for true Christians to do such evil acts. Morton[2] summarized this state of mind as believing the following assertions:

- Everyone at my church is safe and responsible.
- Childhood sexual abuse could never be happening in my church or within a family who attends my church.
- Childhood sexual abuse is primarily a Catholic issue: it doesn't happen within evangelical Christian churches.
- Women can't possibly be suspected of childhood sexual abuse.

In order to gather data on church leaders' knowledge about childhood sexual abuse, Morton[3] surveyed 113 men and 100 women who were involved in Christian ministry in ten denominations. All her study participants held a church leadership position and had been expressly selected from all geographical regions of the United States. All leaders were mature and experienced: the average age was forty-three and average ministry

2. Morton, "Church Leaders' Understanding."
3. Ibid.

experience thirteen years. Pastors made up half the sample. To assess the participants' knowledge, Morton gathered the degree of agreement with supposed *facts* about childhood sexual abuse. She also obtained information about the participants' current church response.

In Morton's study, participants not only agreed with truthful *facts* such as both boys and girls being at risk and that child sexual abuse producing lifelong trauma. Participants also agreed with many nonfactual statements (e.g., child molesters begin molesting in their early twenties). Participants also believed that most churches screen their workers to prevent child sexual abuse. Finally, these participants' beliefs were not linked to their own church practices. As an example, virtually all participants asserted that written policies regarding this issue were important, yet fewer than half of the participants' churches had such policies. Having personal reference checks for employees and volunteers was widely endorsed as a desirable part of selection, but only 24 percent of the sample had ever contacted references. When asked why the participants had not implemented steps that they themselves endorsed as necessary, reasons were "cost," "resistance," and "a high likelihood of offending people."[4]

A disturbing recent trend is that children and youth are sexually vulnerable online. Adults typically do not know the degree to which youth are exposed to sexual material online. Children and adolescents may not intentionally seek the types of material that they are exposed to, but studies show that being exposed to sexual materials is frequent among youth. Such exposure happens in chat rooms, among acquaintances and friends *sexting*, and via online sexual solicitation. While experts had previously thought predators posed as someone having the same age as the youth, researchers[5] have found that predators told the victims that they were older males seeking sexual relations. Surveys of juvenile victims of Internet-initiated sex crimes revealed that the majority of victims were willing to meet face-to-face; almost all of those personal encounters involved sexual contact.

"It Was So Long Ago."

There are several ways of viewing what *memory* is. A popular metaphor of *memory* is a file cabinet with individual memory drawers that can be

4. Ibid.

5. For example, see papers from the Crimes against Children Research Center, University of New Hampshire, at http://www.unh.edu/ccrc/internet-crimes/papers.html.

opened or closed—their contents unchanging over time. Alternatively, *memory* can be thought of as a collection of movies with events that had been accurately recorded at one point in time and that can be replayed in the same way at any point in the future. In our current technological society, *memory* might be a supercomputer that is humming away in our brains and storing events for recall at a later time.

In actuality, *memory* is a complex function that is located in several different areas of our brain. Each location holds part of the working group of brain functions that equals our memory. For example, the hippocampus holds neurons that serve as *memory retrievers*—clues or fractional pieces that recall memories. The process that we think of as *memory* is contained in collections of neuron ensembles. Thus, fumbling for the name of an acquaintance whom you run across—someone you haven't seen or thought about for years—is your neuron ensembles working together to retrieve the name. Perhaps something about the person—say, the smile or laugh—suddenly helped you remember the name. That is because memory is stored with emotions. The amygdala and the hippocampus, which are closely associated, are located together in the frontal subcortical area of the brain.

Ornstein, Ceci, and Loftus[6] summarize what scholars know about memory as follows:

1. Not every aspect of an event is maintained in memory. How the person encodes the memory depends on factors that are associated with the event. One of the most important factors is the presence of positive versus negative emotions.

2. Memories have differential ease of recall; some memories remain clear after many years, while others do not.

3. The process by which the memory is retrieved is influential on what is recalled; for example, *asking* questions about an event will bring about a different set of memories than *viewing* pictures of that same event.

4. *Recall* of a memory and the *accuracy* of a memory are not the same. Given the findings, it makes sense that some memories are fully recalled with less than complete accuracy, whereas other memories are completely accurate but only partially recalled.

An important distinction is whether memory of trauma goes through the same process of being encoded, stored, and retrieved as do memories

6. Ornstein et al., "Adult Recollections" (1996, 1998).

that are obtained during normal living. When a pastor hears an adult relate a sexual abuse incident that happened when he or she had been a child, the pastor might think: "It happened so long ago, so why is it still an issue—shouldn't he or she be *over it* by now?" This doubt is an expression of the wrongful belief that traumatic memory operates according to the same rules and processes as normal memory.

In contrast to that assumption, researchers[7] have established that trauma memory differs from memory of normal events in several important ways.

1. Whereas normal memory is adaptable and is integrated with life experiences that follow the original memory, trauma memory is *unaffected* by life experiences. It remains *frozen*, so to speak, in our brains.

2. Normal memory is present in our awareness in a continuous way: we access and interact with our memory. As an example, think of a family discussing over dinner a family vacation that had been taken several years before the dinner. Bringing up the memories and hearing others discuss their memories influences how the individual's memory of the vacation is stored after the dinner. In contrast, traumatic memories— usually only triggered by reminders that are present at the trauma— are re-experienced by the survivor as vividly as if the original event were happening again. This includes much of the distress in the original event.

3. Normal memory consists of words and symbols. In contrast, trauma memory is primarily composed of sensory and emotional experiences such as panic—experiences which are both physiological and psychological in nature.

Because this book involves childhood sexual abuse, it is important to understand that children's memories are different from adults' memories.[8] Developmental psychology scholars believe that first—perhaps around age two—a *behavioral memory system* appears to develop. This means that children can reenact events that occurred to them in the past, even if they cannot tell what happened in words. Between ages two and three, children speak about past events with some accuracy, although usually not with a complete description. After age four, the child's verbal memories may be

7. See van der Kolk, "Traumatic Memories."
8. Lukowski and Bauer, "Long-Term Memory."

spontaneously brought up in conversation with others. Although children may not have the verbal skills that are sufficient to describe a memory, they do form memories at an early age.

Thus, if you hear from a victim about an event that occurred in the distant past, the memories of that event are still as *present* to the victim as if they had happened just that very day. The scholarship on memory development in youth and on the difference between normal memories and trauma memories demands that hearers understand the nature of the report and to react appropriately. An *appropriate* response is one that is empathic to the expressed and implied emotion, and above all, a response that validates the reporter's choice to tell you something very personal and very frightening.

"I Know Someone Who Was Falsely Accused of Abuse; He Lost Everything."

A distressing number of people believe that children and adolescents make up reports of childhood sexual abuse to *get attention*. There was a significant debate[9] among professionals concerning reports of abuse. However, the context of this debate was the then practice (now discontinued) of encouraging children to give reports of abuse through suggestive questioning. More current research—taking place in the context of improved state laws and legal procedures including those giving adequate rights to the accused—has established several circumstances.

First, the number of intentionally false reports is quite low. In a study[10] conducted in 2000, all case reports that had been made in one city were examined. Of 551 cases, 2.5 percent were erroneous. It is important to consider the specific nature of these erroneous cases:

- Three were made in collusion with a parent, most likely during a custody decision.

- Three cases were considered misinterpretation of an event.

- Eight cases were actually false allegations.

That is, false allegations made up only 1.5 percent of all the cases.

There is also the stereotype that recantation of abuse shows that false reporting is frequent. However, research on the recanting of reports

9. See chapter 1.
10. Oates et al., "Erroneous."

typically shows that the family members pressure the victim to recant. In one study[11] in a large urban district of case files from two years of abuse reports of children and youth from ages two to seventeen, the few cases of recanting revealed victims who were vulnerable to family influences, including younger victims and those abused by a parent.

The presumption that a child or adolescent will give a single, detailed account of the abuse is not consistent with research on disclosure.[12] Most typically, a child will imply that something has happened—testing the listener with a hint to determine whether the listener will respond positively. Additionally, research suggests that children often understate the extent of abuse. In one study,[13] twenty-eight children who had tested positively for sexually transmitted diseases were interviewed by a trained social worker using best practice interviewing techniques. Only 43 percent of the children gave any verbal confirmation of sexual contact. Another study[14] involved a single perpetrator who videotaped his encounters with children. Because of the recorded encounters, researchers knew the nature of the sexual activity. When the children were interviewed, some children simply did not want to disclose the experiences, others had difficulties remembering them, and some children were young enough to lack adequate concepts to describe them.

"Do I Have to Inform Someone?"

Let's assume that Tremell is a youth outreach worker for his church. He is excited to be working with the young adolescents, and the youth ministry staff has successfully built a large group of enthusiastic ten- to fourteen-year-olds. One boy in particular seems to be especially involved: he comes early and also stays late to help stack chairs. Tremell notices that the boy is quiet and keeps his head down. One evening, Tremell initiates a conversation by asking the boy how he is doing. After several weeks of their talking after the group, the boy tells Tremell that he is being sexually abused by his music teacher. The boy's parents are pushing him to get a music scholarship at the local university, and he has several private lessons each week. He doesn't feel that he can tell his parents. In fact, he tells Tremell that he

11. Malloy et al., "Filial Dependency and Recantation."
12. Canadian Centre for Child Protection, *Child Sexual Abuse.*
13. Lawson and Chaffin, "False Negatives."
14. Sjöberg and Lindblad, "Limited Disclosure."

knows they wouldn't believe him. Tremell worries after this conversation: does he need to tell someone what the boy said?

Society gives a privilege to several types of professionals—the privilege of keeping secret what is told to them by clients, patients, or parishioners. It is critical to know that who has this privilege is a decision made at the state level. Each state decides for itself which professional can maintain what types of communications as confidential. The state also determines which professionals who come into contact with children (including adolescents) have a duty to report suspected or actual abuse—a duty termed *mandatory reporting*. Many youth workers and pastors live in states with statutes that require them to report child maltreatment under certain circumstances.[15]

As risk managers[16] point out, it is essential that all persons hearing reports of potential abuse ask themselves the following questions:

- Under my state law, am I a mandatory reporter or permissive reporter?

- Does what I have been told constitute child abuse under my state law? Do I have a reasonable reason to conclude that abuse has occurred?

- Do I have a clergy privilege? If I choose not to tell anyone about what I had been told, do I have a risk under state law?

- Should I try to persuade the youth to inform the proper authorities or maybe offer to go with the youth? If I have to or choose to report, what is the proper authority for me to report to?

Let's return to Tremell, the youth outreach worker. In some states, for example, Tremell's individual responsibility would not be fulfilled by merely informing the senior pastor. In those states, Tremell is responsible for reporting the abuse.

"If I Know about It, What Do I Do?"

Dave Orrison, a pastor with thirty-two years of experience in multiple churches,[17] blogged about the dilemma of not knowing the best response, let alone the "right" one to supposed abuse.[18] Orrison described a situation

---

15. Child Welfare Information Gateway, "Clergy as Mandatory Reporters."

16. AG Financial Solutions, "Church Risk."

17. "About," *Grace for my Heart* (blog), https://graceformyheart.wordpress.com/about.

18. Orrison, "Pastors and Reporting," *Grace for my Heart* (blog), August 27, 2014,

that occurred during vacation Bible school: a girl from a family who was new to the church showed him her injured foot and told him that her mom had "hit her with a board." After much thought, he ultimately called child protective services. As a result, the girl was placed in foster care, the family went to court, and there was no further contact between the family and the church. [19] So what thoughts did he have while he was deciding what to do?

Orrison[20] listed the thoughts that went through his mind: was this event part of a pattern or a one-time event? Was it abuse or an accident? Did the girl do something to aggravate the mother? Would calling the police be a disproportionate response? Would getting involved possibly damage what appeared to him to be a family's new relationship with God? What more traumas would the girl and her family experience if he did call the authorities?

This list of doubts and questions could well be that of any Christian worker who is told by a child or an adult about his or her experience of sexual abuse. As Orrison traced through his thinking about the decision for or against calling the authorities, he identified several dilemmas that he had faced as pastor. Most of the dilemmas involved his making decisions in situations that he did not know whether he had the right or responsibility to choose the next steps in a process.

It is unfortunately true that the reason that many abusers avoid detection and appropriate consequences is that the people in charge hesitate. So why would they hesitate? They might not know enough to determine an appropriate response. Perhaps they care for or are on familiar terms with the alleged perpetrator: they know the person. Maybe they hesitate to go outside the church.

In an alternate approach,[21] Peacemaker Ministries believes that Christians should turn first to God before making use of legal authorities. The justification is provided in Matthew 5:23–24 and 18:15–20. In these biblical passages, Matthew presents processes for Christians to use in conflict situations with one another. These appear to be underlined by Paul in his letter to the Corinthian church (1 Cor 6:1–8) in which members who are involved in a lawsuit are said to have already been defeated.

---

https://graceformyheart.wordpress.com/2014/08/27/pastors-and-reporting.

19. Ibid., para 5–6.

20. Ibid., para. 8.

21. Oppenheimer, "Turn to Jesus."

So, how would this approach work? If a youth worker were a member of a church that used this decision process, a Christian worker—told of childhood sexual abuse in a context in which the abuser is identified, still living, and within the church—may avoid calling the appropriate authority.

It is important to keep in mind that *mediation* or any similar process can only occur between persons who are equal in power. For that reason, using a process such as the Peacemaker approach is a wrongful decision when one party is a child. This is also true even when the child is represented by a parent. Although a parent's power may appear to be equal to that of the alleged offender, a parent cannot be equally present in the mediation process because of the parent's attachment for this child.

If mediation processes are going to be followed by a church, it is critically important for that church to have great transparency in its self-presentation to potential members, so that its use of this process is known. Also, note that the use of this process does not protect the church from litigation.[22]

"Should I First Deal with the Victim or with the Perpetrator?"

It has been said[23] that if an error is to be made, it must be "made on the side of protecting the child." A conflict is at the heart of this barrier to response: who is prioritized—the victim or the offender?

What happens after abuse is discovered? Van Loon[24] details the "predictable arc" of the coverage of high-profile cases in which children had been abused by church leaders. The progression of responses is as follows:

1. First is *shock*, usually accompanied by a recital of the offender's outstanding achievements.

2. Next come *suspicions*: I always wondered if the offender were really as good as he seemed. I had my doubts, but I didn't feel I could say anything.

3. Finally, there is the loyalty-based *circling of the wagons* around the ministry that must go on despite the loss of the offender.

22. Howerton, "How Churches."

23. graceformyheart, August 28, 2014 (3:54 pm), reply to comment on Orrison, "Pastors and Reporting," *Grace for my Heart* (blog), August 27, 2014, https://graceformyheart.wordpress.com/2014/08/27/pastors-and-reporting.

24. Van Loon, "Voice of the Victims," para. 2.

Van Loon's point is critical: Nowhere is there any concern for the victim.[25] In publicized and unpublicized circumstances, it is noted[26] that the victim and the family too frequently are treated as outcasts by a church; they are blamed for somehow having caused the victimization and then told to *get over it*—as though the abuse were a trivial matter that can now be overlooked. In fact, traumatic abuse simply cannot be *gotten over* without assistance.[27]

We are reminded that a relational ministry[28] provides a committed adult who loves and cares for the person[29] who is being ministered to. If carried out in trust and genuine presence, the relationship will create momentum for the person to share deep secrets. How then should the minister respond? There must be a caring response—one that focuses solely on the victim—to help that hurting person. That response may be an assessment that a Christian professional counselor must be involved and then a referral to that person. Additionally, it is critical to have appropriate policies and procedures already in place.[30]

Then I Realized …

So what happened at the meeting that was described at the beginning of this chapter? After both my husband and I read our letters, the atmosphere was tense. Both pastors looked shocked. For several minutes, no one said anything. I went into that meeting with considerable preparation. I had prayed with friends; I had discussed the meeting at length with my therapist and my husband.

As I had expected, one pastor's first response was to apologize. I turned to him and said directly, "I do not accept your apology now. You are only apologizing because you know that's the *right* thing to do and because you feel bad. You haven't had time to consider what your actions have done to me, nor have you considered your own motivations and attitudes. I'll consider your apology at a future time." The meeting ended shortly after that exchange.

25. Ibid., para. 3.
26. Ann post, Jan 31, 2013, comment on Van Loon, "Voice of the Victims."
27. See previous discussion.
28. Zach, "Relational Youth Ministry."
29. In this blog post, that person is a youth. The person might be an adult as well.
30. This will be considered later in this chapter.

Several years after that meeting, I contacted my pastors and asked whether they would meet with me again. Before this second meeting had begun, we exchanged pleasantries while we made coffee.

When we sat down in the office, I began by saying that I wanted to bring them up to date on my own journey. Then I wanted to hear from each of them what their thoughts and feelings were in response to our first meeting. Since the time of our first meeting, God had brought me through difficult times, given me much insight, and guided many changes in my life. Therefore, I had many updates for them. I placed emphasis on the astonishing turns in my life and on God's grace in providing me with abundance and joy. One pastor told me how much joy it gave him to see me healed and whole.

The other pastor told me that he had avoided interacting with me after church because he hadn't wanted to do further damage by "saying the wrong thing." He acknowledged that my intentions had been clear to him when I was maneuvering around him during that coffee time with the hope that he would approach me and that he had deliberately avoided those contacts.

Then the pastor went deeper. He told me of his shame over our confrontation and of his great distress at his own actions. He had prayed, opened his heart to God, and realized that the reason for his not wanting to say something wrong was only a façade. His real reason for avoiding me had been that he was embarrassed. He didn't know what to say, and he was frightened of his feelings and of me. He talked about several recent incidents that involved responding to parishioners when my words in his mind helped him be a different person in challenging interactions.

I told him that I accepted his apology, and we prayed together. I hope that his journey will inspire you to begin your own journey by saying your first response, but then going deeper—accepting the truth of the second response and determining how that deeper response is a barrier to ministering to persons who had been sexually abused as children.

Toolkit

The tools in this chapter are for the companion to serve as an *advocate for the victim* in the larger culture—whether it is a church, a ministry, or an organization that ensures appropriate policies and procedures for prevention and reporting of childhood sexual abuse. The typical foundation for these polices or procedures in the secular world is *ethics*—a term that is typically not used in a Christian setting.

Ethics in the Secular World

Codes of ethical conduct are widely promulgated among professions that exist to serve the public. In fact, the sign of a profession is the adoption of a code of ethics, the development of a process to educate the members in the ethical code, and the creation of another process to sanction members for failure to adhere to that code. Thus we expect that our doctors, our lawyers, our accountants, and even our funeral home directors to have and to follow a code of ethics.

An ethics code may be based on one of three philosophical systems—deontology, utilitarianism, or principle-based ethics. The systems are as follows:

1. A code of ethics may be based on *deontology*, which is a system that focuses on our duty to those we serve. Our most moral actions occur when we fulfill our duties or responsibilities. This philosophy under-lies *Good Samaritan laws*, which are there to protect passersby who encounter people whom they presume to be in need of assistance, such as someone who is injured. Good Samaritan laws encourage by-standers to deal with an emergency without their having to fear arrest or facing lawsuits or other legal consequences. This is *deontological* in that the helper is attempting to fulfill a duty to assist someone out of moral or civic responsibility.

2. Another philosophical system is *utilitarianism*. In contrast to deontol-ogy, the moral value of an action within *utilitarianism* is determined by the consequences of the act on everyone who is involved. For ex-ample, people who decide to participate in a clinical trial of a new drug or medical procedure go through *informed consent*—a process that is centered on the notion that what is *risked* in any procedure or drug is *outweighed* by the increased knowledge that is to be *gained* by that clinical trial. The objective is maximizing the benefit or good for the greatest number of people.

3. Finally, in *principle-based ethics*, certain values (*principles*) are seen as central to the most ethical choice. Some principles may be those of

- *nonmaleficence*—do no intentional harm or do not engage in actions that risk harm to others;
- *beneficence*—commit to promote human welfare and growth; and
- *justice*—treat all persons equally (that is, fairness or impartiality).

Thus, within a principle-based system of ethics, the most ethical choice is that which upholds the principles the most strongly.

Ethics in a Christian Setting

Rarely does a faith-based organization require staff to sign an agreement to adhere to a code of ethics. Doctrinal standards are virtually universal. However, a code of ethics—one that is meant to promote best practices (*aspirational code*) or to govern behavior (*standards*)—is rare.

The National Association of Evangelicals[31] developed and released an ethics code for pastors in 2012. Church leaders were asked to sign and uphold this code. The code was intended to cross denominational lines and thus focused on five primary ethical guidelines: pursue integrity; be trustworthy; seek purity; embrace accountability; and facilitate fairness.[32]

Although it would seem that these five *guidelines*—not specific rules or even descriptions of infractions—would be universally received, that was not the situation. Although some pastors signed the code, other pastors refused and indicated that their behavior was predicated only on teachings in the Bible and others argued against a code altogether.

The reasons put forth by those arguing against the code of ethics are remarkably similar to what Morton[33] found. In a study that examined why policies and procedures to prevent and respond to child sexual abuse were not in place, participants gave the following reasons: *resistance* and *fear of offending people*.

It is instructive to set these reactions against Paul's instructions to Timothy for his church—instructions which are not doctrinal but rather concern pastoral behavior. Paul exhorted Timothy to keep his focus on the gospel (1 Tim 1:3–17), know the qualifications for deacons (1 Tim 3:1–13), be alert to those who will abandon the true faith and follow false teachings

31. "NAE Releases."
32. National Association of Evangelicals, "Code."
33. Morton, "Church Leaders' Understanding."

(1 Tim 4:1–5), serve effectively as the leader/pastor (1 Tim 4:6–15), and treat correctly a variety of persons such as widows in need and slaves (1 Tim 5:1–21; 6:1–2).

Why might persons in the church protest against policies and procedures that are meant to keep children safe? The most basic explanation is that people avoid anxiety. We reduce anxiety by avoiding situations that make us anxious. If that is not possible, we *avoid* the situation by distorting, transforming, or otherwise changing it. If we believe that we need to protect the children in our church, that belief must admit the potential of someone whom we know being an abuser. That potential suggests a failure that is anxiety provoking. If faith is not *enough* to keep people from offending, then what is? Our own faith then trembles.

Cornelius Plantinga, a Reformed theologian, speaks to what can be called *the contemporary slippage in the acknowledgement of sin*. As a society, we prefer not to have brakes and curbs on our behavior. This includes in the church. Christians have been very willing to consider certain types of sexual sins, but have been less willing to acknowledge childhood abuse. Christians were less willing to speak publically regarding other types of personal failures, such as use of pornography, but are now more willing to do so. It remains to be seen whether churches will be courageous enough to put forward child protection policies and procedures.

There is an additional system of ethics—*virtue ethics*. The system should resonate with any Christian who wants to *walk uprightly*. As the Old Testament prophet Micah said, "And what does the Lord require of you but to do justly, to love kindness and mercy, and to humble yourself and walk humbly with your God" (Mic 6:8). This system of ethics is based not on rules, standards, principles, or results but rather on the qualities of the decision maker.

Virtue ethics is concerned with qualities. Examples of such qualities or *virtues* are integrity, dedication to justice, fairness, courage, honesty, and generosity. Virtues such as these enable us to become ethical persons. However, these virtues do not simply *show up* when an ethical decision is needed, because the very act of *perceiving* a situation as an *ethical dilemma* is itself an ethical action. Rather, these virtues are *habits* for the good—actions that need to be repeated so many times that they become characteristic of a person under all circumstances.

An additional component of *virtue ethics* is that they embody a commitment to living within community. Unfortunately in today's complex society, even people who are well-meaning and fully informed disagree on the best solution within a particular community when they are faced with decisions that require a solution.

The following two sections will highlight two types of policies and procedures with regard to childhood sexual abuse. The first will be preventing abuse and the second, confronting existing abuse.

Policies and Procedures to Prevent Abuse from Occurring

The following discussion is taken from Model Policies[34] that is disseminated by the Church Pension Group in partnership with the Nathan Network. These policies define a *child* as under age twelve and a *youth* as ages twelve to eighteen.[35] The safeguard to prevent harm from occurring should be developed by the church or organization in five areas as follows:

- Screening and selection of volunteers and employees—this includes a criminal background check, an individual interview, complete reference check, and sexual offender registry check.

- Education and training requirements—this includes education and training in child abuse prevention and reporting.

- Monitoring and supervision of programs—this includes the presence of persons trained to determine that safeguards are being followed.

- General conduct—this term concerns conduct such as hazing, transportation issues, and avoidance of the appearance of favoritism.

- Careful consideration of privacy—for example, not meeting alone with children behind closed doors.

Policies That Confront Existing Abuse

Reporting abuse is governed by state law. Thus, any policy or procedure must comply with the laws of the state as well as any policies of the denomination or parent organization. In general, a report must be made to the appropriate state authorities—most typically, a local child protective service, a hotline, or law enforcement agency. It is critical to remember that investigation of the alleged abuse belongs to that agency and that those

34. Applewhite et al., "Model Policies."
35. Ibid., 3.

in the agency are solely responsible for determining the factuality of the report. However, a parallel report should be made to the relevant church authority.

The Child Welfare Information Gateway[36] contains extensive information on how to protect children as well as provides a series of reports. Most relevant to this chapter is the report on *Clergy as Mandatory Reporters* that can be found there. There are also a series of helpful publications about how the child welfare system works (e.g., what happens after a report is "screened in" or what happens in substantiated cases).

How should an organization deal with the event of a founded report of abuse? Having a perpetrator simply disappear—leaving the victim and family to suffer in the wake of rumor and innuendo—is simply wrong. No matter how difficult, there must be transparency in the congregation, prayer for and attention to the victim, prayer for and attention to the perpetrator, and a reconsideration of the adequacy of the screening/hiring/monitoring systems in place. An advisory committee might be named to review those systems to avoid the appearance of a conflict of interest. It is essential that all actions be discussed with the victim and family before they occur. It is possible the victim and family will decide to leave the church, or they might stay. However, resources must be put in place to support them in the immediate aftermath of the event, and in later times as well, if the victim and family continue to remain with the church.

Case: Trisha

Trisha is a recent college graduate, who is eager to begin her new job as a children's programming coordinator for your church. You know that Trisha has felt God's calling in this area for a long time. Her college double major was recreational services and theology. During her first week, Trisha receives training in the church computer system, which includes how to reserve space in the church. She also meets with church staff to hear their expectations for children's programming—an area of concern to many of them because the number of participating children has fallen significantly over the past few years. In fact, the previous coordinator was encouraged to find another position, because parents reported that he didn't really seem enthusiastic about his work. Trisha had no opportunity to meet Peter, the

36. A service of the Children's Bureau, Administration for Children and Families, US Department of Health and Family Services, https://www.childwelfare.gov.

previous coordinator, who left suddenly to work for another church in the denomination in a nearby city.

Trisha dives into her work with enthusiasm. She continues several previous programs and also creates new ones. Her excitement and exuberant love for Jesus attracts many children, and the numbers of children begin to grow. This change is welcomed by church administrative staff. She is creative, she has excellent ideas for incorporating new media, and her first year performance review was quite positive.

Trisha notices that a coworker's child, Mia, doesn't appear to really participate in events. Mia is there because her mom works alongside Trisha, but Mia hangs back from games and activities. She is not oppositional at all, just withdrawn. Finally, Trisha summons up the courage to ask her coworker whether Mia is having some difficulties outside the church, such as at school. Her coworker tells her that Mia over the past year has become increasingly withdrawn in school as well as at home. The coworker took Mia to their doctor who gave her a complete physical. Mia is healthy, so her mother and doctor decided that Mia must be "going through a phase."

One night, the coworker was unable to stay for the evening's activities. Trisha is asked to give Mia a ride home. In the car, Trisha engages Mia in conversation. Trisha says that she has noticed that Mia seems unhappy and asks whether there is anything that Trisha can do to help. Mia responds by crying and says that she doesn't want to go to church anymore, but she can't tell anyone why. Trisha tries harder to persuade Mia to provide the reason. Trisha finally promises that she won't tell anyone if Mia says why. Mia says that Peter, who had had Trisha's job before, touched Mia sexually on two occasions. They arrive at Mia's house; Mia reminds Trisha that "she promised" and gets out of the car. Trisha sits in the car, stunned. Then she thinks that at least he is gone and that they won't have to deal with him anymore.

1. What stands out to you in this case? What emotional reactions are you having?

2. What questions would you want to ask Trisha? What about Mia?

3. Trisha promised Mia that Trisha would not tell. Can she keep that promise? Why or why not?

4. What are your concerns about the larger denomination? What additional information would you like to know about denominational policies and procedures?

5. What should Trisha do?

4

Is the Church Complicit?

Chapter Objectives

1. Honestly label the deliberately wrongful actions of powerful persons with respect to childhood sexual abuse.

2. Become committed to the development of a theology of healthy Christian sexuality.

3. Learn how to help victims establish healthy boundaries between themselves and others.

4. Learn how to help victims develop positive identities.

> For once you were full of darkness, but now you have light from the Lord. So live as people of light! For this light within you produces only what is good and right and true. Carefully determine what pleases the Lord. Take no part in the worthless deeds of evil and darkness; instead, expose them. It is shameful even to talk about the things that ungodly people do in secret. But their evil intentions will be exposed when the light shines on them, for the light makes everything visible. (Eph 5: 8–14 NLT)

God and I walk down the alley. God has a candle

But I wish he didn't.

Roaches scurry at the edge of the light.

Rats cross our paths.

Garbage is piled on both sides.

Buildings are dirty and worn.

I'd rather not see where I am walking because I am afraid.

And as the alley goes on, and on,

I am terrified.

IN THE PREVIOUS CHAPTER, possible responses of persons who hear about childhood sexual abuse were considered. Those possible responses were

- the belief—or more accurately, the *assumption*—that the hearer would know about childhood sexual abuse if it had been happening in his or her church;

- a wrongful understanding of *memory of traumatic events*;

- confusion over the necessary responses, such as *mandatory reporting*, to a report of childhood sexual abuse; and

- concern over whether the victim or the alleged offender should be prioritized in responding to the allegations.

These responses are understandable, in that they reflect a lack of knowledge, which can be remedied, or confusion over legal and church policies, which can be clarified. However, the current chapter examines deliberately wrongful responses to childhood sexual abuse, along with potential reasons why these responses occur. These reasons are malevolent and perverted. However, they must be considered, because a healing response from the collective church to the collective victim population can only change when the darkness is confronted by the truth.

The Dark Shadows of Denial

This chapter is about *denial*. Denial can be personal—a person shutting off necessary acknowledgement of responsibility for a problem, its solution, or both. Yet denial can also be corporate, collective, and even systemic. The church is not immune from collective and systemic denial.

How an organization—including Christian organizations so inclined to denial—engages in systemic denial[1] is described as follows:

- First, the organization will do anything to minimize exposure of an embarrassing failure: it will cover up reports or fail to provide transparency regarding them.

- Next, the organization will marginalize accusers by defaming and denying them and by suggesting that a victim is exaggerating or overstating the problem: marginalizing Christian accusers often happens by accusing them of ill-defined *sin* to reduce their credibility.

- Last, the organization will engage in a variety of actions to manipulate public opinion: it will repress negative coverage and produce positive coverage (e.g., obtain support from prominent Christians) and will essentially *redefine* the accusation.

According to Cozzens, denial reveals a predisposition to somehow altering *reality* in face of a threat:

> While denial and minimization are common and understandable foibles evident in mischievous children seeking to avoid parental disciplining, as well as adults defending themselves against embarrassing mistakes or scandalous behaviors threatening loss of face or more serious consequences, they unmask a fundamental inclination to defend one's sense of self-worth or corporate-worth with often torturous bendings and twistings of reality. The conventional wisdom that denial often makes bad situations worse holds little currency when individuals or institutions are threatened and the dynamics of denial kick in.[2]

Social media in 2014[3] was awash with collective denial from the evangelical church about childhood sexual abuse. To illustrate the presence, scope, and impenetrability of this problem, three examples will follow.

1. Orrison, "The Organization Apologizes," *Grace for my Heart* (blog), March 27, 2015, www.graceformyheart.wordpress.com/2015/03/27/the-narcissistic-organization-apologizes.

2. Cozzens, *Sacred Silence*, 26.

3. This was at the time of writing this book.

Article by Former Youth Minister

The first example is that of the online publication[4] in 2014 by *Christianity Today* in the *Leadership Journal* of an article that had been written by a former youth minister about his "easy trip"[5] from his former position to his current incarceration in prison. The person describes his own personal achievements at his ministry—growing numbers of students, mission trips, and ministry success—and other accomplishments that had led to his admitted self-admiration. Also detailed was his frustration with what he viewed as a growing lack of attention from his wife, which led to his seeking a relationship outside marriage. This relationship began, he reports, as a friendship which led to an affair. When the affair was discovered by his wife, their marriage and his job ended. The crux of the matter is that while this situation is unfortunately common when it involves two adults, his so-called affair was actually a sexual relationship with one of his youth group members, a *child* in the eyes of the law.

Reader response to this article was immense and aggressive but not solely against the now felon. The critical voices were also directed against the journal editors who did not understand that publishing this article gave voice and support to a child predator. Clearly the writer of the article was still not ready to acknowledge his abusing a minor child, and thus described the sexual relationship as a *consensual* affair that ended his marriage. The reality that this event was *sexual abuse* was denied by the editors in their selection of his words for publication. Here are some of the many comments[6] that had been posted online at the time:

> I am shocked and horrified to read this author's assertion that he had an "extramarital affair" with a teen. It is not an "affair" when he is in a position of power and authority over her—it is abuse. It is sexual abuse, and it is abuse of power and authority.

> This article is in LEADERSHIP JOURNAL and its focus there is on LEADERS within the church. This article shows the downward slippery slope when a leader has zero accountability, a high amount of admiration, and no reality check.

4. The original article has since been removed. See http://www.christianitytoday.com/le/2014/june-online-only.

5. Name Withheld, "My Easy Trip." The original article is no longer available. The version from the Internet Archives has an editorial introduction and revised language.

6. Comments along with the article have been subsequently removed.

How many editors did this article go through? Were they all men? Where was any concern for the child (though the word child was conveniently never used in the whole post)? The author shows no concern for how his actions may have affected her or her family.

So what happened? Rather than acknowledging its own guilt, *Christianity Today* embarked on a process that can only be described as *institutional denial*. The editors first deleted over sixty comments. They then edited[7] the article. Finally, they removed the article. Now in place of the article is their response, a portion of which is as follows: "The fact that we published [the original article], its deficiencies; and the way its deficiencies illuminate our own lack of insight and foresight is a matter of record. . . ."[8]

Sovereign Grace Ministries

The second example is the lingering problems of Sovereign Grace Ministries, an association of Reformed Church plants. There is currently a lawsuit that alleges church leaders covered up child abuse by asking parents not to report child sexual abuse by church personnel to the proper authorities and to further require victims to forgive their abusers in a personal supervised encounter.

The response of many in positions of Christian leadership has been to support Sovereign Grace, that is, to "withhold judgment until the facts have been determined." The history of this situation, almost two years to date, is detailed by Etttinger[9] and others. As Ettinger notes, now that one pastor has been convicted for criminal sexual abuse of children while in Sovereign Grace and another pastor has confessed under oath that he knew of abuse but hadn't reported it, "people are paying attention" and the "fringe of New Calvinism is unraveling and the more it unravels, the uglier the underbelly looks."[10]

7. Name Withheld, "My Easy Trip." See the version from the Internet Archives website.

8. Shelley and Smith, "From Youth Minister to Felon."

9. Ettinger, "A Guide"; see also the *Wartburg Watch*, thewartburgwatch.com/category/sovereign-grace-ministries.

10. Ettinger, "A Guide," para. 20, 22.

The Duggars

The third episode is the series of revelations concerning Josh Duggar, the oldest son of the Duggar family—widely known from their reality TV show and from their prominent role in conservative Christian circles. In May 2015, *USA Today*[11] and other media outlets publicized Josh's acknowledgement that he had been investigated for molesting underage girls during his teen years in Arkansas. Those alleged victims included four of his sisters.

At that time, Josh confessed to his father, who waited a year before contacting police. The police report, which had been supposedly destroyed, was given to *InTouch* magazine. Prominent Christians, including a candidate for President of the United States,[12] supported the family in the wake of the media reports. Defending their actions taken at the time of the abuse, the parents indicated that they had not considered the sexual touching to be abuse—"it wasn't rape"—and that Josh had obtained counseling.

The counseling was allegedly from the Institute of Basic Life Principles's Little Rock Training Center. This facility was developed and run by Bill Gothard, who himself had been forced to step down from a leadership role because of charges of sexual abuse. Perhaps most telling is that two of the sisters who had been molested by their brother came to his defense. They appeared in an interview with Fox News anchor Megyn Kelly. Jessa, one of the sisters, said in the interview: "I do want to speak up in his defense against people who are calling him a child molester or a pedophile or a rapist."[13]

Denial is a problem markedly faced by a particular type of church organization. In today's world, megachurches[14] have come to play a prominent role in American religion. These churches combine aspects of the entertainment world with social media, an emphasis on young adults, and seeker-friendly theology and rituals. Such large churches gained prominence in the 1980s and the 1990s when their growth was fueled by a combination of technological advances with a growing disinterest in traditional, liturgically based worship services and a consumer-driven culture that was focused on what can be gained as a church member (e.g., programming for children).

11. Puente, "Duggars Reeling."
12. Jackson, "Defends Duggar."
13. Ohlheiser, "Jill, Jessa Say."
14. Thumma and Travis, *Beyond Megachurch Myths*.

A megachurch typically has one leader who serves as minister, pastor, and overseer of a large staff of paid and volunteer adults. The image of this leader is critical to the growth of the church, because the leader is essentially the *brand product*. Thus, personality features of megachurch pastors typically include charisma, ability to influence, and status in the local community. It can be an immense temptation to use this power for personal gain, influence, and respect.

In a for-profit business of this size, there would be layers of administration, legal accountability, supervision, and monitoring. However, both megachurches and very large Christian organizations lack these layers. That may be due to finances, because persons with legal backgrounds or evaluation responsibilities would need to be salaried employees. It may also be due to a misbelief that because we are "all Christians," there is no need for such monitoring. Because of the immense size of these churches, much can be hidden—which should make us leery and watchful. Moreover, Starks[15] argues that this combination of factors—size, lack of monitoring and oversight, overtrusting—creates an organizational climate in which sexual misconduct including extramarital affairs, use of sex workers, child sexual abuse, and sexual harassment can occur unchecked.

Just by its nature, *denial* is an experience that we are extremely uncomfortable examining closely. Not only do we deny, *we deny that we deny*—a *misplaced confidence* in which we fool ourselves that we aren't being fooled.[16] However, denying that something exists when we know it does—and continuing our everyday life as if it didn't exist—causes guilt and fear. When the fear of confronting reality is so great, the act of denial is *transformed* into a positive action—*supporting* something or someone else. An example is denial that is transformed into intense loyalty to a person or to an organization. The reality in any organization is that people's personalities play critical roles in organizational function. Neither the church nor any ministry is immune from this reality. When powerful people are perceived as being under attack, they are often supported first by people whose self-worth is dependent on the approval of others.

Then, personal experiences—such as being abused by a member of a church staff within this type of environment—that do not match the *culture* of the institution are redefined. An example of this reversal is Jessa's

---

15. Starks, *Sexual Misconduct*.

16. Freyd and Birrell, *Blind to Betrayal*.

characterizing the examination of her brother's actions as *revictimization*[17] of the Duggar family. Other people then are drawn in—thus reinforcing those who are in denial.

Last, the *troublemakers*—disloyal persons who refuse to participate in denial—are shunned, silenced, and shamed. Take, for example, what had happened at Bob Jones University.[18] Of the victims who reported their sexual abuse to university staff, only 7.6 percent were encouraged to report the abuse to the police. In contrast, 47 percent were actively told not to do so and 55 percent reported that the university's attitude to their abuse reports was "blaming." Women, for example, were invited to "confess what they had done to entice the abuser" such as wearing revealing clothing.[19]

Even more tragically in cases of child sexual abuse, perpetrators have used a religious defense to justify their actions.[20] Discovery of sexual abuse—rather than provoking the appropriate involvement of authorities and necessary attention to the victim—has triggered a deeply perverted process in which the child is required to confess his or her own *sin* in being sexually abused, even to an entire congregation.[21] This "confession" within a church context violently repeats the abuse, puts the child at the highest possible risk of psychological disintegration, and increases the likelihood of the child abandoning his or her faith at the earliest possible opportunity.

Breaking a Child's Will

My life is a fractured fairy tale.

The white horse was actually carrying the Black Sorcerer

And Death stood beneath the castle window rather than the handsome prince.

And the wicked witch really was wicked

Not just sort of.

And there were no fairy godmothers around to fix the damage.

Mortification has a long tradition within the Catholic Church. The theological framework is that human beings because of original sin are

17. Jackson, "Defends Duggar."
18. Michaelson, "Rooted in Theology."
19. Ibid., para. 3.
20. Vieth and Tchividjian, "Abuser Has a Bible."
21. "Shattered Faith," ABC News video. See also Goldberg et al., "Forced Confession."

in a state of "disorder" or sin. *Mortification*, either physical or mental, is viewed as a means by which self-sanctification can be promoted through the reduction of self. Mortification helps us (Christians) armor ourselves "against faults in present and future by weakening our striving for lust, the source of our sins"[22]

Body mortification by *withholding* (e.g., sleep or food deprivation) or by *administering* (e.g., self-flagellation or wearing painful apparel such as a hair shirt) was practiced individually. This practice was a means by which the individual *killed off* (mortified) the sinful self.

There is a direct link between this theology of mortification and current theories of authoritarian parenting that promote "breaking a child's will." A popular but controversial parenting manual, *To Train up a Child*,[23] advocates the use of spanking a child with PVC pipe[24] in order to reduce rebelliousness and induce behavioral conformity. The Pearls put forward an overall parenting approach that focuses on obedience and conformity among children. This is an *authoritarian* approach. The parent is the authority, the child is the subject of that authority, and children are submissive to that authority. For this parenting approach, the source that is cited is Proverbs 23 in the Bible. There is also a significant appeal to tradition. Supporters of authoritarian parenting note that they *themselves* were raised by parents who used such methods. The Pearls point to the "wisdom of those who have gone before."[25]

Current scholarship on child maltreatment provides us with information about the consequences of authoritarian parenting practices. These include practices sanctioned by Christian authors and speakers. Examples of such practices and their advocates are hitting a child with PVC pipe or a rod (the Pearls) or forcibly putting hot pepper sauce into a child's mouth (Focus on the Family).[26] Note that the latter practice is called *hot saucing* and is considered a biblical approach to discipline.

For the purposes of this chapter, *spanking* is relatively mild physical punishment using an open hand on the child's bottom either clothed or

---

22. In Adolphe Tanquerey's *Handbook of Ascetical and Mystical Theology*, published as *Précis de théologie ascétique et mystique* in 1923 in Paris by the Société de s. Jean l'Évangéliste, Desclée et Cie (quoted in Bosgraaf, "Breaking the Will"). For another translation, see also Tanquerey, "Spiritual Life," 362.

23. Pearl and Pearl, *To Train Up a Child*.

24. Bayer, Alicia, "Another Couple," para. 3, 5.

25. Pearl and Pearl, "Who is No Greater Joy?"

26. Whelchel, *Creative Correction*, 149. See also Buckholtz, "Feeling the Heat."

unclothed. *Corporal punishment* includes hitting the child with an object that results in bruises or welts, slapping the child on the face, and forcing the child to drink vinegar or to receive hot pepper sauce in the mouth. *Highly injurious child abuse* is defined as resulting in lacerations and/or broken bones, often using extended physical restraint.

One outcome of research[27] on discipline is that *spanking* does not appear to have negative outcomes—with the exception of its use on *older children*, that is, children who are above school age. Use of corporal punishment,[28] however, is associated with several negative outcomes:

- Children become more aggressive and antisocial; in other words, extended use of corporal punishment has an effect that is the *opposite* of what the parents had intended.

- When parents use corporal punishment, the likelihood of the punishment crossing into abuse increases over time.

- When children receive corporal punishment, they experience anxiety and depression and report feeling separated from their parents.

Corporal punishment creates an erosion of the family structure that extends over multiple generations and results in maintaining child maltreatment. A family system that relies on corporal punishment has several characteristics. Parents are less physically and emotionally affectionate toward their children and more emotionally distant. This emotional distance is often an intentional means to increase conformity, in that children experience parents' love and affection as conditional on their obedience. Scholars have also established that parents who are authoritarian in their practice experience less enjoyment of parenting.[29]

A family that values total conformity to parents, that frightens children into submissive obedience, and which prides itself on complete lack of individual expression may appear to conform to scriptural dictates. Yet, that legalistic dictate may be covering a dark heresy—the belief that God alone does not have the ability to bring children into a saving relationship with him without parental assistance. Thus parents must break the child's will, so that God is more able to save the child.

Approaches that attempt to break the child's will do not in and of themselves cause childhood sexual abuse. Rather, they rely on a philosophy

27. This has been established by many scholars; see Ferguson, "Meta-analytic Review."
28. Gershoff, "More Harm."
29. Howes et al., "Maltreating."

that denies that the child has rights. The healthy development of children—understood correctly—is that children do have *rights* in the sense that they are separate from the adults (their parents) and should be able to increasingly make separate decisions. For example, a toddler might choose between one of two outfits or which three toys to bring to bed. An older child might express interest in a topic that he or she wishes to be included in a homeschooling curriculum, such as *dinosaurs* or *medieval history*. A young adult may choose a career that is not to his parents' liking, but that matches his or her skills and interests.

The relationship of authoritarian parenting approaches to childhood sexual abuse is the denial of the child's own appropriate emotional needs and desires, the substitution of the parents' own needs and desires, and the failure to recognize and honor the boundary of the child as he or she grows and matures. These situations can lead to expressions of control that become sexualized and then sexually abusive.

Subjugation of Women

Another darkness underlying the sexual abuse of children is the belief that women are inherently evil, that they should be subjugated by any and all means, and that such subjugation is *scriptural*. Let's look at two examples from the Bible. One is from the Old Testament:

> To the woman he said, "I will greatly increase your pains in child-bearing; with pain you will give birth to children. Your desire will be for your husband and he will rule over you." (Gen 3:16 NIV)

The other is from the New Testament:

> I also want the women to dress modestly, with decency and propriety, adorning themselves, not with elaborate hairstyles or gold or pearls or expensive clothes, but with good deeds, appropriate for women who profess to worship God. A woman should learn in quietness and full submission. I do not permit a woman to teach or to assume authority over a man; she must be quiet. (1 Tim 2:9–12 NIV).

Old Testament

On the Genesis verse, Ellicott's[30] comments are as follows. The serpent was cursed as the primary (first) sinner. Although the woman was not *cursed*, she was "punished as next in guilt" in two ways. In her role as a mother, she would experience the pains of childbirth. In her role as a wife, she had been a prime actor in yielding to the temptation and the man had yielded to her entreating. From now on, she would be subject to the husband.

Thus, the man would have the power in the relationship. A social organization with a set of beliefs that men have the right to power, have control over women and children, and have the right to enforce that control (including physical means) is a *patriarchy*.

In a patriarchy, the relationship between a man and a woman—and between man and children—is characterized by power and submission; men have power over women, who in turn submit to this power. The relationship of this social organization to sexual abuse was stated most strongly by Heggen: "As long as patriarchy is supported and male dominance is considered the appropriate model for human relationships, sexual abuse of children will continue."[31]

New Testament

The New Covenant[32] reveals an indwelling by the Spirit, which leaves out no one. Earthly distinctions of rich and poor, Jew and Gentile, male and female, slave and free are abolished.[33] Jesus exemplified a return to God's original intention for relationships in which Eve was seen as Adam's *helper*. The word[34] that is used for that term is also employed to speak of *God* (Ps 70:5 and Ps 121:2). Rather than a *subordinate*, a *helper* is someone who works alongside the person being helped on a *collegial* basis.

What seems to contradict this radical reordering of humanity are the *limiting passages* of 1 Corinthians 14 and 1 Timothy 2, which are used to offer additional argument for the subjugation of women. However, Fee[35] pro-

---

30. Ellicott, ed., *Old Testament*, 25; also Ellicott, *Commentary* (Genesis 3:16).
31. Heggen, *Sexual Abuse*, 87.
32. Viola, "Role," 3.
33. Ibid.
34. Noted by Van Leeuwen, *Gender and Grace*, 42.
35. Fee, *Timothy*.

vides the relevant context: Paul's letter to Timothy appears to be addressing a situation in which the church is being led astray by some of its own elders. Fee also notes that 1 Timothy and 2 Timothy suggest that false teachers had found particular ground among some women—apparently young widows—who had opened their houses to the false teachers and perhaps had helped spread their teachings. By instructing the women to learn quietly, Timothy is being encouraged to control false teaching within the church, both by the false teaching elders and by the women. Rather than having the women foolishly debate or instruct, they are to learn quietly. In a parallel vein, Paul in verse 8 instructs the men to pray without engaging in angry disputing, particularly about and with the false teachers.

Theology and the Bible

Stackaruck[36] addresses how Christians use theology to misuse the Bible. He points to theology as the study of the Bible's life-giving and transforming truths. Christians figuratively *kill* theology when they engage in three approaches to the Bible.

- First, these Christians go to Scripture to hear and to have *supported what they already know*. They have "hermeneutical strategies" for the hard passages; for difficult things in the Bible, there are well-rehearsed excuses.[37] The damaging result of this approach is that Scriptures will eventually stop speaking new truths and providing challenges.

- Another approach is to read the Bible *only to find certain answers*. The questions that aren't asked then become questions that aren't answered but that need asking.

- The last approach is to assume that the Bible teaches *only one system of theology*. The Bible becomes divisive when *one* way of understanding becomes *the way* and when those who disagree become wrong.

Girls and Women are the Cause of their Abuse

Another deeply perverted notion is that women—and even girls—are the cause of their abuse. The movements that are variously titled *sexual purity*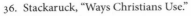

---

36. Stackaruck, "Ways Christians Use."
37. Ibid., para. 8.

or *modesty culture* teach that female bodies are the source of sinful lust.[38] If men sin sexually, it is because women have *caused* men to lust and then sin. The woman who is the victim is as much at fault as the offender.

Growing up in our culture, both men and women experience the hypersexuality of media messages. In the church, there are messages concerning sexuality as well. The most obvious one and the most clear-cut prohibition is that sexual relations are reserved for married, heterosexual couples. Unfortunately, there is widespread confusion around other areas of healthy, *biblical* sexuality. Here are some examples of that confusion:

- Single Christians are not sexual.
- Sexual purity is only a problem when you are single.
- Sexual purity is only about whether or not you are having sex.
- Your temptations define who you are.

With regard to confusions, there are resources to help Christians truly accept sexuality as a *good gift* from God and one that is to be embraced appropriately throughout life.[39] A healthy view of human sexuality embraces both men and women, promotes consent and equality within sexual relationships, and shows how healthy sexuality is grounded within authentic relationships.

Unfortunately false beliefs become ingrained, which in turn leads to the boundary violation of men blaming women for the men's own attitudes, actions, and sin.

- Thinking about sex is *lust*, and lust is as bad as having sex.
- Female bodies are the *source* of sinful lust.
- Men have sexual desire, *good* women do not.
- *No outlets* for sexual feelings are acceptable until marriage.

These statements reflect views that can lead to the belief that victims contribute to their own assault. This is a culture-wide attitude that begins with the historic legal stance that victims be physically and visibly wounded in order for them to prove rape and currently expresses itself in the "What were you doing?" questions that are posed to victims of rape.

---

38. See Schaeffer, "Truth about Christian" and Kylie, "Body Shame."

39. See Balswick and Balswick, *Authentic Human*; Slattery, "Five Lies"; Wilson, *Unburdened.*

Institutional Betrayal

As noted by Freyd,[40] *betrayal trauma* arises from the belief that the abuse perpetrated by persons in close relationship to the victim is a greater violation of trust. Scholarly research reveals that betrayal trauma is associated with greater impairment among victims, which includes increased rates of psychiatric disorders such as depression, post-traumatic stress disorder, and dissociation.

Why does abuse within a relationship cause greater harm? Freyd[41] notes that most victims are constrained to stay within that relationship. Children remain in an abusing family, athletes remain on teams with abusing coaches, and young people continue in youth groups with abusing pastors. When victims are bonded to their abuser, coping strategies must allow the relationship to exist, and so victims deny the abuse, even to the point of become *blind* to the trauma.

Smith and Freyd[42] analyzed institutions that foster *institutional betrayal*. First, these institutions create a strong sense of trust among their members, trust in the institution itself, and a degree of dependence on the institution. Families are the primary such institution, but members of the armed services speak to the degree of attachment that is created by serving together in combat.

Second, members of these institutions fail to recognize that their responses to victimized individuals are negatively influenced by their lack of awareness of appropriate institutional responses. An example was the practice of relocating abusing Catholic priests to other parishes rather than the appropriate reporting to authorities and removal of the priests from active ministry.

It is possible, then, to understand the total *disconnect* between victims of sexual abuse and high-placed members of a church who publically declare that they will support the alleged offender "until all the facts are in." This response demonstrates an appalling lack of appreciation for the situation of the known victim, and more importantly, unknown victims who hear of the response. This response puts victims on notice that their reports are unsubstantial, disbelieved, and disregarded. The victims within

---

40. Freyd, *Betrayal Trauma*, 9–10.
41. Ibid.
42. Smith and Freyd, "Dangerous Safe"; "Institutional."

the Sovereign Grace[43] situation were likely deeply harmed when prominent evangelicals gave public support to the ministry.

Rachel Held Evans[44] speaks of the abusive theology of deserved tragedy, which contributes to wrongful responses to tragic and traumatic events:

> What's worse than the world seeing Christians disagree with one another is the world seeing Christians remain silent when their own go on TV and tell the parents of children lost in a tornado that those children and their families got what they deserved. What's worse than the world seeing Christians disagree with one another is the world seeing Christians remain silent and supportive when their own are accused of multiple counts of child abuse and appeal to the first amendment to try and avoid investigation. What's worse than the world seeing Christians disagree with one another is the world seeing Christians perpetuate an abusive theology that teaches people that whatever abuse they are suffering, whatever pain they are enduring, whatever violence they have been subjected to, is deserved and perpetrated by [God].[45]

When an institution fails to respond immediately and affirmatively to victims, likely one or more of the following characteristics is present:

- First is a failure to prevent abuse. As the previous chapter noted, in a study of knowledge about and response to childhood sexual abuse, many church staff endorsed certain policies and procedures as necessary; but they also reported failure to follow and adhere to them.

- Second, abusive contexts are normalized. *Too close* relationships without boundaries had been redefined as *mentoring* or *pastoral care*. Allowing contact outside the appropriate boundaries of the youth group, church camp, or team fosters ambiguity among youth about how much contact is too much and thus great confusion over the intentions of the potential abuser.

- Third, reporting is difficult and the process is harmful. How many church members would feel comfortable informing the pastor that the youth minister is sexually abusing youth group members? There must be a neutral person to receive and respond to such reports in church contexts.

43. See chapter 4.
44. Evans, "Abusive Theology."
45. Ibid., para. 22.

- Last, the culture and prestige of the institution is maintained by covering up the report, by misinformation, and by the punishment or shunning of victims and other reporters.

During my lifetime, the church as a collective has effectively responded to challenges that I would not have thought would occur. I have heard sermons about addiction to pornography, about lust, about gambling, about financial failures, and about many other problems that in my childhood the church would never have been mentioned. I believe that the church can—with God's help and in humility—come out of the shadows and confront the challenge of changing the culture from one of denial and betrayal to one of acceptance and healing.

How can this change occur? As Smith and Freyd[46] recommend, every church and Christian organization needs to carefully review its own institutional history, culture, and any occurrence of past abuse events. *Transparency* to all members is the goal of this review.

The next step is *valuing reporting*. Institutions can honorably applaud reports within other churches and organizations. By doing so, these institutions will signal to members that such reports are welcome within the church or organization. Policies regarding abuse reporting must be developed and promulgated, and training of all staff is mandatory.

Last, *changes* such as these and others must be committed to over time. Thus, facing up to, acknowledging, and correcting the culture will create opportunities for ministry and healing.

The dark crew was out to get me last night.

And one was named Boundary Blurring

And one was named I Can't

And one was named You Should

And one was named He Did

And one was named the Dark Sorcerer

And together they came and surrounded me.

---

46. Smith and Freyd, "Institutional Betrayal."

Toolkit

The tools in the toolkit for the companion are *boundary building*. The journey tool that the companion can offer to the victim is *identity building*. The red flag is the presence of signs that the victim cannot achieve a separation from his or her victim identity and that the struggle to do so is causing harm.

Boundaries

What are *boundaries*? In the poem "Mending Wall" by Robert Frost, the neighbor says to the narrator that "good fences make good neighbors." Whereas in a poem the narrator may wonder about the necessity of repairing a stone boundary wall, it is certainly true in human life that boundaries are necessary to mental health.

Henry Cloud has written in service of the importance of boundaries within the Christian life in particular. He has addressed such issues as the lack of boundaries resulting in a life out of control or the difficulty of saying no to others and thus being disadvantaged. Cloud and Townsend[47] speak to boundaries in four areas:

1. *Physical boundaries* exist around our bodies and allow us to determine who may touch us, violate our body boundary, and for what reason.

2. *Emotional boundaries* help us separate our own emotions from the emotions of others who often attempt to have us take responsibility for another person's emotional state.

3. *Mental boundaries* exist around our thoughts, attitudes, and beliefs, and allow us to be able to hold our own beliefs and also to dispassionately examine them if we wish to do so, but not under the control of others.

4. Finally, *spiritual boundaries* allow us to separate our will from God's creative plan and to understand and accept disappointment when our *needs and wants* are not met in spite of our prayers.

Companions can note the instances in which *boundary violations* in the lives of victims have occurred and can talk about them. It would be better to start with minor violations, because even minor violations that

47. Cloud and Townsend, *Boundaries*.

are accepted will create conversations about why the victims had not been enforcing his or her boundaries. Here are reasons that Cloud[48] cites for boundaries not being enforced and the reasons that companions can listen for.

- I am bad and don't deserve love.
- People will disapprove of me.
- People will control me.
- God only wants *good Christians*.

Here are the types of relationships that the victim needs.

- First are the relationships in which the victim is lead toward the likeness of God, not away from it.
- Next, the victim needs relationships that have limits—people who accept that *being with* and *not being with* each other is fine.
- Finally, victims need to make choices concerning their own actions; relationships that take those choices away are unhealthy.

Identity Building

The victim's journey skill at this point is *identity building*. That is exactly what healthy boundaries are meant to create. Taking ownership of oneself, one's actions and choices, one's feelings and desires, and one's past and future is the essence of building identity.

- *Positive focus*: Increasing positive focus is essential. One example is that of gratitude. Maintaining a gratitude journal, doing *appreciation walks* in which nature's beauty is illuminated and appreciated, and experiencing sensory pleasures such as listening to music and viewing art will help increase a positive focus.

- *Mindfulness*: Being in the *present* is also essential. The past involves revisiting the trauma, depression, shame, and regret. The future contains anticipatory anxiety, catastrophic thinking (e.g., "I know that I will fail"), and worry. The present is the best place to remain.

---

48. Cloud, *Changes that Heal.*

Many verses in Scripture speak to this attitude. For example, "Be still, and know that I am God. I will be exalted among the nations. I will be exalted throughout the earth" (Ps 46:10 ESV).

The story of Elijah is also amazing for its witness to quiet presence. Elijah (1 Kgs 19:9a, 11–13a) is fleeing for his life. He begins a long journey, finds difficulties along the way, and finally gets to the Mount of Hora. First there is an earthquake. Next there is a wind. Then there is fire. In the Old Testament, each of these natural events have been on occasion signs of the presence of God, and likely Elijah looked for God in each of them. However, God finally arrived in "a tiny whispering sound."

- *Live life responsibly*: Maturity comes as the victim stops blaming others, accepts the need to challenge distorted thinking, accepts the unpleasant reality that setting boundaries will mean that some people will have to be set outside his or her life, and begins working with God to build a new identity.

- *Rejecting shame and stigma*: The new positive image must overcome the stigma of past actions, experiences, beliefs, and responses. Overcoming stigma and shame is hard. There are ministries that are directed to this task: one example is Fresh Hope for Mental Health.[49] While these resources frequently speak to the stigma that is involved in mental health, they also apply directly to the stigma of experiencing childhood sexual abuse.

Red Flags

Maybe the victim cannot take responsibility for him- or herself because of repeated boundary violations. This problem will be evident if the victim cannot stop having others make choices for him or her, cannot stop believing guilt messages, allows him- or herself to be repeatedly manipulated, and fails to set limits on his or her own behaviors and the behavior of others. In such a case, companioning might not be occurring at the best time in the victim's relearning of identity building. If the victim is not seeing a professional mental health counselor, this red flag might be the best evidence for the need for that resource.

---

49. For example, Petersen and Hoefs, "Overcoming" is a podcast on stigmas.

Case: Bill

Bill is a retired high school teacher who volunteers as a teacher for the ninth grade Sunday school class. He enjoys challenging the teenagers with content that provokes thoughtful discussions, although he is also distressed that sometimes he has difficulty handling the group. This year, he has seven students; five are girls and two boys. Unfortunately, they are often rowdy and require a large amount of structure in the class. Still, he believes that they are all *good kids* and going through a normal teen phase of rebelliousness. He remembers his own children at that age, who are now faith-filled adults. Those memories help him through some difficult Sundays.

Before class this week, while he is getting organized and children are arriving, he witnesses one of the girls, Kim, telling another girl that she *knows* that Tamara's been in Mr. Arnold's office after school *a lot*. Kim uses a sneering tone and laughs as she says this to Tamara. Tamara then flushes and looks down at the floor.

Thinking that this is malicious teasing, Bill asks Kim how God would feel about her being cruel to another girl. Kim responds: "I don't know. How *does* God feel about what Tamara and Mr. Arnold *do* after school? No *wonder* she's getting an *A* in Algebra." Bill reminds both girls that malicious teasing is an offense against God as well as against the other person and asks Kim to apologize, which she does reluctantly.

Bill is somewhat taken aback by this exchange. He decides that it's best to go forward and to avoid further discomfort or embarrassment. He decides to arrive early, so there is no time that is not structured in the classroom. As the weeks go by, Bill sees that Tamara is participating less and less. He thinks that this may be because of what Kim said, but he just can't believe the snide reference about a high school teacher whom he knows personally. Bill is not sure what the expected protocol for this problem is. He figures that because he has no real information that there isn't a problem to solve.

Over time, Tamara drops out of Sunday school. The remaining teenagers rarely refer to her. Eventually, Bill feels better and thinks of the incident as an uncomfortable event that has long passed. Sometimes he does see Tamara with her family after church, but she always avoids eye contact with him. A knot ties up in his stomach every time this happens, but he doesn't know what to say or even to whom to say it.

1. What seems clear about this situation? What still seems unclear?

2. By serving as a Sunday school teacher, Bill is part of the church organization. Do you see Bill's actions as those of an agent of the church?

3. Why do you think Bill is feeling and behaving as he is?

4. What do you think Tamara is feeling?

5. What would you do, if anything? Why would you do what you decided to do or not do?

5

Forgiveness: A Knife's Edge

Chapter Objectives

1. Learn how true forgiveness can restore health and healing.

2. Distinguish between true forgiveness and false forgiveness.

3. Discover a model of forgiveness that the companion can follow with the victim.

4. Understand how to promote greater hope within the victim.

5. Learn the journey skill of managing the tension between emotional processing and emotional regulation.

SOME CONCEPTS ARE SO familiar that they are actually ill defined. The concept is at the same time *known* and *unknown* and *understood* but also *confused*. Jesus responded to a question about identifying one's neighbor:

> A man was going down from Jerusalem to Jericho, when he was attacked by robbers. They stripped him of his clothes, beat him and went away, leaving him half dead. A priest happened to be going down the same road, and when he saw the man, he passed by on the other side. So too, a Levite, when he came to the place and saw him, passed by on the other side. But a Samaritan, as he traveled, came where the man was; and when he saw him, he took pity on him. He went to him and bandaged his wounds, pouring on oil and wine. Then he put the man on his own donkey, brought him to an inn and took care of him. The next day he took out two denarii and gave them to the innkeeper. "Look after him," he said,

"and when I return, I will reimburse you for any extra expense you may have." (Luke 10:30–37 NIV)

This parable was spoken to an *expert in the law*. You have probably not considered that part of the parable. Perhaps the phrase seems familiar, because these persons materialized to test Jesus on many occasions (Matt 22:35, Luke 10:25). Experts on religious law can be dated back to the scribes in the Old Testament who served as official secretaries (2 Sam 8:17, 20:25). After the Israelites returned from captivity in Babylon, the scribes devoted themselves to adding their own opinions and traditions to the *Law*. Although they were experts in the Scriptures, they failed, however, to recognize Jesus as the Messiah. John reports Jesus' comment on their expertise: "You study the Scriptures diligently because you think that in them you have eternal life. These are the very Scriptures that testify about me, yet you refuse to come to me to have life" (John 5:39–40 NIV).

Defining *forgiveness* is akin to defining a neighbor. While the Levites and priests would have considered themselves *a neighbor*, they failed miserably at the test of giving mercy. The Samaritan, a despised outsider, would certainly have not defined himself as *a neighbor*, but he administered mercy. Similarly, Christians consider themselves experts in forgiveness. However, particularly when speaking to deeply and traumatically wounded persons, they may fail to show mercy.

This chapter considers forgiveness as the *knife's edge*. A *knife's edge* is a situation in which success and failure are equally likely—a situation in which a slight change can have disastrous consequences. Wars, elections, and athletic events balance on a knife's edge. Within this chapter, we consider forgiveness as a Christian response to childhood sexual abuse to be equally likely a weapon as it is a cure.

Defining Forgiveness

What is forgiveness?

It is letting go of the anger.

It is releasing its hold.

It is loosening its grip.

But does it need forgetting?

Are some things too embedded to be forgiven?

Like the branches of a tree that have grown together

And you can't figure out where one starts and the other stops?

Can you untangle the untangleable?

A response to being hurt or wounded by another person is *forgiveness*. The exact nature of the response is the difference among definitions. For example, *forgiveness* is seen as a process that unfolds over time as the victim replaces negative *thoughts* about the offender with positive thoughts.[1] Alternatively, *forgiveness* is considered to be a change in *motivation*: the victim abandons the desire for revenge against the offender and instead adopts more conciliatory motivations.[2] Last, *forgiveness* is viewed as an *emotional* change—that is, when the victim exchanges negative feelings toward the offender (e.g., anger, bitterness) with positive feelings (e.g., empathy, good will).[3]

For the purposes of this chapter, *forgiveness* will be defined as the victim releasing one set of feelings, beliefs, *and* behaviors and adopting another set. The *released set* includes anger, intent to revenge, avoidance of the offender, bitterness, rumination over the offense, and fear of future harm by the offender. The *adopted set* includes empathy, good will, benevolence (acting in a kindly way toward the offender), and resolution. Also for this chapter, forgiveness will be considered within the context of interpersonal relationship. Although there are many words for the person who was wounded and for the person who was the actor, the terms *victim* and *offender* will be used, respectively, in this chapter.

Psychologists have significantly expanded scholarship on forgiveness, its likelihood, and its effects. Only 210 scholarly articles and books were published on forgiveness between 1990 and 2000. In contrast, 2,832 publications appeared between 2000 and the first half of 2015. Why are psychologists so interested in forgiveness?

- It is seen by many as a virtue—an integral part of living a *good life*.[4]

- Second, Christian psychologists began to have their work noticed in the larger academy—a tribute to those who have studied these topics without much attention for many years.[5]

1. Enright and Fitzgibbons, "Model of Forgiveness."
2. McCullough et al., "Interpersonal."
3. Wade and Worthington Jr., "Unforgiveness."
4. See Seligman, *Flourish*.
5. For example, McCullough and Worthington Jr., "Models."

- Third, public attention has been attracted by acts of terrible violence that were followed by acts of forgiveness in other countries. Among these were personally forgiving responses by Nelson Mandela and Bishop Desmond Tutu of South Africa after years of apartheid and the events inspired by the Truth and Reconciliation Commission that was established in 1995 in South Africa. Other examples are various forgiveness projects that came about after the 1994 genocide in Rwanda.

- Last, forgiveness has been shown to have significant effects on physical well-being.[6] Perhaps the most interesting research[7] with respect to forgiveness was conducted using 1,232 persons interviewed over a three years. Persons who believed that God *unconditionally* forgave them and who also forgave others had lower *mortality* (rate of death) than might be expected for their age and other physical conditions. Persons who had a *conditional* view of forgiveness—that apologies, amends, and assurances were needed before forgiveness could be granted—had a higher mortality than expected.

What is Not Forgiveness?

Victims experience significant harm when forgiveness is misunderstood. Three misunderstandings are as follows:

One misunderstanding equates forgiveness with *condoning*. When a third party tells the victim that it's no big deal or that it really wasn't *that* bad, the third party unfairly attempts to reduce the impact of the transgression on the victim and will make it more likely that the victim will mask his or her true feelings. *Condoning* refers to the victim's response rather than the offender's actions in its attempts to minimize the victim's feelings of hurt and anger. The message is that you the victim should not be feeling the way that you do.

A second misunderstanding equates forgiveness with *justification*. This misunderstanding attempts to undo the harm of the action by a focus on the offender. "He was just having a bad day" and "She didn't really mean it" are statements that try to give an acceptable reason or excuse for why the offender engaged in the offensive action. Justification denies the right of the

---

6. See Worthington Jr. et al., "Review of Evidence."
7. Toussaint et al., "Forgive to Live."

victim to be hurt because of the supposed lack of motivation of the offender to inflict the pain.

A third harmful misunderstanding of forgiveness is that forgiveness always results in *reconciliation*. The process of reconciliation restores a broken relationship to a renewed status: *reconciliation* is the re-establishment of trust and caring between two persons. Yet reconciliation is a *two-person* process with necessary actions and responses on both parts. A victim can forgive an offender without reconciling with him or her and without necessarily needing to.

Thus, forgiveness is not condoning or a justification. Forgiveness does not always include reconciliation. Also, forgiveness is not any of the following situations:

- *Fear of confronting the offender*. Forgiveness can happen without contact with the offender. If the victim needs to talk with or confront the offender but avoids doing so because of fear, forgiveness may not have actually been attained.

- *Unwillingness to admit to anger*. The victim does not label the offense as a *transgression* because he or she is unwilling to allow or admit anger at being harmed. Many Christians misunderstand and fear anger. Acknowledging anger at being harmed is an essential part of the forgiveness process. Thus, Christians who believe they *cannot be angry* will voice forgiveness without the true process of understanding the harm that had been done to them.

- *Legal actions*. Forgiveness can still occur even when legal processes are used to obtain restitution or justice. Forgiveness can accompany those legal processes or go beyond them. To pursue a legal remedy is not a failure to forgive.

- *Simply stating that "you are forgiven" without an actual belief and consideration*. Apologies that do not acknowledge responsibility for harm and victims who say "yes, I forgive you" when the process has not been completed are both examples of false forgiveness.

How Does Forgiveness Work?

The Enright Process Model of Forgiveness[8] is a central model in the study of forgiveness. In this model, there are four phases.

8. Enright, *Choice*.

1. *Uncovering.* During this phase, the victim works toward understanding the nature and consequences of the injury. This phase involves thinking about *who did what to whom.* It is important in the uncovering phase that the victim is honest with him- or herself. While thinking about the offense, victims may experience difficult emotions and beliefs such as shame, anger, change in one's view of God, or intrusive thoughts about the event and/or the offender. To forgive, the victim must acknowledge the actual reality of the offense, which includes both "justifiable" realities and the "unjustifiable but actually experienced" realities. For example, a victim who fantasizes about revenge against the offender must acknowledge the reality of these fantasies even though they cause shame and guilt.

2. *Decision.* The victim—with an accurate understanding of the offense and his or her own responses—makes a decision to forgive the offender. This decision may be strong or feeble, but it represents a necessary step. In this phase, the victim understands that whatever has been tried regarding the transgression is not *working* and that he or she will gain from this decision to forgive. This decision belongs to the victim. It cannot be made by a third party and cannot be forced to occur.

3. *Work.* In this phase, victims have to work on forgiving, particularly with severe offenses. Usually this work involves a deeper understanding of the offender and thinking differently about him or her. Accepting the pain that was caused by the offense also takes place. Essentially, the victim gives the offender the "gift of forgiveness." The work phase may involve a conversation with the offender. It might be that the victim invites the offender to talk about motives, details about the situation, and explanations, so that both the offender and the victim can jointly construct the meaning of the offense.

4. *Deepening.* In this phase, the victim creates a new meaning for the offense. As an example, a victim can come to see that the experience of another's betrayal and the gift of forgiving the betrayal has made it possible for her to better empathize with others in a similar situation. Enright believes that deepening creates a greater capacity in the victim to forgive in the future. Further, Enright states that victims discover greater ability to ask for forgiveness in the future from those whom they have harmed. The latter may be true because the victim has come to a complex and complete appreciation of the harm that is

done by interpersonal offenses and realizes that he or she has needed the forgiveness of others in the past.

What Factors Influence Forgiveness?

A meta-analysis[9] was conducted on 175 research studies about forgiveness that involved 26,006 participants. A meta-analysis is a statistical method that allows results from different studies to be transformed into results that can be directly compared to each other; an analogy would be changing a comparison of apples versus oranges to one of apples versus apples. Meta-analysis allows more confidence in the conclusions because they are based on many published studies.

This meta-analysis found that forgiveness was less likely to take place when the victim believed that the offense had been intentional, when the harm was severe, when the victim was very angry and depressed, and when the victim engaged in *ruminative* thinking about the offense. *Ruminative thinking* occurs when we think about something over and over but without any resolution; an everyday term would be *dwelling on it.*

In contrast, the meta-analysis showed that forgiveness was more likely to take place when the offender apologized for the offense, when the victim was in a close relationship with the offender, and when victims described themselves as more religious. Because this was a study of studies, we cannot know exactly how apologies were measured. It does makes sense that forgiveness is more likely if the offender took responsibility by apologizing for having caused the offense.

An additional influence on forgiveness is if the victim sees him- or herself as also having done wrong to others. In a study by Exline[10] and others, the results of seven studies that were based on hypothetical scenarios and on actual recalled offenses among college students and community living adults were presented. The combined results show that people are more likely to forgive an offense when they see themselves as capable of committing that same offense against another person. This result is likely due to *perspective-taking*—I experience someone offending against me, but I know that I have also offended against someone else in a similar situation.

9. Fehr et al., "Road to Forgiveness."
10. Exline et al., "Not So Innocent."

What about Knowing Why?

Mona Lisa is on her stand

And blood drips from the frame.

It may stain the floor but not the picture.

The picture is always intact

But the blood is pooling underneath.

Many persons might believe forgiveness would be easier if they knew *why*. *Why* did this person do this to me? What were the reasons? This question applies across the phases of the Enright Model:[11] in the uncovering phase, in the decisional phase, and even in the work phase. We see this desire in our everyday transactions. In apologizing, we often offer a reason or perhaps an excuse. As an offender, we want to justify our actions to the victim by offering a reason.

As Christians, we must accept that God does not always allow us to know why. I recently attended a women's coffeehouse—a beautiful fall evening with coffee and treats, songs and worship, and testimonies on the theme of surrendering to God. Speakers challenged us: what did we need to surrender? What were we holding that we needed to give up to God? One of the songs was "I Surrender All" (Judson Van DeVenter)—a beautiful traditional hymn that I last sang with only women and girls at a Christian girls' camp around a campfire fifty years before. Here is the first verse and chorus:

All to Jesus I surrender, All to Him I freely give;

I will ever love and trust Him, in His presence daily live.

I surrender all, I surrender all; All to thee my blessed Savior, I surrender all.

The testimonies of the coffeehouse were often about not knowing why, such as a woman dying of brain cancer. So the *why* question may not ever be answered. Yet in the forgiveness process, we can ask that it be revealed at the best time for our own growth.

---

11. The phases are described in the "How Does Forgiveness Work?" section in this chapter.

The Benefits of Forgiveness

Forgiveness is not simply in the mind; rather, it ripples across the body and creates physical benefits. In one study, Witvliet[12] and others compared four groups—an unforgiving ruminating about the offender, an unforgiving nursing a grudge toward the offender, a forgiving attempt to empathically understand the offender, and a forgiving releasing of hurt and angry emotions. *Unforgiving* was associated with higher heart rate and higher blood pressure—both risk factors in many chronic diseases. In another study, Lawler[13] and others demonstrated that positive emotions that accompany forgiveness contributed to better physical health. The reverse was also true: lower levels of forgiveness were associated with higher blood pressure and higher cortisol (stress) levels, both of which are associated with heart diseases.

Forgiveness also creates positive psychological changes. One example is that forgiveness may result in the victim finding benefit after a difficult situation. In a study of college students who had been wounded in a relationship,[14] students reported greater forgiveness of the offender when they also considered positive outcomes of the offense. In a study of adults who lived independently, Schultz, Tallman, and Altmaier[15] examined the responses of 146 persons who had experienced a severe transgression such as sexual assault, infidelity, and slander. Adopting positive feelings toward the offender was found to be associated with a sense of closeness to others and having compassion for others.

Spiritual gain is also a product of forgiveness. Persons often experience a change in spirituality(spiritual transformation) following a highly stressful life event; these changes—either positive (spiritual gain) or negative (spiritual decline)—show up in one's worldview, sense of self, goals and priorities in life, and relationships with others.[16] In a study by Schultz, Altmaier, Ali, and Tallman,[17] adults who had been personally wronged reported on their forgiveness toward that person as well as their experience of

12. Witvliet et al., "Implications."

13. Lawler et al., "Change of Heart."

14. McCullough et al., "Writing."

15. Schultz et al., "Pathways."

16. Cole et al., "Assessing Spiritual," 112.

17. Schultz et al., "Posttraumatic Spiritual."

spiritual transformation. The adults in the study who had lower forgiveness experienced spiritual decline.

Christian Paths to Unforgiveness

Perhaps because of the very great gift of God's forgiveness to us, as Christians we believe that we know a lot about it. In fact, we read and write about it with great frequency. However, in spite of all that reading and writing, Christians often misunderstand forgiveness.

Stoop[18] described wrongful beliefs about forgiveness that are often expressed by Christians. Here are some of those beliefs:

- With forgiving, I ought to always try to forgive and forget.

- It's wrong to get angry when I am trying to forgive.

- I should try to forgive others quickly and completely.

- Over time, my hurt will go away and my forgiveness will take care of itself.

- If I have forgiven, I will never have angry feelings against those who have hurt me.

- If I forgive, I am saying that what happened to me did not matter.

All these beliefs are false and can lead to one of two pathways that are not forgiveness.

The first pathway is the *path of denial*. On this pathway, the wrongful offense occurs. The victim then experiences a range of negative responses, usually dominated by hurt. However, the victim decides to deny that the offense has occurred[19] or to blame him- or herself for the offense. The victim then shuts down emotionally. The final step is depression. This path of denial exists because we are trying protect ourselves from painful truth.

The second pathway is the *path of bitterness*. On this pathway, after the offense, the victim tells and retells the story. For Christians, this telling is frequently masked as requests for prayer support or requests for ideas for *the most Christian response*. Not only does this pathway fail to achieve forgiveness, it also can be the case that the victim can get caught up in trying

---

18. Stoop, *Forgiving*, chap. 2.

19. Perhaps because of third-party intervention, perhaps because of an inaccurate understanding of Scripture.

to understand *why*. "If I only knew why she did this, then I could forgive her." This pathway leads to bitterness, revenge, and avoidance.

In his sermon on "Be kind to one another, tender-hearted, forgiving one another as God in Christ forgave you" (Eph 4:32), Pastor Sam Storms[20] contrasts four falsehoods with four truths about Christian forgiveness.

Falsehood	Truth
Falsehood 1. Forgiveness is followed by forgetting the offense and no longer feeling its pain.	*Truth 1*. Pastor Storms notes that God forgave us by absorbing the consequences of our sins. When we forgive another, we too absorb and live with painful consequences.
Falsehood 2. If we forgive the offender and do not obtain justice, we will stop longing for the justice that did not occur.	*Truth 2*. Pastor Storm noted that God does not require the *justice* that should be required for our many sins. When God cancelled the debt, he also promised to never bring it up again. As humans, it is difficult to stop *bringing it up* either to God or to another person. Yet God set an example of cancelling the debt and burying it forever, and we must work to do the same.
Falsehood 3. If we forgive an offender, that act equals our trusting again in the offender.	*Truth 3*. Protecting ourselves against an offender who continues to have a presence in our lives is important. Healthy boundaries are consistent with forgiveness. Reconciling does not automatically follow forgiveness. The offender has a necessary role to play in reconciling, and part of that is helping to rebuild trust with the victim. Also, trust takes considerable time to establish after a serious wrongdoing.
Falsehood 4. Forgiveness is a single event, a moment in time.	*Truth 4*. For less serious offenses, that characterization may be true. However, for serious, traumatic interpersonal wounds, there will be long-lasting effects in our lives.

20. Storms, "From Forgiven."

In the last section of Romans, Paul provides instructions about living a holy life. In his letter, he cautions against *vengeance*:

> Do not repay anyone evil for evil. Be careful to do what is right in the eyes of everyone. If it is possible, as far as it depend on you, live at peace with everyone. Do not take revenge, my dear friends, but leave room for God's wrath for it is written: "It is mine to avenge. I will repay," says the Lord. (Rom 12:17–19 NIV)

The letter to Romans continues with an encouragement to do good to the person who is seen as the enemy. In terms of forgiveness, *doing good* might be an actual deed—adopting more compassionate attitudes toward and developing empathy for the offender. It might begin with a single event of choosing to forgive, but the process is ongoing.

The Machete

At one time, I was in a position to counsel a student who had been raped by another student. The circumstances that put her in this position were common on a college campus. She had been drinking. She was invited by people whom she trusted to a party at the home of another student. People started leaving; there were few persons around when he held her mouth to stop her from screaming and brutally sexually assaulted her. She was injured, and she then called a friend to take her to the emergency room, where they did a rape kit and treated her.

There were unusual circumstances to her violation. She was a student athlete, and her rapist was another student athlete who was among the stars of his team. She was a Christian and attended a Bible study group that was led by a person who represented a national campus ministry on her campus. In her crisis, she turned to that person and his wife. Here is what she heard:

- "He didn't rape you. You had sex with him."
- "Because you are a Christian, you must forgive him right away."
- "To show that you have forgiven him, you must not press charges or even tell your side of the story to the police."

When I met with her, she was deeply traumatized. She had been raped, she had been victimized and abandoned by the Christians to whom she looked for help, and she was publically humiliated and shamed. We talked on multiple occasions, and she finally asked me whether I thought God required her to forgive both her rapist and the campus representative. I told her that I believed that he did, but that he did not specify a timeline. She could work with God over time, and she would find him honest to his promises—that she would be able to forgive. She could make the first feeble decision, and she could hold God accountable to work with her until forgiveness was present. Still, she had no responsibility to work toward reconciliation with any other party until any persons acknowledged their roles in her trauma, displayed repentance and true change of behavior, and humbled themselves with God and with her to restore trust.

This illustration returns to the concept of forgiveness as a *knife's edge*. For this young woman, to have believed what she was told by the leaders of the Christian organization—that she was to blame for the rape, that she must forgive immediately to attempt to recover their good will toward her, that she must not file charges to demonstrate that she had forgiven—would have been false forgiveness. It would have set her on a path to *unforgiveness* rather than true forgiveness. Her future ability to forgive, in turn, might have been negatively affected. Rather than the incremental improvements that are caused by forgiveness, she would have experienced the deterioration of false forgiveness. Christians put other Christians on a similar knife's edge with misunderstandings and wrongful actions.

The Christian Path to Forgiveness and Reconciliation

As Stoop[21] describes, the Christian path to forgiveness begins when we make the choice to forgive, however weak and feeble and trembling that choice is. We choose to follow God's command for radical forgiveness, even as we have no idea how we will carry it out.

"If you forgive those who sin against you, your heavenly Father will forgive you. But if you refuse to forgive others, your Father will not forgive your sins" (Matt 6:14 NLT). When Peter asks how many times he should forgive someone, Jesus replies not seven times, but rather seventy times seven. "No, not seven times," Jesus replied, "but seventy times seven" (Matt 18:21–22 NLT).

In radical forgiveness, we become like the father of the possessed child who answers Jesus, "I do believe; help my unbelief" (Mk 9:24 NLT). We

21. Stoop, *Forgiving*.

decide to forgive at the same time that we know that we are dependent on God to help us achieve that which seems impossible.

Forgiving is *hard work*. It begins with the work of assigning *blame*, of accurately understanding the transgression, and of letting in the searing hurt and pain of the offense. For adults who had been sexually abused as children, their location for blame most likely has been themselves. They commonly believe that they should have done something different, behaved better, or been a more obedient child. The developmental trajectory is significantly interrupted by childhood abuse.[22] The child-now-adult must see and acknowledge that he or she did not deserve the abuse and is not, nor ever was, at fault.

Work then moves to *grief*—deep, horrible, sundering grief. This part of forgiveness focuses on the self who was harmed. I once cried so hard and so long that our golden retriever, who was sitting on the couch with me, actually got up, jumped off the couch, and left the room. He could *not* stay with me anymore in my grief. For people who are companioning victims, a challenging task is to help the victim deal with emotions. Specific suggestions for how to accomplish this task will be discussed in the toolkit section.

Along with the pain of betrayal, deep shame, the sense of dirtiness that will never be clean, and brokenness that will never heal, grieving after childhood sexual abuse is for innumerable losses. Markus and Nurius[23] introduced the concept of *possible selves*: these are the ideal self, the self that we would like to become, and the self that we are afraid of becoming. For grievers, lost possible selves need to be defined and given up. While some aspect of the possible selves may be achievable in the future, some are truly gone.

Grief also involves anger, and *anger* at the offender must be part of the work. So many Christians see anger as wrong, that this step of forgiveness can be difficult. As Stoop[24] reminds us, anger can be productive or unproductive. He describes *healthy anger* as involving a sense of justice—being disciplined in its expression. We have a sense of justice, because God "wrote it on our hearts."[25] Anger with respect to our having been wounded reflects our deep emotional response to an unjustified wrong.

22. See introductory chapters.
23. Markus and Nurius, "Possible Selves."
24. Stoop, *Forgiving*.
25. C. H. Spurgeon's sermon is worth reading in regard to the way that our hearts

Forgiveness leads to many beneficial outcomes. One outcome is that the work of forgiveness leads to the victim acquiring forgivingness.[26] *Forgivingness* is the tendency to be more forgiving across multiple situations.[27] As an ongoing aspect of one's character, it is a positive aspect of personality that promotes relating with others, gratitude, and empathy. *Forgivingness* is related to purpose in life (meaning), being able to tolerate negative emotions, accepting oneself more completely (including forgiving oneself more easily), and forgiving others more willingly. Forgivingness appears to be what is described as love in Corinthians:

> Love is patient, love is kind. It does not envy, it does not boast, it is not proud. It does not dishonor others, it is not self-seeking, it is not easily angered, it keeps no record of wrongs. Love does not delight in evil but rejoices with the truth. (1 Cor 13:4–6 NIV)

Of all the positive outcomes of forgiveness, one of the best is the emergence of a new self whose character has forgivingness.

Reconciliation

Reconciliation is a separate process from forgiveness. When forgiveness takes place, the victim adopts forgiveness. Nothing further is owed to the offender, and nothing further is owed to the victim. Forgiveness cancels the debt. Yet we live in a network of relationships with others, and it is possible that the victim and the offender will continue to have contact. In that case, there may be a mutual process that is entered into by both the offender and the victim that leads to reconciliation.

Reconciliation begins with the offender being humble and repentant toward the victim, *after* the offender has done his or her own work with God. The offender's attitude must be one of humility, sorrow, and vulnerability. The offender must communicate that attitude to the victim, so that the victim can decide whether he or she wants to participate in reconciliation. If the victim is willing, the offender can create an atmosphere of openness by acknowledging the offense, confessing his or her role in it, and adopting an attitude of patience while the victim relearns to trust the offender.

---

contain God's law. See Spurgeon, "God's Law."

26. See Corrie ten Boom's story at the end of the chapter.

27. Hill and Allemand, "Forgivingness."

In the Catholic Church, the sacrament of *confession* is also the sacrament of *reconciliation*. The believer confesses the wrong to God, who restores sanctifying grace in the soul of the believer and reconciles himself to the believer.

> For I know the thoughts that I think toward you, says the Lord, thoughts of peace and not of evil, to give you a future and a hope. Then you will call upon Me and go and pray to Me, and I will listen to you. And you will seek Me and find Me, when you search for Me with all your heart. (Jer 29:11–12 NKJV)

Father Jonah[28] comments on the relationship between forgiveness and reconciliation. Forgiveness leaves open the idea of reconciliation, which he terms *forgiveness in action*. The offender may not be willing to reconcile, it may not be wise for the victim to restore a relationship with an abuser, or the offender may be gone or dead. Forgiveness can take place in all of those circumstances. Yet reconciliation occurs when the offender humbly seeks forgiveness from the victim, accepts the forgiveness, forgives himself or herself, and repents and begins to have the love of God and the forgiveness of the victim transform his or her life and soul.

Corrie ten Boom[29]

> It was in a church in Munich that I saw him—a balding, heavy-set man in a gray overcoat, a brown felt hat clutched between his hands. People were filing out of the basement room where I had just spoken, moving along the rows of wooden chairs to the door at the rear. It was 1947 and I had come from Holland to defeated Germany with the message that God forgives.
>
> It was the truth they needed most to hear in that bitter, bombed-out land, and I gave them my favorite mental picture. Maybe because the sea is never far from a Hollander's mind, I liked to think that that's where forgiven sins were thrown. "When we confess our sins," I said, "God casts them into the deepest ocean, gone forever...."
>
> The solemn faces stared back at me, not quite daring to believe. There were never questions after a talk in Germany in 1947.

28. Jonah, "Forgiveness and Reconciliation."
29. ten Boom, "Forgiveness."

People stood up in silence, in silence collected their wraps, in silence left the room.

And that's when I saw him, working his way forward against the others. One moment I saw the overcoat and the brown hat; the next, a blue uniform and a visored cap with its skull and cross-bones. It came back with a rush: the huge room with its harsh overhead lights; the pathetic pile of dresses and shoes in the center of the floor; the shame of walking naked past this man. I could see my sister's frail form ahead of me, ribs sharp beneath the parchment skin. *Betsie, how thin you were!*

[Betsie and I had been arrested for concealing Jews in our home during the Nazi occupation of Holland; this man had been a guard at Ravensbruck concentration camp where we were sent.]

Now he was in front of me, hand thrust out: "A fine message, Fräulein! How good it is to know that, as you say, all our sins are at the bottom of the sea!"

And I, who had spoken so glibly of forgiveness, fumbled in my pocketbook rather than take that hand. He would not remember me, of course—how could he remember one prisoner among those thousands of women?

But I remembered him and the leather crop swinging from his belt. I was face-to-face with one of my captors and my blood seemed to freeze.

"You mentioned Ravensbruck in your talk," he was saying, "I was a guard there." No, he did not remember me.

"But since that time," he went on, "I have become a Christian. I know that God has forgiven me for the cruel things I did there, but I would like to hear it from your lips as well. Fräulein," again the hand came out—"will you forgive me?"

And I stood there—I whose sins had again and again to be forgiven—and could not forgive. Betsie had died in that place—could he erase her slow terrible death simply for the asking?

It could not have been many seconds that he stood there—hand held out—but to me it seemed hours as I wrestled with the most difficult thing I had ever had to do.

For I had to do it—I knew that. The message that God forgives has a prior condition: that we forgive those who have injured us. "If you do not forgive men their trespasses," Jesus says, "neither will your Father in heaven forgive your trespasses."

I knew it not only as a commandment of God, but as a daily experience. Since the end of the war I had had a home in Holland for victims of Nazi brutality. Those who were able to forgive their former enemies were able also to return to the outside world and rebuild their lives, no matter what the physical scars. Those who nursed their bitterness remained invalids. It was as simple and as horrible as that.

And still I stood there with the coldness clutching my heart. But forgiveness is not an emotion—I knew that too. Forgiveness is an act of the will, and the will can function regardless of the temperature of the heart. ". . . Help!" I prayed silently. "I can lift my hand. I can do that much. You supply the feeling."

And so woodenly, mechanically, I thrust my hand into the one stretched out to me. And as I did, an incredible thing took place. The current started in my shoulder, raced down my arm, sprang into our joined hands. And then this healing warmth seemed to flood my whole being, bringing tears to my eyes.

"I forgive you, brother!" I cried. "With all my heart!"

For a long moment we grasped each other's hands, the former guard and the former prisoner. I had never known God's love so intensely, as I did then.

Toolkit

The tools in the toolkit for the companion are those that help maintain hope and work with the victim to allow him or her to hold distressing emotion. All the active listening skills discussed earlier in this book certainly apply to difficult conversations. The best gift that the companion can give to the victim at this point in his or her journey is a *renewed focus on hope*. Much of the work that the victim needs to do will occur outside of conversations with the companion. In fact, it may feel more like the victim is *reporting in* on his or her journeys somewhat like a travel blog.

Renewed Focus on Hope

There are specific techniques that have been found useful to promote hope among people as they explore difficult issues. The techniques that are described here were presented by Howell, Jacobson, and Larsen:[30]

1. *Poetry and other literary passages.* It is helpful to hear how others have experienced life building hope. Poetry and other *third items* are useful for that activity. A *third item* is an item that has no personal

---

30. Howell et al., "Enhanced Psychological Health."

relationship to either the victim or the companion. Therefore, it can be considered and discussed objectively.

2. *Building a hope collage.* Using various media, the companion and the victim can build a hope collage. This product may be finished or may be returned to as the victim continues work. Sample items are newspaper stories, pictures, poetry, art, and natural items such as flowers.

3. *Using personal strengths*—considered in an earlier chapter—is another way to maintain hope. It is important to remember that the victim is not completely defined by this one wound and his or her struggles to forgive. Rather, the victim is experiencing a whole life, and the companion can remind the victim of personal strengths that were earlier identified. Such topics as *joyfulness* (what is causing you joy right now), *meaning* (what purposes are in your life right now), and *engagement* (what are you doing right now) are relevant for *stretching* the victim's view of self.

Balancing Emotional Processing and Emotional Regulation

The companion is doing intensive work now that involves deep and distressing feelings. Therefore, the journey skills that are important are those that allow painful feelings and thoughts to be *observed*. People who are wounded experience many distressing emotions. Victims must learn the journey skills of *balancing emotional processing and emotional regulation*.[31]

During forgiveness, victims must identify and experience emotions. Still, being overwhelmed with emotions is not helpful. There is a temptation then to tamp down emotions or to stuff them away inside. Yet that is not helpful either, because those emotions must be experienced and identified and properly *taken in.*

Thus, victims must learn to regulate emotions. The tension, if resolved well, will allow the victim to have emotions revealed, to experience and identify them, to process them to gain understanding, and to use those emotions to lead to new identity and meaning. Here are two examples of ways to view emotions:

- You are seated comfortably, and your thoughts are in boxes on a conveyer belt that is running in front of you. You are not in control of the

31. Worthington and Sandage, *Forgiveness and Spirituality.*

speed of the conveyer belt. Each thought passes briefly by in front of you. You observe each thought as it comes into view and then leaves.

- You are sitting on a beach. You can feel the sand near your feet and hear the birds. Your thoughts are on each wave s. You watch as the waves individually roll in to shore. Some waves are small and gentle as they come and go. Other waves are strong and forceful and make louder noises as they come up onto the shore, but they also go.

Methods such as these of *getting distance* from thoughts can help the victim to realize that he or she is more than the contents of the mind and the sensations of the body. In fact, there is a part that exists outside of these thoughts and feelings and sensations.

Another way to include emotions without being overwhelmed by them is by creating a change metaphor and using it to get a different perspective on the process. Everyone's metaphor will be different. Mine was climbing a mountain path. Behind me were pine trees and darkness; the path was dim. The emotions behind me were sadness, pain, loneliness, anger, dread, and shame. Yet I was rounding a corner, and ahead of me was sunlight and a flowery meadow. I could see a few rocks by the meadow, and I could feel myself climbing toward them so that I could rest and view the meadow. The meadow was my emotions of hope, peace, well-being, life, love, acceptance, and joy.

Red Flags

The red flags that signal the need for more professional help are the same as listed in earlier chapters—interference in life activities. Can the victim focus and concentrate on his or her tasks? Are there times when depression and anger are so overwhelming that the victim has self-harming thoughts or plans or is using substances to cope? Both the loss of focus and the uncontrollable nature of feelings are signs to seek professional help.

Conclusion

In forgiveness of deeply traumatic wounds, there is a gap between the promise and its fulfillment, between the petition and the revelation. The companion can *stand in that gap* between what *now* is and what *will be*—bearing witness and honor to the presence of God in the struggles of the victim.

Case: Penelope

Penelope is a twenty-one-year-old, African American, Christian woman who is single. When she was thirteen, she was sexually abused by a camp counselor at her church summer camp. He was an eighteen-year-old man who was highly praised within the camp for his athleticism and attractiveness. Penelope was initially flattered by his attention. However, the relationship grew increasingly physical while also becoming coercive and secretive, and Penelope felt that she had no recourse. The summer went on without anyone noticing. While he loomed large, Penelope got smaller and smaller.

The next year, Penelope returned to camp at the insistence of her parents, only to find that he was no longer a counselor. Other counselors spoke fondly and sadly of him. They remembered how he had "shined so brightly, despite so much adversity in his life." Penelope was disgusted by their words. She heard an excuse behind their praise, and she felt shamed and resented by their adulation of him. At the same time, she wondered deep down whether their praise meant that she must have been mistaken— that he could not have victimized her and that she must be the one who was wrong. These warring thoughts nagged her. Eventually, Penelope insisted on leaving camp. When she returned home, she attended church services only to please her parents and to maintain their expectations.

Years passed, and Penelope left home. Away from the eyes of her parents, she left the church. When Penelope's younger sister came to visit Penelope at college over a weekend, they argued over Penelope's refusal to attend church. The confrontation ended in tears.

After her sister's departure, Penelope felt overwhelmed by a sense of loss and sadness. She missed her classes that Monday—overcome with memories of the abuse, memories of his touching her, and his words of praise to her as he took advantage of her. She replayed images in her mind of confronting him, of announcing his sins to the whole of the camp, and of shaming him and tearing him down. The day passed with Penelope barely leaving her bed. As she lay in the darkness, she recognized the toll of her anger and the magnitude of her loss. She said quietly to herself, "I can't let this destroy me." She felt resolute in her desire to forgive for the sake of her own life, and yet as the night came on, Penelope felt no less wounded.

1. In what stage of forgiveness is Penelope? Why?

2. Consider the *Enright Process Model of Forgiveness* and Stoop's *Paths to Unforgiveness* and the *Path to Christian Forgiveness* to discuss the following: what elements of Penelope's story indicate that she may have trouble forgiving? What elements indicate increased likelihood of forgiveness?

3. How might Penelope experience change as a result of her forgiving process?

4. How might you be helpful to Penelope in her journey? What things might you say? What things might you take care to not say?

6

Meaning Making after Trauma

Chapter Objectives

1. Understand the loss of meaning after trauma.

2. Appreciate relationships as a space for rebuilding meaning.

3. See reconstruction of meaning as essential in trauma recovery.

4. Learn companioning skills for rebuilding meaning.

5. Learn journey skills for meaning reconstruction.

I lied when I said I could hold it.
Because I can't.
It's too much and I hate the part of me that is weak.
And that is part of the problem because it will take all of me
The strong me
The weak me
The four-year-old
Working together to do this.

WORLD WAR II WAS notable for many reasons. It was the first true world-wide war, and soldiers from virtually every country fought and died for one side or the other. Scientists on both sides devoted years to research in service to the war, and both weaponry and technology advanced dramatically. Finally, World War II contained systematic and horrifying violence—primarily but not exclusively in the concentration camps—by people against people. Much has been written in particular about the Holocaust. The term *holocaust* is rooted in the Greek term *holokauston* which means sacrifice by fire. The Nazi government referred to the camps—concentration, extermination, labor, prisoner of war, and transit—as the *final solution* for the extermination of Jewish people, although the camps also contained political prisoners, gypsies, homosexuals, the disabled, and Jehovah's Witnesses.

The Holocaust itself was notable for its provocation of deep-rooted thinking—by many persons in the camps—about *meaning*. What was the meaning of life in the face of daily unspeakable degradation? What did it mean to be human, when emotions were dead? Looking back at his time at Auschwitz, Viktor Frankl[1] wrote about his search for meaning. In the camps, the human being was controlled by the environment of the camp, which included the physical environment of snow, freezing temperatures, and extreme suffering. The human was also behaviorally controlled—systematically starved and worked to death. The social environment was also controlled by camp authorities who were usually brutal but sometimes unpredictably humane. In spite of all this control, Frankl concluded that the human always retained choice:

> Even though conditions such as lack of sleep, insufficient food, and various mental stresses may suggest that the inmates were bound to react in certain ways, in the final analysis it becomes clear that the sort of person the prisoner became was the result of an inner decision, and not the result of camp influences alone. . . . If there is a meaning in life at all, then there must be a *meaning in suffering* [italics added]. Suffering is an ineradicable part of life, even as fate and death. Without suffering and death, human life cannot be complete.[2]

During my work as a clinical supervisor, I once supervised a trainee who was completing a placement at a community mental health center. At the end of her time there, during which she had successfully treated a variety of

1. Frankl, *Man's Search*.
2. Ibid., 76.

challenging cases, she wanted to give gifts to her patients. Gift giving is an ethical dilemma in psychology. She and I had several serious conversations about the ethics of gift giving to her clients. Yet her plan and reasoning were good, and I agreed with it. For each client, she selected a stone. On that stone, she painted a single word, one that she believed best summarized their work together or a strength that she believed the client had come to achieve.

Each client received that gift in tears. On the one hand, you might think: why are people crying when they are given a rock? Still, each rock had deep meaning: the therapist had chosen the stone, had chosen the exact word, had painted it, and had presented it. The ritual and the gift gave meaning to their work together, celebrated it, summarized it, and enhanced it. The meaning transformed the rock into something far more important and personal.

This chapter is about *meaning* and its re-creation after the destruction of meaning in trauma. The toolkit gives the companion ways of adding meaning to the victim's life as well as to the companioning experience. Journey skills also concern meaning making in the face of darkness.

Development of Meaning

Erikson[3] defines a model of lifelong development in which every person is faced with and then resolves or fails to resolve sequential *crises*. The focus in chapter 1 was on the crisis within infancy and early childhood—resolving *trust versus mistrust*. When that crisis is resolved in favor of trust, the child develops hope.

The crisis of *initiative versus guilt* occurs in what Erikson terms the *play age* (ages three to five). At this age, children begin to experiment on the world and to plan activities and make up imaginary games. Children also push parental limits with their activities. Parents must have rules for safe living, family stability, and family values. How these rules are enforced is an essential part of parenting. Good discipline *both* teaches that a certain response is wrong and that other responses are right. When this crisis is resolved in favor of initiative, the child gains purpose. Purpose is essential to meaning. Purpose in life has been revealed as a major contributor to life satisfaction for children as well as adults.[4]

3. Erikson, *Childhood.*
4. See Heintzelman and King, "Meaningful."

During *school age* (ages five to twelve), the crisis of *industry versus inferiority*, children begin to think about life: what is real, how do we know that something is true or not, what is the purpose of a given thing, and how we manage our responses to events and challenges of life. Children also develop *lay theories* of human life. These *lay theories* are the foundation for our later adult thoughts about *meaning*. Some examples of lay theories are "Good people get what they deserve, and bad people get what they deserve," "Life is fair," and "I am a worthwhile person."

As Christians, many of our reasons concerning why something exists or why things happen are centered in our views of the power and purposes of God. These are *teleological* reasons for meaning. A *teleological* reason for meaning contains final causes and purposes. The method by which we attach and modify final causes and purposes to events as our life goes by is our *autobiographical memory*. We look back and see good things in our lives as *blessings*—gifts from God that gave our life purpose and pleasure. We similarly look back and see bad things as occurring to us for a reason also related to purpose. The Scriptures are full of stories of individuals who suffered bad things, yet knew their suffering was occurring within God's ultimate plans.

However, it is vitally important to separate *information* from *meaning*. For example, Christians often are told information from the Scripture about trials in which they are being tested:

> Consider it pure joy, my brothers and sisters, whenever you face trials of many kinds, because you know that the testing of your faith produces perseverance. Let perseverance finish its work so that you may be mature and complete, not lacking anything. (Jas 1:2–4 NIV)

For a Christian who has not experienced developmental barriers that are posed by childhood sexual abuse, such verses are both informative and meaningful. Persons who had been abused as children cannot grasp[5] the meaningfulness of this and other similar verses, because their faith tenuously stands on the foundation of their own deep insecurity. They cannot *know* that testing produces faith, because they have no foundations for that knowledge and thus it has no meaning.

A psychological view of persons in accord with a biblical worldview is that persons are *agents* who act with purpose on their environment, create

5. See chapter 2.

motivation and plans, and are responsible for the directions of their lives. A critical component of this view of humans is what Singer[6] terms *narrative identity*—individuals' stories about themselves become the literal stuff of self-development and create the means by which they are agents in their lives. We use stories to define meaning about events and persons, and we use them as a basis for plans and for forming beliefs in our success in achieving those plans. We also actively turn our experiences into *narratives* or stories. Most importantly, our ability to build these narratives changes as we age. The meaning of the stories that we tell evolves and changes over time. This lets us create new meanings for old stories even many years after the initial event.

The Effects of Trauma on Meaning

The diagnostic category[7] of *post-traumatic stress disorder* was the formal expression for the expectation that psychological trauma had resulted in significant distress. That distress was manifested in three ways:

- First were emotions—sadness, anger, deep depression.

- Second were thoughts—problems with memory or concentration, views of the self that were degrading or debilitating.

- Third were physical symptoms—sleeplessness, loss of appetite, lethargy, actual physical illnesses such as heart disease and chronic gastrointestinal conditions.

Healthcare providers who were treating individuals with post-traumatic stress disorder presumed that only negative outcomes followed experiences of severe trauma, such as that experienced in combat, after physical or sexual assault, or after captivity.

Psychologists agreed with this viewpoint and described the primary pathway between traumatic events and distressing outcomes. Janoff-Bulman[8] depicted each of us as possessing a series of assumptions—earlier referred to as *lay theories*. Her research established almost universally common assumptions such as that the world is just, the world is meaningful, and the self is worthy. These assumptions are present in everyday

6. Singer, "Narrative."
7. See chapter 1.
8. Janoff-Bulman, *Shattered*.

life through *schemas*—more limited structures that bring the high-level assumptions to the level of everyday living. For example, the schema of "if I am nice to people, they will be nice to me in return" reflects the assumption that the *world is just*.

However, trauma collides dramatically and drastically with these assumptions about the world. Rather than believing that the world is benevolent, trauma survivors fear the world and see it as dangerous and unpredictable. Instead of their seeing meaning in the world, the unexpected and unexplainable overcomes meaning. Rather than their believing the self to be worthy, the self becomes uncertain and unworthy. All these aftereffects of trauma are true for adults who had previously had full meaning in their lives. For children who experience trauma without the firm foundation of mature development, the effect of trauma on basic assumptions is significantly magnified. Aldwin[9] described three patterns of life after trauma for adults in general.

1. *Negative coping* prevents the individual from returning to his or her previous level of functioning. Examples of negative coping are avoiding the problem or self-medicating with drugs or alcohol. These individuals cannot or will not think about their core assumptions or their schemata, because they are stuck in fear and respond with avoidance. Instead, they blame themselves or someone else for the event, they deny the event or its importance, and they avoid any discussion of the event. Distress, depression, and insecurity then take the place of previous normal function; and the individual experiences damage in interpersonal relationships, work, and social life.

2. *Homeostatic coping* leads to a return to previous level of functioning. Examples of homeostatic coping are problem solving and emotion-focused coping. These individuals are able to think about their assumptions and schemata after the event and to modify them in order to cope. So for example, a person who was assaulted and robbed in a large city might continue to believe that the world in general is a safe place but not a large city.

3. Finally, *transformational coping* leads to a future that is an improvement—sometimes a great one—over the pre-trauma level of function. These individuals willingly face the struggle after the trauma. They accept the trauma as a necessary impetus for personal change. They

9. Aldwin, *Stress.*

work on changing their worldviews—a process that requires a certain amount of deliberating over the event. They use social support to help them approach rather than avoid the hardships of the process.

Can There Be Posttraumatic Growth?

In 1998, a book with the seemingly contradictory title of *Posttraumatic Growth: Positive Changes in the Aftermath of Crisis* was published. Tedeschi[10] and other psychologists brought together evidence from many research studies of individuals who discovered or created *enduring positive changes* in their lives after trauma. These positive changes tended to occur in certain areas of life.

- First, there were changes in the person's *sense of self*. A popular expression of this change is the statement that "I learned that I could be stronger than I had expected." People also reported being more aware of and appreciative of life itself—what they had previously thought were *small things*.

- A second change was in *relationships with others*. After trauma, many persons reported improvements in interpersonal relationships. Examples were working toward more harmony in existing relationships or making new friends.

- Third were changes in a person's *life goals*. People changed careers, redirected their lives to new purposes, or became advocates for others who had experienced the same trauma.

- Last was *religious and spiritual* change. After crisis, people reported greater reliance on their faith, more participation in their faith communities, and great spiritual meaning in their own faith experiences.

Did this positive posttraumatic growth always occur? No—while it was common, it is in fact by no means universal. Additionally, Tedeschi and Calhoun[11] documented that people after trauma can experience both growth and decline at the same time. What differences between people account for these different outcomes after trauma? While there are social and environmental characteristics, psychologists often focus on personal characteristics that influence response to trauma.

10. Tedeschi et al., eds., *Aftermath*.
11. Tedeschi and Calhoun, "Measuring."

Perhaps the most important personal characteristic is *resilience*. Resilience[12] is a personal quality of intentional purpose and being. Both children and adults can be resilient. Although resilience may look different at various stages of life, resilient children and adults are optimistic, have self-confidence, know how to gain support from others, and manage their emotions in ways that do not harm themselves. A recent consideration[13] of resilience in the face of trauma argued that resilience is more than an all-or-none quality that is present in the individual, but rather the conversion of trauma into resilience. Resilient individuals *did something* with the trauma and that process of struggle was what caused them to "harness something useful or positive that can be mobilized toward their greater recovery."[14]

It is also essential to note the importance of *time*. Several researchers have demonstrated that *time since trauma* is related to the effects of the trauma on the person. In research on cancer, for example, spiritual transformation was positively related to life satisfaction only after several years following cancer treatment.[15] Similar findings were demonstrated by Barskova and Oesterreich:[16] Spiritual transformations were later important influences on life satisfaction after traumas that were associated with diagnosis and treatment of serious medical conditions.

How Does Being a Christian Contribute to Meaning Reconstruction?

The role of religion and spirituality after trauma is becoming widely recognized even among secular psychologists. Bryant-Davis and Wong[17] summarized the state of psychological research on meaning making in three areas of interpersonal trauma—childhood sexual abuse, sexual assault and sex trafficking, and refugee trauma including torture. This research covered individuals across the world; survivors who practiced a variety of religions and spiritual traditions were studied. The authors documented that religious coping—such as prayer, reading religious texts, and attending worship services—improves psychological response after disturbing traumas.

12. Masten, "Resilience."
13. Brown et al., "Unbraiding."
14. Ibid., 108.
15. Cole et al., "Assessing Spiritual."
16. Barskova and Oesterreich, "Systematic Review."
17. Bryant-Davis and Wong, "Faith."

This includes individuals within underserved communities and those who survived oppression that was based on race, gender, or tribe.

De Castella and Simmonds[18] interviewed ten Christian women who had experienced spiritual or religious growth after a trauma in order to determine how religion helped them. The traumas were varied (e.g., sexual assault, car accident, serious illness, domestic violence); all had occurred one year or more before the interview. These women described several pathways to meaning re-creation.

- One was a need to *struggle over time* to make sense of the incident.

- Another was the process of rediscovering oneself.

- The third pathway was through friendships that held safety and security—people who encouraged the victim to feel safe and to share thoughts and feelings. These latter friendships served a companioning purpose, the central focus of this text.

Finding meaning after trauma is associated with better outcomes across several areas of life. For example, Triplett[19] and others studied 300 young adults after a variety of traumas—including bereavement, violence, medical illness, and accident that resulted in serious injury. The model of the trauma-to-growth process began with the trauma event, which led to deliberate reflection and contemplation among some participants. Participants who reported posttraumatic growth had found meaning of the event and the highest level of life satisfaction. In contrast, participants who failed to make sense of the event or who did not try to engage in the reflection and contemplation process did not find meaning and reported lower growth and less life satisfaction.

Reconstructing Meaning as an Adult after Childhood Trauma

Squares split and reform

and colors change and it is the

kaleidoscope of me.

And the patterns change, and some collide

And why can't the darn thing stop

18. De Castella and Simmonds, "Experiences."
19. Triplett et al., "Response to Trauma."

swirling colors and

tumbling shapes because

I want to be done

and set in a final pattern.

To summarize the chapter so far, some persons respond to trauma in a resilient manner, with enduring personal growth, with a changed sense of self, with enlarged resources of patience and commitment, and often with a passion for helping others who are in the same darkness. Other persons after trauma remain *traumatized*—unable to find resolution and remaining in darkness—often addicted to mind-numbing substances and caught in broken relationships and self-destructive behaviors.

The normal developmental nature of the discovery of meaning was recounted earlier in this chapter. As children become adults, they develop both the awareness of *meaning* and a series of personal meanings as they experience life. However, much of the research on *meaning* speaks of its discovery, not its reconstruction. The essence of trauma is that meaning is shattered: the self is blamed, the dangerousness of the world is sharpened, and a pervasive weakness permeates all thought and action. Therefore, just as childhood sexual abuse influences an adult's psychological and physical self, so too does it saturate the adult's meanings.

Research shows the search for meaning continues, even after it has been unsuccessfully attempted. Silver[20] and others interviewed seventy-seven adult women who were survivors of incest that had occurred on average twenty years before the interview. In spite of that amount of time, over 80 percent of the women reported to the researchers that they continued to search for *meaning*—a way to make sense of their childhood trauma. An equal number reported that this search for meaning was very important to them. Yet only half of the women had been able to construct a personal meaning; and for the others, the ongoing search led to greater personal distress and unsuccessful ruminations (obsessions) about the trauma.

This last section of the chapter interweaves my personal experiences with psychological research to describe trauma response and meaning reconstruction—one that in my case resulted in deep spiritual healing, psychological recovery, and enduring personal meaning. I must be clear that my recovery would share similarities with other survivors of childhood

---

20. Silver et al., "Search."

sexual abuse, but it also has unique components based on my own life and circumstances.

Brown[21] and others interviewed twenty early-recovery adult survivors of trauma in treatment. All these survivors were victims of child abuse, and some had suffered additional traumas as well. The authors remind us that recovery begins in the adult environment that is created by the aftereffects of early trauma. The child-now-adult has great difficulties in managing emotions, views the self as unworthy and unlovable, is unable to gain meaningful support from others, and engages in self-destructive behaviors.

While the participants in the study by Brown[22] and others exhibited all these problems as adults, many also reported a *resilience experience* that occurred while they were children or adults that they believed had been critical to their survival. Most often, this experience was interpersonal in nature. Examples were finding *alternate environments* as children—environments outside where the abuse had occurred and where interactions took place with adults who took an interest in the child. Other adults reported the useful experience of social support—persons who had encouraged them and who became trustworthy resources. Finally and central to this chapter is that many participants had *hope*—hope that persisted despite many desperations. *Hope* is the belief in recovery, the motivation to change, the presence of relationships in which hope is created and grown, the presence of positive thinking, and the dreams and aspirations of a better future.

For me as a child, I had a caring adult neighbor, there were several school teachers who took a personal interest in me, and I was supported by an adult within a Christian girl's organization. Each summer I went to that organization's summer camp, where my Christian college student counselors gave me models of an adult who I could become. However, as an adolescent, my despair was manageable only though complete numbing of my own emotions, risky behaviors around sex and substance use, and suicidal ideation. Again, however, there was a resilience event: those difficulties were recognized by a woman in the retail establishment where I worked as a teenager, and I now see how she tried to understand and help me.

De Castella and Simmonds noted in their detailed study of the lives of ten trauma survivors that they shared an "inner yearning for connection."[23] Much of this connection was directed toward spiritual connection; but it

21. Brown et al., "Unbraiding."
22. Ibid.
23. De Castella and Simmonds, "Experiences," 541.

coexisted with doubt, anger, and retreat. I began psychological treatment as an adult with a deep disillusionment about religion. *Having religion* didn't seem to have been of much help to me. I questioned why God would allow this experience to occur to me and why he had not protected me. I realized that I might not accurately understand God, and I decided to go find out for myself. I then read the Bible twice in its entirety. I kept a journal of what I discovered about God in this reading process that lasted for several years, which provided me with much new information that contributed to my own meaning making.

As an example, I struggled with the concept of a *loving God*.[24] I had to accept that a God who loved me could allow my abuse to occur because God loved us all enough to let us make choices. In my own case, I experienced my abuser's choices, but I also had made many self-destructive choices. If God still loved me and he still loved my abuser, then God's love was much more complex than I had thought. Reading the Old Testament gave this complexity a historical appearance in God's abiding love for the Israelites, who seemed determined to reject both him and his commandments. Repeatedly God "remembered his covenant" (Exod 2:24, Ps 98:3, and Jer 30:10–11), and he acted out of his love for the Israelites.

Scholars tease apart the experience of trauma and its negative effects in order to better understand how to treat persons with post-traumatic stress disorder. One aspect of trauma is its simultaneous damage of both thoughts and feelings. Beck[25] and others studied 109 women in treatment for intimate partner violence. For these women, persistent negative emotions were associated with two kinds of thoughts—*self-blame* and *negative beliefs about the world* (being a bad or dangerous place). We know from research on childhood sexual abuse that both of these thoughts are present in the experience of the child and later in the adult.

These realities were present in my own life in my shame about my own actions as an adolescent and adult—actions that I learned in treatment were shared by virtually all adults who had experienced childhood sexual abuse. However, for me to believe that God could forgive my actions and that I could forgive myself, I had to *approach* rather than avoid those dark spaces in my life and memory.

---

24. See Bishop, *God Distorted*.
25. Beck et al., "Negative Emotions."

That vulnerability is described by Brené Brown.[26] The title[27] of her book is derived from the speech that Theodore Roosevelt gave in 1910 and is predicated on this section of his famous speech:

> It is not the critic who counts; not the man who points out how the strong man stumbles, or where the doer of deeds could have done them better. The credit belongs to the man who is actually in the arena, whose face is marred by dust and sweat and blood; who strives valiantly; who errs, who comes short again and again, because there is no effort without error and shortcoming . . . who at the best knows in the end the triumph of high achievement, and who at the worst, if he fails, at least fails while daring greatly.[28]

An abuse survivor must *dare greatly*—must be not solely willing but rather eager, driven, and passionate to go forward into very dark places. Those dark places include the suffering frightened child, the adolescent who is filled with shame and anger, and the adult who must thrust past a society that is filled with messages of avoidance, such as the society of the church. For me, that meant confronting the dark memories of the past and the equally dark ways in which the past had become entwined in the present. It meant confronting persons in my current life; it meant being rejected and abandoned again; and it meant deliberately deciding on intense emotional pain for the hope of finding meaning at the end of the journey.

Psalm 119 is a beautiful representation of someone who is actively working in relationship to God to find meaning about difficulty. Psalm 119 describes the writer: He is laid low in the dust (verse 25); he is suffering much (verses 50, 107); he is afflicted (verse 71); he is being destroyed like a wineskin in the smoke (verse 83); and streams of tears flow from his eyes (verse 136).

Yet he is interacting with a God whom he is *holding accountable*—he reminds God of his many commitments, and he repeatedly puts his thoughts in the context of what God has promised. "According to your promise," he expects that God will hear him (verses 149, 154); preserve his life (verses 25, 50); strengthen him in his sorrow (verse 28); enable him to respond to taunting from others (verses 41–42); be sustained and have hope (verse 116); and find understanding, or *meaning* (verse 169).

26. Brown, *Daring Greatly*.
27. Ibid., xii.
28. Roosevelt, "Man in the Arena." See ibid.

What is unique about a Christian reconstructing meaning after trauma?

1. Christians have enduring hope in an active, loving God. Their assumptive worlds rest on truth in Scripture, even when that truth appears to be shattered by their own experience.

2. Christians can claim a promise—a verse that meant so much to me that I have an abbreviated version tattooed on my wrist: "For now we see through a glass, darkly, but then face to face. Now I know in part; but then shall I know, even as also I am known" (1 Cor 13:12; KJ21).

3. Christians are in relationship with a God who *wants* to be tested. Survivors such as I can engage in deep dialogue with God without fear of being deemed *bad* or *wrong*. As Dr. Vernon McGee[29] says, "God has never asked any to believe anything that does not rest upon a foundation." God really means business, and that is *most true* for persons who have the most to ask of him.

In summary, our Christian assumptive world has permanence. God has overcome the world (John 16:33). All things work together for good (Rom 8:28). God has a plan for us to prosper us, not harm us (Jer 29:11). In our meaning making, we have to *work back* to those global meanings. That task depends on our being willing to be active, to be vulnerable, and to suffer. It is enhanced as we believe that God is willing to be accountable to us. There is truth in enduring love.

> Now we see things imperfectly, like puzzling reflections in a mirror, but then we will see everything with perfect clarity. All that I know now is partial and incomplete, but then I will know everything completely, just as God now knows me completely. Three things will last forever—faith, hope and love—and the greatest of these is love. (1 Cor 13:12–13 NLT)

Toolkit

The toolkit will concentrate on meaning. Storytelling will be encouraged for rebuilding meaning. Then the focus will be on the meanings that are created during the storytelling process.

29. McGee, "Blind Faith."

Rebuilding Meaning

The tools in the toolkit for the companion are those that encourage the victim to use *narrative discourse* (storytelling) for meaning reconstruction. Schwab[30] analyzed the life stories of fifteen participants who participated in extensive interviews. Analyzing those interviews revealed that three dilemmas were explored by almost all the participants, and these dilemmas will be the focus in the stories of the victim.

First is the dilemma of *continuity or change*. How has change occurred? What is still continuous from the past? For victims of trauma, although much has and will be forced to change, there are still some continuities. Are they experienced the same way as in the past, or are they changing? What aspects of change feel easy, and what feel resistant? Within this dilemma are certainly aspects of faith. How does God feel similar, and how has he changed? What is *living in faith* like now, and has it changed? Identities will be a complex mixture of changes and continuities. Being able to identify each is a valued goal, especially both continuities and changes that reflect a positive self. For example, my lifelong sense of fairness has resulted in my now being a passionate advocate of persons who are being treated unfairly. The fairness concern is similar, but it is no longer me that is the person being considered, rather it is someone else.

The second dilemma is that of *sameness or difference*. This dilemma refers to how the new self-identity is becoming similar to that of others and also different from others. How is the *self* connected to experiences and attitudes of others, and how is it disconnected? Within faith storytelling, this dilemma is especially important. When certain features that are associated in the past with "acceptable religious appearances" come up for discussion, it is complex to consider how those appearances might no longer be part of one's identity or might become more of one's identity. An example for me is religious rituals. Building a new identity that has deeper faith has meant for me an increase in rituals and a change to a church that uses a more ritualized and liturgical style of worship. So I am different from others who worship within today's more casual and individualist style, and I am similar to persons who worship in the long-standing rituals and sacraments.

The third identity dilemma is *agency or non-agency*. A new identity will include components that are both *agentic* (freedom of choice) and *non-agentic* (reduced or eliminated freedom of choice). In everyday words, the

30. Schwab, "Meaning Making."

new identity and meaning will include some choices and some limitations. It might be a misunderstanding that new meaning and new identity will involve only free expression of choices. There will also be limits within the new identify. God puts limits around us to create and continue humility.[31]

Creating Meaning

The companion and the victim will be focusing on new meanings that are developed, built, and created by the victim as he or she tells and retells his or her story. Rather than this retelling being aimless, it will be gently guided by the companion along the identity dilemmas.

It must be noted that this is *not* an exercise in imagination and inventive fiction. Some events, especially those experienced by trauma survivors, have intrinsic meaning. Yet those events also have a new context and may well become connected with a new valence. This change is especially true for survivors who recognize that the original intent—to be wronged by another—has been altered by the providence of God. Recall Joseph telling his brothers: "As far as you're concerned, you were planning evil against me, but God intended it for good, planning to bring about the present result so that many people would be preserved alive" (Gen 50:20 ISV). That realization did not change the fact that Joseph was sold into slavery, was imprisoned for many years, and grew up apart from his beloved father. Rather, those events were incorporated into a narrative with a new meaning.

A specific journey skill is to complete a new *life identity*, the depiction of which is found in the following figure from Diohn Brancaleoni.[32]

Describe your ideal life.

a. What are your living environment and daily habits?

b. How do you spend your time?

c. Who is socially supporting you with affection, guidance, and actual help?

d. What are activities that you use to grow and learn?

e. What gives you meaning and purpose in this ideal life?

---

31. See Scazzero, *Emotionally*, 135–52.

32. Permission to use was provided via email correspondence in 2015.

Describe your ideal self.

a. What do you like most about yourself?

b. What do you do to cope with stress and uncomfortable feelings?

c. How do you treat other people?

d. How do other people treat you?

e. How do you honor and support your ideal self?

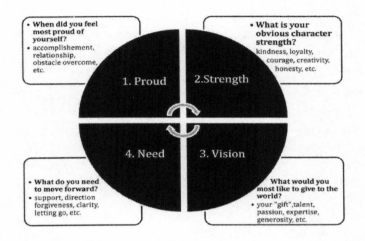

Copyright 2015 Diohn Brancaleoni. Used with permission.

The figure suggests four quadrants of life that can be further discussed and considered by the companion and the victim.

As new meanings are constructed, negative emotions can begin to be used as clues for *positive action*. Rather than dreading sadness or anger, we use those emotions as signs for action—as messengers to us.

- *Anger, irritation*: These give us information about what we need and are not getting. These give us strength and motivation to make a demand, to set a boundary, or to stand our ground on a belief or issue.

- *Fear, anxiety*: These give us information about what we need in order to feel safe. These give us courage to move forward. We also can use fear or anxiety as a sign that we need to increase our trust in ourselves and others. Perhaps they are a sign that we should ask for help in more concrete ways than we have been or to ask for help when we haven't been willing to do so.

- *Loneliness, boredom*: These give us information about how we are keeping the world at a distance from us. These give us the *push* to create opportunities to engage in activities and experiences that will reward us.

- *Grief, sadness*: These encourage us to consider healing and cleansing. They also promote compassion in us for these emotions in others.

- *Hurt*: Hurt promotes resilience when we allow it to be present. Hurt promotes self-care and participation in activities that will nurture us and our lives. Hurt also promotes our compassion for others who are hurting and increases our empathy for that emotion in others.

Each of these messenger emotions can provoke a process of consideration. As an example, fear can tell us what we need to feel *safe*. We can respond with a specific affirmation, such as "I deserve to be treated with respect." Fear motivates *action*, and we can respond with a request for help: "I will ask for what I need even if asking for help scares me." Last, fear promotes *trust* in others: "I am not alone in this, and I know that [person/God] will help me in this problem."

To conclude, meaning in life provides two key parts. One is *purpose*—meaning gives us various purposes, and a *meaningful life* is a life with a strong sense of purpose. The second is *significance*—meaning creates significance beyond the trivial or momentary, and a *significant* life is one of potential and achievement.

Case: Cecelia

You are a campus minister for a small liberal arts college—a job that you love because you do spiritual counseling for students on campus and you plan activities, events, and worship services to promote faith and community. Cecelia is a freshman who just turned eighteen and who is in her first year of college. In late September, she comes to your office and tells you that she's having trouble adjusting to school. You have seen her around the student center and at your events with student groups, and she appears quiet and reserved but is funny when given an opening. In your office, she appears very uncomfortable—she sits frozen for long periods of time and then will suddenly shift her weight, shake her foot, or wring her hands briefly before settling back into a rigid posture.

Cecelia asks repeatedly if you will tell anyone what she tells you. After significant reassurance that you will work to respect her privacy, she reveals that she has been cutting herself to relieve "painful memories." You ask Cecelia to tell you more about the situation. She says that she has only been doing it for the last couple of months, but the memories are from a "really long time ago." She isn't comfortable telling you what happened to her, other than "an older man did things to her" that she "thought she was over." She is perplexed to have such intense memories and feelings about these events so far after the event, as are you.

Cecelia tells you that she's from a small town, has known and been friends with the same people her whole life, and generally felt *safe* in that town. Making the adjustment to campus appears to be her main explanation for her distress. Cecelia tells you that she has few friends here and doesn't feel comfortable talking to them about these things. She said sadly that "they probably don't like me anyway and are just being nice." This characterization doesn't feel consistent with what you've seen of her interactions in the campus ministry center.

You notice that you are feeling sad, confused, and more than a little bit incompetent. You consider telling her to take comfort in God and trust his plan, but that somehow doesn't feel quite right. Instead, you remind her of God's love for her and reassure her that others including you like her and believe in her. She smiles sadly and thanks you. You offer to continue meeting with her, tell her that you are worried about her safety because she is cutting, and you suggest that she may want to speak with a therapist.

After that day, you still see Cecelia around the ministry center. At one point, you ask her to come into your office and you talk with her about how she is doing. She tells you that talking about it only made things worse for her, and she apologizes to you for causing you trouble and being a nuisance.

1. How is Cecelia making meaning? How is she making meaning of herself, of others, of the world?

2. Recall previous chapters: how do you feel about ensuring efforts to respect her *privacy*? Are there reasons you might consider breaking that promise?

3. What do you make of her apparent rejection of your reassurance that God loves her and that you and others genuinely like her?

4. What other information would you want or need to have?

5. What other things would you want to do in this situation?

7

Companioning on the Journey toward Healing for Victims and Their "Others"

Chapter Objectives

1. Understand the effects of childhood sexual abuse on relationships that the adult victim has with family and friends.

2. Expand your appreciation of your companioning contribution to the victim's journey.

3. Learn a model of change.

4. Learn journey skills that promote positive emotions in the midst of difficulties.

VICTIMS OF MANY TYPES of trauma often refer to their healing as a *journey*. That is an apt metaphor because a journey involves planning, a destination, and effort. Journeys are rarely completed without interruptions or delays. Cars have flat tires, plane flights are delayed or cancelled, weather complicates travel, and traveler fatigue mounts up.

A victim of childhood sexual abuse is also on a journey. We have established that victims have two destinations among others—forgiveness and meaning making. The relationship of forgiveness to meaning making is different for every traveler. For some travelers, one will be a stopping point on the way to the other; for other travelers, both will occur in tandem. Still, all travelers needs companions on their journeys.

Previous chapters have established a knowledge foundation about childhood sexual abuse for persons in positions in which they will likely hear from victims, have described why certain beliefs about childhood sexual abuse are helpful or harmful, and have explained *forgiveness* and *meaning reconstruction*. Because almost all adults who had experienced childhood sexual abuse live within extended circles of spouse/partner or ex-spouse/partner, children, and siblings, these persons also participate—either for good or for ill—in the victim's healing. If the victim is currently married, then the spouse will especially be involved in the journey. In this chapter, we will turn to victims and these other persons and will consider the effects of the victim's childhood family background on his or her adult relationships with others.

Family Characteristics

There is no single model for families in which childhood sexual abuse has occurred. That is also true for families with children who report their abuse to parents, but the family fails to appropriately respond. However, these families share features that likely contributed to the environment in which abuse occurred or was not responded to appropriately. Trepper and Barrett[1] describe three such features: cultural characteristics, family of origin history, and unspoken rules.

- The first influence is *cultural characteristics*. One relevant cultural characteristic is that females are considered subservient to males. There are many families with male dominant models that are not abusive or abusive-tolerant, so that model is not in itself a causative factor. Rather, since virtually all abuse that occurs in a family is done by male family members to female family members,[2] female submission to male dominance is often noted among abusive or abusive-tolerant families.[3]

- Another cultural characteristic is the degree to which the family is isolated within itself instead of regularly interacting with the social

1. Trepper and Barrett, *Systemic Treatment*.
2. See Finkelhor, "Prevention," and Russell, *Secret Trauma*.
3. See Finkelhor, *New Theory*.

environment. A strictly isolated environment in which the family keeps everything "inside the family" is common in an abusive situation. That may be physical isolation or isolation as the family builds a wall of appearances by which they look fine to outsiders but are actually deeply troubled within the family. As an example of this turning inward, Finkelhor[4] studied child sexual abuse in a sample of families. In families in which the parents were informed, 75 percent of the parents who did not report the abuse to anyone outside the family gave as a reason that the abuse was "no one else's business."

- The parents' own *families of origin* are a second influence on the occurrence of childhood sexual abuse. If one or both parents experienced attachment problems during their own childhoods or were parented in harmful ways, their current parenting styles and practices will be damaged. Russell[5] notes that in order for abuse to occur, certain factors must override the social inhibition of sexuality with a child. Some of these factors—such as inability to identify with the needs of the child or a need to feel overly powerful and controlling—may have been created within the parent's own difficult childhood.

- The third influence is the problematic *unspoken "rules"* that govern communication. Some families have the unspoken rule that there will be no conflict within the family or that there will be no upsetting the father or mother. Another unspoken rule is that nothing is said directly to the person who is the actual subject of a communication. As an example, a teenager may be told by her aunt that her mother is upset with her. The mother does not talk to her teenager directly, and the indirect style of dealing with the problem through the aunt is not likely to lead to effective problem resolution. Other families have an unspoken rule that one parent is the single communicator. This family's communication structure looks like a wagon wheel with all spokes going toward the hub. The communication equivalent is that all family members tell everything to that one dominant parent, and that parent then passes along information to other family members as he or she chooses.

A study of forty-eight families in treatment for incest provides additional information about the characteristics of families in which childhood

4. Finkelhor, *New Theory.*
5. Russell, *Secret Trauma.*

sexual abuse occurs. Trepper[6] and others assessed individual and family characteristics among families in treatment for incestuous abuse. Within this group, offenders were the natural father of the victim (48 percent), the stepfather (19 percent), an adult male friend of the family (17 percent), the brother of the victim (4 percent), and the mother of the victim (3 percent). Victims were primarily girls (92 percent); the majority of the victims were abused at ages twelve to fifteen (31 percent) or eight to eleven years (19 percent).

A frequent finding in the families that were being treated for incestuous abuse was family enmeshment (72 percent). *Enmeshment* occurs when family members have unclear or permeable boundaries. As an example, a teenage daughter gets anxious and depressed, and her mother, in turn, quickly becomes anxious and depressed simply because the daughter is anxious and depressed. This mother then becomes overinvolved in her daughter's life—trying to "help" her daughter by stepping in and solving what the mother sees as problems. This style will create difficulty for the daughter who is becoming developmentally independent and responsible for her own choices. Another characteristic of enmeshment among families is the almost complete lack of privacy. Only 11 percent of families in this study allowed privacy to family members.

Carrying These Characteristics Forward

Because the adult victim carries the damage of childhood sexual abuse into adulthood, it is inevitable that the adult victim's marriage, parenting, and work are affected. The influences—cultural characteristics, family of origin problems, and unspoken rules—come forward in time and reoccur in the victim's own family. For example, a male adult who had been abused during his childhood copes by obsessively watching pornography. Because conflict was not allowed to be expressed in his family during childhood, the same rule of *no conflict* applies to his current family. His wife is angry and bitter about his obsession with pornography; but going along with the rule to not confront her husband, she mistreats the children and turns her anger on them. They, in turn, become alienated from both parents and act out in ways that are age-appropriate but problematic. Examples might be academic failure, crimes such as shoplifting or vandalism, or substance abuse.

---

6. Trepper et al., "Characteristics."

Symptoms of family dysfunction when one parent is a survivor were detailed by Allender.[7] These symptoms might be depression, sexual problems, compulsive behavior, or low self-esteem.

- First, the survivor is depressed. As Allender notes, depression is not always a sad mood; it can also appear as mood swings, hopelessness, a deep sense of injustice, and shame.

- Second, sexual dysfunction and addiction are likely a longtime concern between spouses. In some cases, though, there may have been a satisfying sexual relationship that will degrade as the victim attempts to deal with the abuse. Abused victims may have no interest in sexual contact. This can range from avoidance to disgust. Alternatively, they may have sexual addictions or might engage in multiple affairs.

- Third, there will often be a pattern of compulsive behaviors. These include alcoholism, workaholism, eating disorders, and perfectionism.

- Last, victims experience very low self-esteem and see themselves as ugly, dirty, stupid, and worthless. This self-image creates problems in the victim's current family as the victim attempts to deal with the self-degradation. For example, a mother may treat her children unequally to foster ongoing competition for her affection or a father might alternate between parenting that is overly harsh and overly affectionate.

Courtois[8] notes that when a victim seeks professional treatment, he or she will eventually start catching up on the delayed developmental tasks of separation and individuation. Unfortunately, these did not occur in the family of origin, but will occur in the victim's current family. Here are two examples:

- A female victim may not have formerly acknowledged and accepted her anger. She now creates confusion in her current family when family members experience her anger. Because they had not caused it, they feel that the anger is misdirected at them.

- Perhaps a victim may experience a great need to be independent. The victim works that out by avoiding her family life, which troubles her husband and children. They then feel wronged because they rightfully

---

7. Allender, *Wounded Heart*, 148.
8. Courtois, *Healing*.

want to keep the same relationship with the mother and wife, but believe that she is "turning into a different person."

If a victim is in treatment, the therapist can consult with the family. The therapist can explain the course of treatment, meet with family members to help them with their own emotional concerns, and develop family strategies for living with the victim as he or she continues on the journey to healing. Because so much of the disability in adulthood involves relationships, the spouse is the most vulnerable person in the network and will benefit from individual sessions with the therapist.

Are the victim's children to be informed? Courtois[9] believes that children should be informed of the parent's past trauma and that the information should be presented to the child with both parents present and in an age-appropriate way. However, both parents need to be in agreement that the disclosure should be made and their children should be provided with support in the months that follow the disclosure. There are two reasons to consider disclosure.

1. The children may be victims of the same perpetrator.

2. Their childhoods were inevitably affected by the abuse.

The older the children, the more they will understand how their own childhood experiences were affected by the long-term consequences of abuse for their mother or father.

This extended discussion of the victim's likely experience in his or her family of origin—and current family function—is meant to *widen the window* of understanding the complexity of the victim's experience. The abuse most likely did not happen in isolation, but rather within a family or a close interpersonal relationship. The layers of secrecy about the abuse both in the past and present contribute to the victim's ongoing inability to be open and transparent. This includes within his or her current family and friend networks. The companion can be a resource who recognizes the difficulties in communication but continues to provide an interpersonal relationship that follows "different rules" in being open and genuine.

9. Ibid.

The Complexity of Companioning

Dr. Alan Wolfelt founded the Center for Loss[10] over twenty years ago. He noted how persons who interacted with mourners attempted to *treat* grief. Rather than *treating*, Wolfelt[11] proposes *companioning* the bereaved. Based on its derivation, *companioning*[12] is essentially "sharing a meal with." Hence, *companioning* is being present with the other by sharing and communing. The companion creates a safe place for the griever to share stories, to mourn, to remember, and to search for meaning.

In his model, Wolfelt[13] outlines eleven specific tenets of companioning. If his companioning model is used for adult victims of childhood sexual abuse, five are especially pertinent. *Companioning* is about

- being present to another person's pain—not about taking it away.

- listening with the heart—not about analyzing with the head.

- bearing witness to the struggles of others—not about judging or directing these struggles.

- the gift of sacred silence—not about filling up every moment with words.

- respecting disorder and confusion—not about imposing order and logic.

We know that Jesus had his crucifixion especially in mind as he resolutely set out for Jerusalem (Luke 9:51). Yet in spite of that knowledge, Jesus asks his disciples to stay awake and to pray with him in the garden of Gethsemane just before the crucifixion. He desired their companionship. For the victim, the experience of a companion creates hope for a new future, capacity and motivation to become involved in the regular activities of living, and the joy of a renewed and redeemed self in relationship with God.

Adult victims of childhood sexual abuse are rightfully frightened of their past, its horrors and losses. Hence, the companion follows five core principles:

---

10. www.centerforloss.com.

11. Wolfelt, *Handbook*, 2–3; "Tenets."

12. From the Latin prefix *com-* "with" and *pan(is)* "bread" with *-ing*.

13. See Wolfelt, *Companioning, Handbook*, "Tenets."

1. *Safety*—the victim must have physical and emotional safety. It might be the case that the companion suggests a referral to a professional to ensure that safety.

2. *Trustworthiness*—the companion must have clear and consistent boundaries. The second principle is important because victims do not have good boundaries. Their own were violated during childhood, and they don't have experiences that allowed them to construct boundaries. An example of a good boundary is that companions meet with victims at times of mutual choice. The companion is not a resource that is always available. A companion with a poor boundary might repeatedly respond outside their planned meeting to the victim by telephone and text.

3. *Collaboration*—Companions are on the journey with the victims. They work together. Think of two persons who are climbing a rock wall. They share tasks, or they alternate tasks.

4. *Empowerment*—the victim learns to be powerful. The victim identifies strengths, engages in skill building, learns true reliance on God, and uses Scripture for *building up*.

5. *Choice*—the victim makes choices about the journey. The companion is accompanying—not leading—the victim.

Tedeschi and Calhoun[14] discussed companioning a person who was diagnosed with and being treated for a severe medical illness. Their suggestions are also relevant for companioning adults after childhood sexual abuse.

- *Adopt the Attitude of the Companion*. A companion has a unique, honorable role in bearing witness to the struggles of the victim and being a trustworthy ally during times of reflection. The companion is never *the expert* on any topic but rather a humble human. It is acceptable to say "that was truly horrible; I am not surprised that you feel so angry." The victim is learning about him- or herself, and the companion is learning alongside.

- *Appreciate the Paradoxes of the Healing Journey*. Companions, a *spouse*, a counselor, an understanding physician, a pastor—all are important team members for the victim's recovery. However, the victim ultimately feels alone with his or her loss. Companions must

14. Tedeschi and Calhoun, "Clinician."

understand that although they will be beside the victim, giving support and encouragement during difficult times, the victim will often report being "alone." This feeling in no way undermines the importance of any team member. It is simply that the task of reconstructing meaning must be done within oneself.

- *Developing New Beliefs and Goals.* Remember that the adult *survivor* is living with a shattered world. New beliefs and goals must be developed. The best companions know their own process of developing beliefs and goals and share their own struggles. Reading a book or story together and discussing it is an example of how companions might assist in this task. The resources chapters provide ideas for books and readings, and there are many authors who regularly blog on their own faith journeys.

Why Does Companioning Work?
The Psychology of Encouragement

Encouragement is an activity that shows up frequently in the Bible. In fact, *parakaleo*, the Greek term for encourage, is mentioned 105 times in the New Testament. However, our understanding of the concept of *encouragement* is fuzzy. We think of *encouraging* as telling someone in difficult times to "just keep going!" or complimenting someone by saying that "you are such a great friend." We might encourage a group by commenting favorably on their work ethic: "I can't believe how hard you all worked to make this come together." However, those comments, while worthwhile and emotionally supportive, are not actually *encouragement.*

Wong[15] presented a model of encouragement as a character strength with certain features. First, encouragement is an *active* interpersonal process—a give and take between people. Next, encouragement always has a *present or future* orientation, whereas praise has a past orientation. Praise occurs after the observance of an activity and is an evaluation of the activity no matter how well intended. Finally, encouragement has the quality of *affirming* another in order to instill courage, perseverance, hope, and confidence while the recipient is "addressing a challenging situation or realizing a potential."[16]

15. Wong, "Psychology."
16. Ibid., 182.

In order for the victim of childhood sexual abuse to succeed in facing challenge, the companion provides encouragement, which instills bravery and motivation. For the victim to develop new potential, the companion recognizes and communicates the strengths of the victim that match the necessary tasks of forgiveness and meaning making.

Wong elaborates on the characteristics of effective encouragement. For encouragement to be effective, it should focus on the process, be delivered by trusted persons, stimulate a certain type of communication, and focus on strengths.

To be effective, encouragement should focus on the *process*.[17] *Process encouraging* is about a person's effort, not his or her ability; about strategies that had been used, not personal characteristics; and about consistency over time. Thus, to hear "you are really strong" is not as encouraging as to hear "I noticed when you talked about your conversation with him, you were very careful to say to him exactly what you meant to say. You did not avoid using hard words." When encouragement is that specific, it does not seem patronizing.

Additionally, encouragement is effective when it is delivered by persons who are *trusted*—they are seen as sincere, rather than overly effusive and just "being nice." There is also a critical need for encouragers to be *accurate*; it is not encouraging for a person who is trying to achieve a potential to hear unrealistic optimism.

Encouragement is also effective when it stimulates a particular kind of *communication*. How people think about a past trauma has been considered many times in this book. One ineffective way that victims deal with trauma is *rumination*—when people are *stuck* in their words and feelings and continually re-experience the emotions of the trauma. Another ineffective way is *avoidance*. Although people might talk about their trauma, they are actually avoiding it. They do this by using what Combs and Freedman[18] refer to as *thin* stories. These short stories describe few aspects of trauma. Encouragement fosters an atmosphere in which victims retell their stories and with each retelling, the stories become *thicker*—with more details, new perspectives, and a meaning narrative that is more complex.

Last, encouragement is effective because it focuses on *strengths*. Many of us can name a personal strength, but we cannot define it with any detail. As an example of how to counter that deficit, Wong suggests that the person

17. Kamins and Dweck, "Implications."
18. Combs and Freedman, "Narrative Therapy," 1038.

who is being encouraged elaborate what a complete day would be like if he or she were fully *the strength that is named*. There are many lists of character strengths; one list[19] names twenty-four strengths within the categories of wisdom, courage, humanity, justice, temperance, and transcendence.

Most relevant to our Christian churches and organizations is that encouragement can and should be a cultural norm. If victimized persons believe that revealing a particular struggle will be met with encouragement rather than shock, disbelief, denial, or avoidance, they will more frequently talk about their struggles. Unfortunately, our Christian church, *writ large*, is experiencing a crisis of encouragement. Responses to personal struggles that are more frequently seen and heard are criticisms, shaming or shunning, and blocking persons out. These communications are not only painful for the person at whom they are aimed. They also do two harmful things in general. These communications

- foster the sense that all our personhood is available for evaluation by others and
- affirm implicitly that others' evaluations of us matter more than our evaluations of ourselves and God's evaluation of us.

Are There Wrong Reasons that People Want to be Companions?

Unfortunately but understandably, a person may want to participate in an activity that he or she might have chosen for unconscious reasons. Thus, it can happen that people who *themselves* have emotional problems may choose to be involved in helping others. Scazzero[20] wrote extensively of the difficulties of attempting to be spiritually mature while at the same time being emotionally immature. His diagnosis is painfully accurate:

> The problem, however, is that . . . the spirituality of most current discipleship models often only adds an additional protective layer against people growing up emotionally. Because people are having real, and helpful, spiritual experiences in certain areas of their lives—such as worship, prayer, Bible studies, and fellowship—they mistakenly believe they are doing fine, even if their relational life and interior world is not in order. This apparent "progress"

19. "Character Strengths and Virtue Descriptions."
20. Scazzero, *Emotionally*.

then provides a spiritual reason for not doing the hard work of maturing.

They are deceived.[21]

If you are thinking of being a companion, a resource and a filter for your own reasons for companioning is Scazzero's examination of the necessary links of emotional health to spiritual health.[22] Briefly, here are examples of symptoms of unhealthy emotional spirituality.

- *Using God to run from God.* For example, when I do "Christian things" so that people will think well of me or when I use God's truth to judge and devalue other people.

- *Ignoring emotions of anger, sadness, and fear.* Many Christians are taught that emotions are not to be trusted and should essentially be avoided. At some level, that teaching can be incorporated into a Christian lifestyle that *tamps down* strong emotions. A victim cannot avoid these emotions—they must be given over to God in an active, self-aware way. The companion cannot avoid dealing with strong and distressing emotions.

- *Denying the impact of the past on the present.* When Paul tells us that "the old life has gone, a new life has begun" (1 Cor 5:17 NLT), this does not mean that our past lives cease to influence us. Growing in Christ often involves re-examining our past lives for negative and even sinful influences on our present lives.

- *Spiritualizing away conflict.* It is true that very few of us are fortunate enough to have grown up in a family that handled conflict in a healthy way. Rather, most of us have learned ways to effectively avoid conflict or to wrongly engage in conflict.

- *Covering over brokenness, weakness, and failure.* Many Christians suffer under the expectation that their salvation depends on their achievements and feel guilty for what appears to be constant failure. Instead, God welcomes our failures and invites us to put them in his hands so that he can heal us.

- *Living without limits.* There must be limits to what we can give away of ourselves. We cannot say yes to every request for our time, energy, and

21. Ibid., 15.
22. Ibid.

resources. Jesus set a clear example by going away from his schedule to rest, to commune with God, and to talk with his disciples.

- *Judging other people's spiritual journeys.* Our emotional immaturity causes us to fear. So to cope with that fear, we place ourselves above someone else. Comparisons may allow us to feel worthy, but they are wrong. Companions must above all else let people move at their own pace—trusting God to do his work with them in his time.

The Creation of Hope in the Narrative of Restoration

EMILY DICKINSON,[23] 1830–1886:

Hope is the thing with feathers
That perches in the soul,
And sings the tune without the words,
And never stops at all,

And sweetest in the gale is heard;
And sore must be the storm
That could abash the little bird
That kept so many warm.

I've heard it in the chillest land,
And on the strangest sea;
Yet, never, in extremity,
It asked a crumb of me.

Perriman[24] examined the life of Emily Dickinson through family letters and testimony from persons who knew her and her family and concluded that she had experienced childhood abuse, which was likely sexual. Although Emily Dickinson was never able to connect to the outside world, her poetry can be analyzed as exhibiting stages of recovery. This poem that likens *hope* to a bird speaks quietly yet forcefully of the resilience of hope—surviving a storm, a chilly land, a strange sea, and extremity (the furthest

---

23. "Hope is the Thing" (public domain).
24. Perriman, *Wounded Deer.*

point or limit). As we saw, *hope* can be a topic of poetry. *Hope* has also been extensively discussed and studied.[25]

What is *hope*? Hope has certain qualities.[26] It is energetic, *agentic* (focusing on a goal), and confident. It also contains positive emotions.

It is these positive emotions that we will now consider. Perhaps because we consider negative emotions more frequently, our experience of positive emotions is blurry rather than sharp. We tend to say that we are *happy* or *content* or occasionally *joyful*. Positive emotions can be confused with physiological states such as arousal or with moods which are more long lasting.

A useful model for understanding positive emotions is the broaden-and-build model that was proposed by Fredrickson.[27] Consider the effect of a negative emotion such as fear. If a person is suddenly struck by fear, the emotion *narrows* the person's response to one specific action, that of escape. In contrast, positive emotions have the opposite effect of *broadening* an individual's feeling-action response. *Joy* can lead to play, to singing, to creativity, or to worship. *Contentment* creates reflection, rest, appreciation, and self-insight. Positive emotions create circumstances during which we build resources for the future. These resources last longer than the emotion itself; therefore, we experience incremental transformation by "becoming more creative, knowledgeable, resilient, socially integrated, and healthy individuals."[28]

The journey of restoration, then, contains hope and many instances of this broaden-build-transform sequence. Experiencing hope in association with a companion can restore what had been lost to the victim—exploration leading to creativity, life experiences that fuel development. *Small* transformations become foundational to more *expansive* transformations, which then increase resilience and courage. Thus an ever-widening cycle of healing and restoration is created.

a "fellowship"

25. For example, an international database of research on *hope* contains almost 4,500 references from many disciplines. This includes psychology and health-related fields. (See "Hope-Lit.") A quick search on the APA PsycNet database yielded over 2,600 books and articles on the term *hope* alone.

26. See, for example, Snyder et al., "Hope"; Rand and Cheavens, "Hope."

27. Fredrickson, "What Good?" and "Role."

28. Fredrickson, "Positive," 123. (Note that this phrase can be found in several chapters and articles that are written by Fredrickson alone or in collaboration with others.)

The Bible says about this hope: "I will restore the years that the locust has eaten" (Joel 2:25 NIV). Colin Smith[29] comments on the wide applicability of this verse for our lost years—not only lost food but also lost abundance of life. Victims have lost many years to pain, shame, self-destruction, misdirection, and avoidance. By his deepening their relationships with him, by creating benefits and gains in the midst of their unspeakable damages, and by multiplying their blessings, God can restore those *locust-lost years* to victims. What a privilege it is to be a companion to a victim—however long that time is—and to honor that journey from despair to restoration and redemption.

> We don't yet see things clearly. We're squinting in a fog, peering through a mist. But it won't be long before the weather clears and the sun shines bright! We'll see it all then, see it all as clearly as God sees us, knowing him directly just as he knows us! But for right now, until that completeness, we have three things to do to lead us toward that consummation: Trust steadily in God, hope unswervingly, love extravagantly. And the best of the three is love. (1 Cor 13:12–13 MSG)

Toolkit

The tool in the toolkit for the companion is a *model of change* that will incorporate the stages of recovery. The journey skill for the survivor is the *GREAT DREAM*.

Model of Change

It is tempting to think of *change* as a smooth pathway between the *decision* to change and the *achievement* of change. Still, our own personal experiences in changing any habit—however trivial—inform us that change is anything but smooth. As changes are attempted, you can keep in mind the model[30] of change that Prochaska, DiClemente, and Norcross developed. Here each of the four[31] stages of change from their model are described, followed by a companioning response.

29. Smith, "Restore."
30. Prochaska et al., "Change."
31. Ibid, 1103–4. Note that an additional stage before the *contemplation* stage is

1. *Contemplation.* At this stage, the person is aware that a change may be needed; the person might be as far as six months out from making a change. That awareness could be positive ("I am really ready to make a career change") or negative ("I have some symptoms in my body that aren't good. I should make a doctor's appointment and have some tests, but I don't really want to do that"). The person can be tempted to not make a change ("I will just let fate take its course") or can get ambivalent and anxious.

   Companion response. A companion can encourage information gathering to increase knowledge. It's important to remember that action without planning will likely be unsuccessful. Focusing on the future and setting out specific goals that are related to the change will create an understanding of the costs and benefits of the change as well as an accurate evaluation of the victim's readiness to move forward.

2. *Preparation.* The person commits to taking action within the next month. There is awareness and anticipation that is accompanied by uncertainty. Small behavior changes may be made. The preparation stage builds to the action stage.

   Companion response. Encourage the victim to use planning, visualizing, and even mapping to see how steps might occur. Define small steps or subgoals that will lead to the desired change. It's important to plan ahead for strategies to deal with setbacks and failures, because these will occur. Role models of successful changers are important.

3. *Action.* This step is the change! There is investment and energy in the new behaviors, thoughts, and emotions. There may be positive feedback from the environment. There will also be setbacks. It's also during this stage that a new identity begins to be built.

   Companion response. The most encouraging companioning response is support, both emotional and instrumental (tangible). There will need to be adjustments in the plan, and the companion can be an active encourager.

4. *Maintenance.* Making changes is hard, and keeping them continuously implemented is harder! After six months of positive change, a person reaches the maintenance stage. It might now be said that a change has been made. The new behaviors are established, and the person is integrating the change into his or her new identity.

---

identified: at the *precontemplation* stage, the person doesn't feel a need to make changes.

Let's rework the stages according to what we know about recovery from childhood sexual abuse as detailed in the book so far. For each stage, several key phrases are listed.

1. *Contemplation.* Accepting help, begin to create hope. A *turning point.* Moving from being overwhelmed to coping with various disabilities. Beginning recovery. Identifying and coping with difficult—and sometimes overwhelming—emotions. Accepting connection to another person and beginning to make a decision to trust.

2. *Preparation.* Developing insight into the nature of being a victim; identifying and changing sabotaging behaviors (e.g., substance use, isolation, neglected self-care, impulsivity). Making a decision to establish independence. Struggling against despair and being overwhelmed. Belief in the possibility of recovery, and establishing recovery-oriented personal relationships. Having positive dreams and aspirations rather than having despair and disconnection.

3. *Action.* Begin developing a new identity that is set on firm ground of change and recovery. Actions can include journaling, taking new directions in work or family or friendship networks. Learning and discovering new ways to leave behind disability and dysfunction; moving toward engagement and health. Overcoming stigma and shame. Moving toward forgiveness and meaning making. Beginning the new *story.*

4. *Maintenance.* Gaining meaning; giving forgiveness. Becoming more forgiving toward self and others. Learning how to evaluate oneself according to Scripture rather than the dictates of others. Establishing a meaningful ongoing set of spiritual practices that sustain growth and meaning. Establishing a meaningful life with social, occupational, leisure, and service components. Focusing on strengths and personal responsibility. Becoming empowered to advocate for others and to work toward their empowerment in victimizing circumstances.

The Great Dream Acronym

By this point, the victim is becoming a survivor in the truest sense of the word. The victim is relying more closely on and trusting in God to create newness of life and hope after darkness and despair. The Action for

Happiness group—established originally in the United Kingdom—has an excellent set of actions that collectively foster both recovery and post-traumatic growth and change. The acronym for these actions is GREAT DREAM.[32]

G	Giving	Do things for others.
R	Relating	Connect with people.
E	Exercising	Take care of your body.
A	Appreciating	Notice the world around you.
T	Trying Out	Keep learning new things.
D	Direction	Have goals to accomplish.
R	Resilience	Find ways to bounce back from adversity.
E	Emotion	Take a positive approach to life.
A	Acceptance	Be comfortable with who you are.
M	Meaning	Be part of something bigger than you are.

Henri Nouwen was a Dutch Roman Catholic priest who left his academic career to work with people with mental disabilities. For the last ten years of his life, he was pastor to L'Arche Daybreak community in Canada. Nouwen wrote extensively on his thoughts and experiences. On peace, Nouwen[33] wrote:

> Keep your eyes on the prince of peace, the one who doesn't cling to his divine power; the one who refuses to turn stones into bread, jump from great heights, and rule with great power; the one who says, "Blessed are the poor, the gentle, those who mourn, and those who hunger and third for righteousness; blessed are the merciful, the pure in heart, the peacemakers and those who are persecuted in the cause of uprightness" (see Matt 5:3–11). See the one who touches the lame, the crippled, and the blind; the one who speaks words of forgiveness and encouragement; the one who dies lone, rejected, and despised. Keep your eyes on him who becomes poor with the poor, weak with the weak, and who is rejected with the rejected. That one, Jesus, is the source of all peace.
>
> Where is his peace to be found? The answer is surprising but it is clear. In weakness. Few people are telling us this truth, but there is peace to be found in our own weakness, in those places of our hearts where we feel most broken, most insecure, most

32. "Ten Keys to Happier Living."
33. Nouwen, "Path of Peace," 78–80.

in agony, most afraid. Why there? Because in our weakness our familiar ways of controlling and manipulating our world are being stripped away and we are forced to let go from doing much, thinking much, and relying on our self-sufficiency. Right there where we are most vulnerable, the peace that is not of this world is mysteriously hidden.

Case: You as Companion

One case vignette for this chapter is *you*! Think through answers to the following questions slowly and prayerfully, and share them with your group members. As you share, allow yourself to be open to feedback and to giving it.

1. In what ways have your experiences helped you to be an effective companion?

2. In what ways might your past experiences be a barrier to effective companioning?

3. What are your fears about companioning?

4. What are your hopes for companioning?

5. Who has been a companion for you? What did you learn from that experience about companioning?

6. What Bible verses speak most directly to you about being a companion?

7. As you were reading this book, what did you learn about companioning? What have you learned about yourself?

Case: Developing a Companioning Ministry

The other case vignette for this chapter is your church, organization, or faith community. As a group, identify one or two aspects of companioning that appeal to you. Describe those aspects together. Then formulate an action plan for how to develop a companioning ministry that fosters those aspects.

1. Who do you see participating? Why?

2. How will the participant(s) be selected or trained and by whom?

3. What are pushbacks/challenges that you will encounter? What barriers will be put in place by other people? An example of such a barrier would be the following remark: "We don't have anyone in our church who had been sexually abused. I would know if we did."

4. What would be evidence that your plans are ready to implement?

5. How can you enrich the environment of your church, organization, or faith community so that silencing and shaming victims occurs less frequently? What actions might be necessary?

6. How would you measure *success*? What would be a *successful* program?

8

Resources for Pastors and Caregivers

There are many excellent resources for information about childhood sexual abuse and for *best practices*[1] concerning policies and procedures within churches and Christian organizations. The resources provide a solid starting point for additional information gathering by the interested reader. This chapter is organized as follows: policies and procedures, text resources, and digital resources such as advocacy groups and other websites.

Policies and Procedures

The first denominations to develop and disseminate official policies and procedures with regard to childhood sexual abuse and to provide educational and programming resources to their members were the Roman Catholic, Episcopal, and Baptist denominations. This section will start with a discussion on the Southern Baptist Convention. Next the Episcopal and Roman Catholic Churches will be covered. Some information from governmental agencies will be included.

Baptist

The Southern Baptist Convention[2] passed several resolutions that pertain to sexual abuse. The initial resolution "On the Sexual Integrity of Ministers"

1. *Best practices* means that the method or procedure has consistently shown better results than alternatives.

2. Southern Baptist Convention, "Resources." See Southern Baptist Convention,

149

was passed in 2002. Clear steps toward addressing childhood sexual abuse were the resolution "On Protecting Children from Abuse" in 2007 and "Responding to the Evil of Sexual Abuse" from the executive committee in 2008. Such steps, however, were not undertaken without dissent. For example, an attempt to establish a database of pedophile clergy was rejected.[3] The most recent resolution "On Sexual Abuse" is as follows:

> WHEREAS, The Bible is clear in its affirmation that children are a gift from the Lord (Psalm 127:3–5); and
>
> WHEREAS, The Lord Jesus demonstrated His love for children by encouraging them to follow Him, correcting those who hindered them, and condemning those who harmed them (Matthew 18:3–6; Mark 10:13–14); and
>
> WHEREAS, The sexual abuse of children remains an ever-increasing criminal offense with more than 1.8 million reported victims of sexual abuse by more than 750,000 child abuse perpetrators identified in the United States alone; and
>
> WHEREAS, Tragically, instances of sexual abuse have been perpetrated within Southern Baptist congregations, churches of other denominations, and other Christian ministries; now, therefore, be it
>
> RESOLVED, That the messengers to the Southern Baptist Convention meeting in Houston, Texas, June 11–12, 2013, call upon Southern Baptists to stand with our Lord Jesus in loving and protecting children as He does; and be it further
>
> RESOLVED, That we remind all Southern Baptists of their legal and moral responsibility to report any accusations of child abuse to authorities in addition to implementing any appropriate church discipline or internal restoration processes; and be it further
>
> RESOLVED, That we likewise call upon all Southern Baptists to cooperate fully with law enforcement officials in exposing and bringing to justice all perpetrators, sexual or otherwise, who criminally harm children placed in our trust; and be it further

---

"Integrity"; "Protecting"; "Sexual Abuse" and Southern Baptist Convention, Executive Committee, "Responding."

3. Southern Baptist Convention, Executive Committee, "Responding," 2–3. See also Foust, "Wrap Up," para. 14–18; Chapman, "Light," para. 18; Fitzpatrick, "Database."

RESOLVED, That we strongly urge Southern Baptist churches to utilize back checks like those provided through Life Way Christian Resources (www.lifeway.com/backgroundchecks), databases of sexual predators such as the US Department of Justice sex offender database linked at SBC.net (www.SBC.net/localchurches/mnistryhelp.asp), or other relevant resources in screening all potential staff and volunteer workers, particularly those to minister to children and youth, and be it further

RESOLVED, That we encourage pastors and church leaders to develop and implement sound policies and procedures to protect our children; and be it further

RESOLVED, That we encourage all denominational leaders and employees of the Southern Baptist Convention to utilize the highest sense of discernment in affiliating with groups and or individuals that possess questionable policies and practices in protecting our children from criminal abuse; and be it finally

RESOLVED, That we urge all Southern Baptists to pray for children who are victims of abuse, to stand for their protection from abuse, and to support safe and healthy children's ministries in our churches and communities.

These resolutions can be found at the Southern Baptist Convention[4] webpage that contains resources and links to material for training leaders, for preventing child sexual abuse within organizations, and for balancing defense against sex offenders and ministry to sex offenders. It is correctly noted that state laws contain provisions for reporting to authorities that differ across states. Thus, each church or organization must be familiar with the laws of its own state and must use policies that are in compliance with the requirements of the state in which the ministry is located. The Southern Baptist Convention defines the key components of child sexual abuse prevention that are to be addressed in the context of state law as the following: guidelines for screening and selecting employees and volunteers; guidelines for interactions among individuals; monitoring behaviors; ensuring safe environments; responding to inappropriate behaviors, breaches in policy, and allegations or suspicions of child sexual abuse; and training about child sexual abuse prevention.

4. Southern Baptist Convention, "Resources."

Episcopal

In 1991, the Episcopal Church[5] created a committee to address sexual exploitation. The committee conducted a survey of church members that revealed a need for additional formal attention to the topic within the denomination. A Conference on Pastoral Standards was held in 2001 which called for the development of more informed policies. A committee created the policies with the help of the Church Pension Group.

In 2003, the House of Bishops passed Resolution B008, "Protection of Children and Youth from Abuse, 74th General Convention (2003)." That resolution established that "times and circumstances"[6] demand that the church articulate a clear commitment to the safety of churches and urged dioceses to develop and adopt policies to protect youth against abuse. Here are two necessary policies from the resolution:[7]

- Screening and selection process for all clergy, lay employees, and volunteers who work with children is to include a written application, a public records check, a personal interview, reference checks, and the provision that volunteers not work with children until the volunteers have been known to the clergy and congregation for at least six months.

- Behavioral standards are to be defined and include respect for the privacy of children and youth by not putting them in unsupervised one-on-one situations, using age-appropriate arrangements for activities such as sleeping or showering, the prohibition of any sexually oriented materials in the presence of children except for preauthorized educational programs, guidelines for physical contact, a prohibition for self-disclosing the worker's own sexual activities or fantasies, and a prohibition on being under the influence of any substance.

Roman Catholic

The Roman Catholic Church has been significantly affected by media coverage of childhood sexual abuse by priests as well as by the lack of

---

5. Applewhite et al., "Model Policies," i–ii. See also Prichard, "Church (1990–)," 389–392; Fontaine, "Confronting."

6. Ibid., 33.

7. Ibid.

disciplinary action against priests when abuse was suspected or revealed. In the United States, the John Jay Report[8] was commissioned and funded by the US Conference of Catholic Bishops. The report was based on over 10,000 cases or allegations made between 1950 and 2002. Among other findings, the report noted that the incidence of abuse increased after the 1960s and peaked in the 1970s; incidents then decreased through the 1980s and 1990s. Victims have not hesitated to pursue legal remedies for their experiences: an online archive estimates that over 4,000[9] civil lawsuits have been filed against the Church.

The Catholic Church began in the 1980s to move from a policy that deemed child sexual abuse a *spiritual* problem to defining abuse as a *criminal* problem. [10] In 2002, the US Conference of Catholic Bishops adopted a *zero-tolerance* policy[11] that required a series of reforms for selection of church employees, creation of a safe environment for children, cooperation with civil authorities, and healing and reconciliation of victims and survivors. In the United States, the National Review Board[12] requires dioceses that are faced with an allegation to contact legal authorities, cooperate in an investigation, and remove the accused person from duty.

The language is significant in its acceptance of responsibility. The *Child and Youth Protection Charter*[13] is introduced as follows:

> Since 2002, the Church in the United States has experienced a crisis without precedent in our times. The sexual abuse of children and young people by some deacons, priests, and bishops, and the ways in which these crimes and sins were addressed, have caused enormous pain, anger, and confusion. As bishops, we have acknowledged our mistakes and our roles in that suffering, and we apologize and take responsibility again for too often failing victims and the Catholic people in the past. From the depths of our hearts,

---

8. John Jay College of Criminal Justice Research Team, *The Nature and Scope.* For additional studies from the John Jay College research team, see United States Conference of Catholic Bishops, "Reports."

9. BishopAccountability.org, "Circumstances," para. 4.

10. Merz, "History," 3–4.

11. Ibid., 9–10. See United States Conference of Catholic Bishops, *Charter*, 11 (Article 5).

12. Ibid., 6–22. See also United States Conference of Catholic Bishops, "Board"; "Protection."

13. Booklet, full-page version, and Spanish version are available at United States Conference of Catholic Bishops, "Charter."

we bishops express great sorrow and profound regret for what the Catholic people have endured.

Again, with this 2011 revision of the *Charter for the Protection of Children and Young People*, we re-affirm our deep commitment to creating a safe environment within the Church for children and youth. We have listened to the profound pain and suffering of those victimized by sexual abuse and will continue to respond to their cries.[14]

Governmental Agencies

Governmental agencies also provide resources to assist organizations that serve youth. For example, *Preventing Child Sexual Abuse within Youth-Serving Organizations* is available from the Centers for Disease Control and Prevention (CDC).[15] This guide was created by experts with the assistance of an advisory group. In the guide, components of child abuse prevention are defined; specifically, the challenges to child sexual abuse prevention within youth-serving organizations are addressed. These challenges are outlined explicitly as follows:

- *Beliefs* that hinder child sexual abuse prevention include denial; fear that people will assume that something is wrong, should the organization focus on preventing child sexual abuse; attitudes about sexuality; lack of buying in or support; and fear of actually uncovering incidents of abuse.[16]

- *Structural issues* that hinder child sexual abuse prevention include limited or inadequate resources; employee turnover that is high; organizations that tend to rely on a single strategy, rather than making use of multiple strategies; the difficulty of internal communication; and the need for partnerships.[17]

Note that often the efforts that these denominations made proceeded within a context of pushback and denial. The denominations should be

14. United States Conference of Catholic Bishops, *Charter*, 3.
15. Saul and Audage, *Youth-Serving Organizations*.
16. Ibid., 29–30.
17. Ibid., 31–32.

commended for their commitment to improving both prevention and re-mediation responses[18] with respect to childhood sexual abuse.

Why Aren't All Churches and Organizations Using These Policies?

Unfortunately, policies and procedures by themselves can neither prevent nor mitigate the damage from child sexual abuse. Rather, the *motivation* to implement them must be present. This topic[19] creates a climate of denial, misunderstanding, and fear. Ministry staff and workers must all be personally committed to implementation of these policies and procedures and to related solutions for prevention.

It is a great temptation for churches to rely on mechanisms that are already in existence with respect to Christian sexuality as a means of preventing childhood sexual abuse. In many churches, there are either *accountability partners* or *accountability groups*.

This practice began about the same time as the Promise Keepers[20] organization was founded by Bill McCartney, who at that time was head coach of the University of Colorado football team. The original Promise Keepers conference was held in July 1990. From then, Promise Keepers grew rapidly—with many conferences and events that culminated in 1997 with the Stand in the Gap: A Sacred Assembly of Men in Washington, DC, that was attended by approximately 800,000 men. The organization lists seven core beliefs.[21] That is, a Promise Keeper is committed to

1. honoring Jesus through worship, prayer, and obedience to God's word in the power of the Holy Spirit;

2. pursuing vital relationships with a few men and understanding that he needs brothers to help him fulfill his promises;

3. practicing spiritual, moral, ethical, and sexual purity;

18. Prevention policies are, for example, adequate screening of staff and volunteers who work with children and careful development of response to allegations of abuse (including full disclosure of relevant state laws). Remediation policies include identification of appropriate ministries to former victims.

19. This is clear from the challenges that were previously stated and also considered in previous chapters.

20. https://promisekeepers.org

21. Lutz, "Promise Keepers." See also Claussen, *Promises*.

4. building strong marriages and families through love, protection, and biblical values;

5. supporting his church's mission by honoring and praying for his pastor and by actively giving time and resources;

6. reaching beyond racial and denominational barriers to demonstrate the power of biblical unity; and

7. influencing his world and being obedient to the Great Commandment (Mark 12:30–31) and the Great Commission (Matt 28:19–20).

One outgrowth of the movement—explicit in the second core belief that vital relationships with other men will assist men in keeping their promises—was the increased use of accountability partners in local churches. An *accountability relationship*, whether a partnership or a group as described by Easley,[22]

- helps each member submit every part of life to the will of God,

- acts as a safeguard against adulterous relationships and lustful habits by bringing such thoughts and behaviors into the open, and

- provides a regular time for prayer and encouragement.

In today's technology-driven world, computer software[23] has also been used to produce reports of one's online behaviors for accountability relationships. Computer access is a means of committing a range of problematic behaviors and that through use of software reports, accountability activity is grounded in actual data.[24] Using this process, the person would define the problem for which accountability is needed—whether pornography, online gaming, online shopping, or another problematic or addictive behavior. Together with the partner, the data can be used to direct the accountability discussion. Some questions might be "What was the most tempting thing that you encountered online this last week?" and "What would in your accountability report would draw my attention?"[25]

Unfortunately, as with most external checks on behavior, the mere existence of accountability partners is not a reliable guard on wrongful sexual

---

22. Easley, "Accountability," para. 2.

23. For example, CovenantEyes, http://www.covenanteyes.com.

24. See Gilkerson, "Finding."

25. Ibid., #4.

or other behaviors. Jacobsen[26] noted, in fact, that accountability groups actually let men off the hook from confessing sexual sin to their wives: as he[27] says, "there's a safe comfort in the fellowship of failure." His question regarding confession to the accountability group rather than to one's wife is provocative: is it really that you want to spare her the pain, or is it that you would rather spare yourself the shame?[28]

An even stronger confrontation of this method was made by Klenck.[29] In his perspective, regular complete confession of all sins to an accountability partner or group leads to a shift away from the biblical notion of accountability to God. Additionally, the person may be concerned more about what the accountability partner will think or say about the confessed behavior or thought than the actual sin itself. Klenck[30] acknowledges that James 5:16 commands us to confess our faults to each other, but he draws a distinction between humble admission of our sinful nature to others and the ongoing confessional relationship of believer to God clearly described in Scripture. His concern about accountability groups is the substitution of confession to others for confession to God.

Finally, churches using this method must be particularly sensitive to train accountability partners on their responsibilities to the larger church and communities with regard to child abuse issues. If an accountability partner or group becomes aware of threats to children's safety or trust, there must be a procedure and policy to follow. For example, an immediate policy-driven response must be made if websites that include child pornography are on an accountability partner's software report.

Overall, the message of this chapter section is that every church, every Christian organization, and every youth ministry must have and use policies and procedures that directly relate to their organization's purpose, that apply in the state or states in which the organization is located, and that emphasize the protection of children and their safety.

26. Jacobson, "Real."
27. Ibid., para. 10.
28. Ibid., para. 7–9.
29. Klenck, "Wrong." See Discipleship section.
30. Ibid.

Text Resources

This section has a list of excellent texts that can be used to educate ministry workers about childhood sexual abuse and appropriate responses by those who hear reports from victims. These texts are not written for victims: material that is directed toward victims can be found in the next chapter.

Every pastor and ministry worker should have educational texts for personal study as well as for lending to new staff. The texts have been selected because of their quality of writing, their availability, and their inclusiveness. Each text is briefly described and its basic publication information is listed. Each of the included texts has reference lists that can be consulted for further reading. The list in alphabetical order by author is as follows:

Boyle, Lance A. *Wounded Churches, Wounded People: A View from the Trenches and Recovery Guidelines*. Mustang, OK: Tate, 2005. (177 pages)

The author is an ordained pastor who served in seven churches over a thirty-year period. His role was that of *after-pastor*—a pastor who serves on an interim basis because the previous pastor has been accused or charged with sexual misconduct. The after-pastor is there to act in response to the crisis in the church and to prepare church members for a new pastor. Hence, the experiences of this pastor are uniquely from the *trenches*. For privacy reasons, the author chose to write under a pseudonym and obscured details of events and persons that he discusses in the book. The writing is explicit and straightforward. He begins with his understanding of the symptoms of a violated church—distrust of the pastor and the denomination, poor communication, symbolic fights over what appear to be trivial issues and lack of confronting actual issues, and memory lapses with respect to the church's history. By covering such topics as forgiveness, shame, and justice within traditional Christian theology, he outlines how these problems—and the actuality of the sexual misconduct—can be healed.

Rev. Boyle graduated from an accredited seminary with a Master of Divinity (MDiv) degree; he also majored in pastoral counseling. His bachelor's degree was in human care services, and he received specialized training in critical stress debriefing and emergency response. He has facilitated a range of services from workshops to response and intervention teams.

Courtois, Christine A. *Healing the Incest Wound: Adult Survivors in Therapy*. 2nd ed. Norton Professional. New York: Norton, 2010. (748 pages)

This book is a revised version of the classic psychological examination of the effects of incest on adults and the ways in which treatment can provide growth and healing. Written for psychologists, the book is so clearly presented that nonpsychologists can benefit from the author's research and clinical experience. There are also many resources, which include workbooks for survivors, resources for survivors and their supporters, and websites.

Dr. Courtois is an authority in the field of trauma and incest. She is a psychologist in private practice and is also past president of the Psychological Trauma Division of the American Psychological Association. She conducts training workshops nationally and internationally on issues that are related to traumatic stress and its treatment.

Cozzens, Donald. *Sacred Silence: Denial and the Crisis in the Church.* Collegeville, MN: Liturgical, 2002. (199 pages)

Although Roman Catholic in its focus, this book is a forceful examination of the role of denial in continuing destabilization among church members, who are overwhelmed by mistrust of the church as an institution. Cozzens promotes and describes the "redemptive honesty"[31] that is needed to regain a role for the church in modern culture. His argument for retrieval of spirituality and for candor and honest dialogue relates to all Christians.

Rev. Cozzens teaches religious studies at John Carroll University. He served as a priest for several years and as president-rector of St. Mary Seminary. He leads workshops and retreats for priests. In 2009, he was given the Priest of Integrity Award by the Voice of the Faithful, an organization that is devoted to support survivors of clergy abuse and priests of integrity and to create and shape structural change in the Catholic Church.

Finkelhor, David. *Child Sexual Abuse: New Theory and Research.* New York: Free, 1984. (260 pages)

This academic text is a classic examination of research on childhood sexual abuse by a leading scholar of family violence. Conditions that lead perpetrators to commit abuse are described and extensive statistical information is provided on abuse itself and on public perceptions and beliefs about abuse. Although some chapters are more technical in nature, Professor Finkelhor

31. Finkelhor, *New Theory*, 18.

provides an overview in his preface to assist the reader in locating the most personally relevant information.

Professor Finkelhor is a sociologist who has devoted his academic career to the study of child sexual abuse and related topics. He currently directs the Crimes against Children Research Center and is co-director of the Family Research Laboratory at the University of New Hampshire. The center's website[32] contains extensive resources about a variety of child-related topics such as bullying, sex trafficking, child abuse in several domains, and prevention.

Franklin, Cynthia, and Rowena Fong, eds. *The Church Leader's Counseling Resource Book: A Guide to Mental Health and Social Problems*. New York: Oxford University Press, 2011. (494 pages)

In the foreword to the book, Ruth Graham notes the growing need for pastors to confront mental health problems in the congregation. In her words, "God longs for us to be healthy emotionally (Luke 4:18–19; John 10:10). He has called you to minister to His wounded flock." A wide range of disorders may occur in congregations. Thus, problems or issues that affect children and adults are discussed: some examples are autism, defiant youth, addiction, domestic violence, marital issues, and financial problems. Resources include self-help books and a glossary of mental health terms.

Professors Franklin and Fong are internationally known scholars on mental health concerns. They worked with an editorial board of authors and pastors to select topics and chapter contributors. Each chapter was written to provide an informed perspective on a particular problem and instruction on pastoral care with a mental health emphasis.

Heggen, Carolyn Holderread. *Sexual Abuse in Christian Homes and Churches*. Eugene, OR: Wipf & Stock, 1993. (208 pages)

This book was the first to present childhood sexual abuse as a lived experience in Christian homes and churches. Dr. Heggen is a Christian psychotherapist who wrote the book based on her experiences with clients who had abuse histories within the church. She includes their accounts in her analysis of why the church is so resistant to admitting and dealing with the problem of childhood sexual abuse, which in her opinion relates primarily to the patriarchal nature of most churches. Her book also includes

32. www.unh.edu/ccrc/about/index.html.

resources for making worship sensitive to survivors of abuse (e.g., in liturgies and responsive readings).

Dr. Heggen has served on Mennonite church boards and committees. Her focus is on trauma recovery. She is a frequent speaker and workshop leader on personal and communal healing.

Jones, L. Gregory. *Embodying Forgiveness: A Theological Analysis*. Grand Rapids, MI: Eerdmans, 1995. (333 pages)

This study of forgiveness crosses theology, contemporary culture, and Christian traditions to confront what forgiveness really is—a "tough, distinctive, hard-won accomplishment" (to quote from a reviewer) and what Jones considers a *craft*. Jones presents the cultivation of reconciling forgiveness within community, in which trust and dialogue are engaged rather than avoided. Jones also addresses critical issues such as forgiveness in the absence of reconciliation; he discusses the roles of God's forgiveness, our forgiveness, and God's vengeance. Jones creates a challenge for the complexity of *embodying* forgiveness.

Dr. Jones currently serves as provost at Baylor University. He served as dean of the School of Divinity and is currently senior strategist for the Fuqua/Coach K Center on Leadership and Ethics at Duke University. He has written extensively on forgiveness, Christian ministry, and pastoral leadership.

Langlois, Tish. *Fault Lines: Incest, Sexuality, and Catholic Family Culture*. Women's Issues. Toronto: Second Story, 1997. (236 pages)

In this book, interviews that were conducted with eight women who were incest survivors and also deeply grounded in Catholic culture are described. Although the author writes from a feminist perspective, her understanding of theological tradition and her straightforward writing style would make this book excellent reading for persons outside the feminist tradition. It also relates to the evangelical tradition, in that the Catholic theology of the family closely resembles the evangelical theology of the family. The term *fault line* describes the demarcation between a woman's experience and the reality that she learned from her faith-filled upbringing and current life.

Ms. Langlois is an advocate for women. She was the first recipient of the Master of Women's Studies at Memorial University of Newfoundland.

Lord, Janice Harris, Melissa Hook, Sharifa Alkhateeb, and Sharon J. English. *Spiritually Sensitive Caregiving: A Multi-faith Handbook.* Burnsville, NC: Compassion, 2008. (208 pages)

Many of the readers of *Push Back the Dark* may have a ministry opportunity that involves working with persons of other faiths. Evangelical churches are increasingly involved in ministries to refugees, and the United States itself is increasingly diverse. The authors of this book discuss beliefs and rituals, issues around death and dying, and issues of justice among the following faith groups—Native American, Hindu, Buddhism, Judaism, Christianity, and Islam. There are many resources that are provided in the book for victims and targeted to sexual abuse among children and adults. The book is rich with information, and there are summaries for each chapter.

Each of the authors is experienced in healthcare, law enforcement, education, and justice; and each has held positions of authority in their separate fields. Janice Harris Lord was National Director of Victim Services for Mothers Against Drunk Driving (MADD); Sharon English is a hearing officer for the California Youthful Offender Parole Board; and Melissa Hook is director of the Office of Victim Services for the District of Columbia. Sharifa Alkhateeb, who was president of the North American Council for Muslim Women, died before the book's publication.

Plantinga, Cornelius, Jr. *Not The Way It's Supposed to Be: A Breviary of Sin.* Grand Rapids, MI: Eerdmans, 1995. (216 pages)

Plantinga returns to *sin* as it is historically understood in his examination of sin as the major human trouble. One result of sin is its distortion of our character and its creation of our intentionality to sin more. *Sin* is also a major human trouble because it results in misery which creates more sin. His example[33] pertains to childhood sexual abuse:

> A father who sexually abuses his daughter corrupts her: he breaks all the little bones of self-respect that hold her character together. Filled with shame and anger at her treacherous father and conniving mother, grieving for her lost and innocent self, the corrupted child is extremely likely to abuse *her* children or to assault her central nervous system with large quantities of alcohol or to make and break one rickety marriage after another.

33. Plantinga Jr., *Breviary*, 3.

His book recovers our awareness of sin in a culture that seems overly focused on grace.

Professor Plantinga is president emeritus of the Calvin Theological Seminary. He earned his doctorate from Princeton Theological Seminary. He has served as pastor for several churches and on the faculties of two colleges and three seminaries.

Russell, Diana E. H. *The Secret Trauma: Incest in the Lives of Girls and Women*. Rev. ed. New York: Basic, 1999. (426 pages)

This text remains the classic study of the effects of incest on girls and women. Russell is a sociologist whose work was federally funded by several agencies. In this book, she reports at length on her study of a large number of women who experienced incest as a child. Her scholarship was among the first to provide data on the experience of abuse (e.g., frequency and duration, severity of abuse) and the relationship between incest and social factors (e.g., face, social class, religious upbringing). The research was considered exemplary because of the number of women in her sample[34] who represented a wide range of socioeconomic variables and because of the technical details of the study (e.g., extensive training of interviewers). Her book presents cases and scholarly material in a way that is understandable by an educated lay reader.

Diana E. H. Russell is currently professor emeritus of sociology at Mills College in Oakland, California. She is the widely recognized expert on the study of sexual violence against women and girls, and her works have received multiple international awards. *The Secret Trauma* itself received three National Book of the Year awards.

Scazzero, Peter. *Emotionally Healthy Spirituality: Unleash a Revolution in Your Life in Christ*. Nashville: Nelson, 2006. (228 pages)

A consideration of the assertion that spirituality cannot be healthy and mature without an accompanying emotional healthy maturity is the foundation of this book. Focused on pastors and ministry staff, its content is both challenging and comforting: it is possible to confront areas of emotional immaturity and disease within oneself and to experience changes in one's approach to ministry to others as well as relationship to God.

---

34. There were 930 women.

Peter Scazzero is a founder and senior pastor of New Life Fellowship Church in Brooklyn, New York—a large multiracial church. He holds a doctoral degree in ministry to marriage and family and graduated from Gordon Conwell Theological Seminary. Peter and his wife Geri co-founded Emotionally Healthy Spirituality[35] to bring the precepts of emotional health and contemplative spirituality to pastors, church leaders, and staff.

Starks, Glenn L. *Sexual Misconduct and the Future of Mega-churches: How Large Religious Organizations Go Astray*. Santa Barbara, CA: Praeger. 2013. (161 pages)

A recent development in American religious life, megachurches have become established as a permanent component of evangelicalism. By definition, *megachurches* have 2,000 or more attendees and may have upwards of 10,000 or more.[36] They exist in stark contrast to historically smaller Protestant churches. Across Protestant churches, the average attendance on Sunday is seventy-five participants. Only 5 percent of the churches in the United States have an average attendance of more than 500.

Starks notes that the administrative structure in megachurches—with its emphasis on a single leader—differs dramatically from that of large businesses or organizations. While businesses have a chief operating officer, they also have other administrative staff with authority and typically an external board or advisory group as well. His argument, which is supported by multiple case data, is that the overreliance in a megachurch on a single person with significant power and authority creates an environment that resembles a business without the accompanying oversight that is intentionally present in most large businesses. The book details how this organizational climate promotes a culture of secrecy that allows acts of sexual abuse as well as financial misdeeds and other problematic behaviors that occur unchecked.

Glen L. Starks holds a PhD in public policy and administration. He has written books and articles on leadership and management and has worked in the federal government for over twenty years.

---

35. www.emotionallyhealthy.org

36. Starks, *Sexual Misconduct*, 6-7; Thumma and Travis, *Beyond Megachurch Myths*, 8.

Tracy, Steven R. *Mending the Soul: Understanding and Healing Abuse.* Grand Rapids, MI: Zondervan, 2005. (270 pages)

This book is a thorough and biblical analysis of abuse in all its forms—emotional, physical, and sexual. Professor Tracy has a background in both theology and counseling; he writes knowledgeably on the nature of abuse, the effects of abuse on the child or adult, and healing from abuse. The text contains many clinical examples that are analyzed in the context of Scripture. Appendices include a child protection policy, an application for employment in children's and youth work in a Christian church or organization, an interview protocol for use during selection of employees and volunteers, a compendium of characteristics that are often possessed by abusers, and a collection of Bible passages that directly address the issue of child abuse.

Professor Tracy is on the faculty of the Phoenix Seminary. Before his academic employment, he had been pastor of three churches. He and his wife are founders of Mending the Soul Ministries.[37] Tracy conducts research and ministers in areas of gender, sexuality, and abuse.

Volf, Miroslav. *Free of Charge: Giving and Forgiving in a Culture Stripped of Grace.* The Archbishop's Official 2006 Lent Book. Grand Rapids, MI: Zondervan, 2005. (247 pages)

This deeply moving book explicates *God Who is a Giver* and *God Who is the Forgiver*. How do we as his disciples respond to his actions? First, Volf considers our weak attempts at giving within the radical and sacrificial giving of God. He then draws a parallel between God's radical giving and God's equally radical forgiving. Our own attempts at forgiveness are weaker than our acts of giving—likely because we are clinging to our pride and rejecting humility. Volf notes that forgiveness for Christians always involves the triangle of the person who did the wrong, the person who is forgiving the wrong, and God. Without God, the relationships become fragile and will crumble.

Miroslav Volf is the Henry B. Wright Professor of Theology at Yale University. His book *Exclusion and Embrace* won the Grawemeyer Award in religion in 2002.

37. See the digital resources section in this chapter.

Digital Resources

Many digital resources have been mentioned in this and other chapters. Resources that have been previously mentioned will not be repeated in this section. Rather, this section notes online groups that are centrally positioned to educate and to assist readers in creating new approaches for responding to childhood sexual abuse within the church. These resources are listed in alphabetical order. As with the text resources, there are many more than can be listed in this chapter. This list was chosen for the quality and quantity of information that is provided by the organization and by its duration and intensity of involvement in the issue of childhood sexual abuse.

Godly Response to Abuse in the Christian Environment (www.netgrace.org)

Godly Response to Abuse in the Christian Environment (GRACE) has an active presence on social media such as Facebook and Twitter. Their website contains information about the mission of GRACE, which is to "empower the Christian community through education and training to recognize and respond to the sin of child abuse." There is a board of directors and a series of partnerships. The website provides extensive information in prevention, response assistance, consultations, and investigations and answers common questions about abuse. There is a list of resources and a blog.

The Hope of Survivors (www.thehopeofsurvivors.com)

The Hope of Survivors was founded to serve men and women who had been sexually abused by clergy. There are many resources for victims, churches, and pastors. There are international divisions of Hope for Survivors including Latin America, Australia, Canada, and Romania; the website content is available in a range of languages.

Joyful Heart Foundation (www.joyfulheartfoundation.org)

The Joyful Heart Foundation was founded to focus on domestic violence and sexual assault. Thus, their resources pertain to adult victims. The goal of the organization is to create opportunities for healing through programs, educational resources, and media coverage. Their programs cover three topics: healing and wellness, education and awareness, and policy and advocacy. They are widely present on social media, such as Facebook, Twitter, Pinterest, YouTube, Instagram, and FeedBurner.

Mending the Soul Ministries (www.mendingthesoul.org)

Mending the Soul Ministries is an organization that is devoted to training church leaders around the world to restore broken persons and rebuild community. The website provides models of community healing, offers books and curricula, provides resources, and presents data on ongoing training. The training model is precise and grounded in both theology and psychology—understanding the theology of suffering and compassion; understanding the effects of abuse; how *Mending the Soul* groups operate; and leadership training. The organization is present on social media with Facebook, Twitter, and FeedBurner and also has offerings in Spanish.

National Child Traumatic Stress Network (www.nctsn.org)

The National Child Traumatic Stress Network was established to consider childhood traumas such as natural disasters, community and school violence, and neglect and physical abuse. Their resources on sexual abuse include information that is available in Spanish. The network is a federal effort—funded by several governmental agencies and coordinated by two universities. They are also on social media through Facebook and Twitter.

Patheos (www.patheos.com)

Patheos hosts conversations on faith through faith channels, blogs, columns, and a book club. Their blog authors are widely recognized and write on a wide variety of topics and views. (Patheos Press publishes books through several imprints.) Patheos is also on social media—Facebook, Twitter, and FeedBurner.

Rape, Abuse, and Incest National Network (www.rainn.org)

The Rape, Abuse, and Incest National Network (RAINN) is one of the largest online organizations for sexual assault survivors. The website offers information and extensive resources on topics such as state-by-state laws, policies, strategies for family members, and relevant news reporting. They are on social media: some examples are Facebook, Twitter Tumblr, Pinterest, StumbleUpon, and LinkedIn.

Stop It Now (www.stopitnow.org)

Stop It Now is an organization that was founded in 1992 to prevent sexual abuse of children. Their specialty is training programs for parents and caregivers, although they also have resources for survivors. The unique approach of Stop It Now is that it frames *abuse* as a preventable public health problem—encouraging adults to take responsibility to prevent abuse and to create effective programs to accomplish those goals. Stop It Now believes that adults can stop abuse with accurate information and tools and that communities will mobilize around prevention initiatives. Particularly relevant to readers, there is a separate section for faith communities that outlines safety planning and prevention within faith organizations. There is also a section that directly addresses mandated reporting.

Survivors Network of those Abused by Priests (www.snapnetwork.org)

Survivors Network of those Abused by Priests (SNAP) is the oldest network of sexual abuse survivors. It was organized in 1989 to support survivors of clergy abuse and their allies. Currently SNAP has a global presence, with groups in over thirty countries. This network is also active in social media on Facebook and Twitter. The website is large and well organized. There is a list of resources that includes recommended reading, FAQs, support groups, and several resources that address issues of victims such as choosing a therapist. A blog, stories of survivors, and extensive coverage of news is available.

9

Resources for Survivors

My Letter to You, a Survivor

Dear Sister or Brother:

I have not met you; but I know you deeply, intimately, and in a way that no one else knows you. I have experienced your shattered displacement of losing truth and reality. I along with you have confronted the God who "loves me" and struggled with you to know why in that love there was no protection. I along with you have lived a life that has been divided—lived on two or more levels at the same time. I have your symptoms—being alienated from my own body, feeling the demand to be perfect, being abandoned over and over, and knowing myself to be dirty beyond any hope of becoming clean. Yet I have walked far along the path of healing, and so can you.

Here are three pleas from me. First, consider in an ongoing way when you need professional help and when you don't. As a psychologist, I urge you to seek professional help if you are self-destructive (such as cutting, or engaging in risky sex with strangers); if you have times that you cannot account for (what psychologists would call dissociation); if you are so frightened that you are perfectly compliant with every demand that everyone places on you; and if you see no ending but ending your own life. There are many counselors, treatments, and medications that can help you. It is not weakness to get help. It takes amazing strength to walk into a stranger's office and to sit down and say "I am having problems."

Second, understand that recovering from childhood sexual abuse is not an event. It is a process. Processes take time, energy, and patience. Your goal is not a finish line. Your goal is a pathway along which you walk, run, crawl, and sometimes stop. Those actions are okay; when you stop or fall, you will learn to pick yourself back up and start moving again. You will also do better when you have at least one partner on the path. Early in my own journey, I hesitatingly disclosed my abuse history to a Christian friend. It happened that she also was an abuse survivor. She had spent more time on the path than I, and she became a valued touchpoint for questions such as "Is what I am experiencing normal?" and "What did you do about this situation?" (By the way, you will be amazed how many Christian women have experienced childhood sexual abuse.)

However, I need to warn you about disclosure. During my journey, I changed from not telling anyone to slowly telling people, to aggressively telling people, and to not telling people anymore. Be wary about disclosing and realize that it's helpful to have friends who know and friends who don't. Some people who I had most trusted responded most destructively to my disclosure. Yet sometimes there was wonderful affirmation: I remember when I told our small group—they were stunned and confused but supportive. I received the most loving email from one member the next day that simply said, "I don't know what to say. I have never met anyone who experienced that, but I want you to know we love you and we will pray for you."

Third, I can guarantee that God loves you more deeply than you can imagine: you can tell him, shout at him, or scream at him—anything you want, and he will still love you. He knows already how you feel; you aren't hiding anything from him when you don't own up to feelings that you think aren't "right." I had to resolve many issues with God: where was he when this was happening to me? Was my abuser really a Christian? When I sinned extravagantly, because that is what abuse survivors do, was that still sin?

His presence only deepened for me as I opened my heart and gave him so much pain and hurt. At this point in my journey, his presence is as much a part of me as breathing; I now see my abuse experience as a gift, but that took me a very long time of complete honesty with God.

You can start a process of healing by talking only with God. As you begin to open up to him, you will find that he helps place resources in your hands. Trust him with your healing. Know that I and every other survivor I know pray every day for you and your healing journey.

This chapter will begin with information about providers of professional treatment and best practices[1] in mental health treatment. The chapter will then cover digital resources and end with text resources.

Providers of Professional Treatment

Survivors may be considering seeking professional treatment. This section of the chapter describes community-based treatment providers including their background, training, and credentialing. These providers are listed in order of the amount of training that is required to identify oneself as belonging to that profession. The alternative to community-based providers are institutionally based providers; in which case, survivors may have less ability to select specific types of services.

This section also briefly describes the most commonly used treatments for trauma related to childhood sexual abuse. Each of these treatments has been investigated for its effectiveness and has been shown to be effective. Because of space limitations, not all treatments that might be available are described. Patients who are considering treatments that are not listed should use websites from professional associations to query for specific treatments.

There is a widespread misunderstanding that needs correction before providers are described, and that pertains to state licensure. Some such as Abundant Life[2] have argued that state licensure is incompatible with a Christian commitment:

> Each individual must decide if he or she wants to be an agent of the state or a servant of GOD and the Church (Body of Christ). If you have a Divine call on your life to counsel and minister to the hurting, then a state licensure and certification will inhibit such ministry because "No man can serve two masters: for either he will hate the one, and love the other; or else he will hold to the one, and despise the other. Ye cannot serve God and mammon," Mt. 6:24.[3]

---

1. *Best practices* means that the method or procedure has consistently shown better results than alternatives.

2. http://www.abundantlife4me.org.

3. http://abundantlife4me.org/career.

Abundant Life goes on to assert that a state-licensed professional counselor would be forbidden to pray, read or refer to the Holy Scriptures, or counsel against homosexuality. They argue that in most states, a counselor cannot promote his or her personal religious beliefs.[4]

This overall description of the limits to what treatments can be offered by state-licensed therapists is simply wrong—with one exception that will be discussed next. State-licensed health providers have complete freedom to offer treatments that seem best to them and for their clients. That freedom is balanced by an informed consent process that occurs before and during treatment. This process allows the client to understand the nature of his or her concern as defined by the provider, the intended treatment (including its length), whether there are alternate treatments that might be also considered, and any other relevant factors. Clients typically sign informed consent forms which are kept on file by the provider.

Why is informed consent so important? A legal case[5] involved Dr. Osherhoff, who received psychoanalytic treatment from a private facility, Chestnut Lodge, for his depression. The treatment was unsuccessful, and Dr. Osherhoff left Chestnut Lodge and consulted another provider who recommended antidepressant medication. Having experienced significant financial and personal loss during the year of unsuccessful treatment, Dr. Osherhoff sued Chestnut Lodge. In court, Chestnut Lodge providers argued that their choice was protected by the doctrine of *respectable minority*, that is, that their choice of treatment would have been approved by a respectable minority of health providers. The difficulty with their argument is that it requires informed consent by the patient, which Dr. Osherhoff had not provided.

A state-licensed Christian provider can offer virtually any treatment to a patient as long as the patient completes an informed consent process and understands the potential risks that are involved. As an example, a provider might wish to try a new and relatively unproven treatment. It is *ethical* and *proper* if the client—after understanding its experimental nature—consents to receiving that treatment. Of course, if the treatment is being paid for by third party coverage (such as insurance), the treatment must be justified to those payers.

4. Ibid.

5. See *Osheroff v. Chestnut Lodge* for the case or Klerman, "Osheroff," for case details and implications.

Consequently, persons who seek treatment should seek it from persons who are licensed and/or credentialed by the state. In some cases,[6] providers who have completed their degree must also complete a certain amount of supervised work. The best parallel to this situation is student teaching: the student is teaching but that teaching is supervised by the teacher of the classroom. If you are receiving treatment from a provider who is receiving supervision, that provider will inform you of that fact and tell you the name and credentials of the supervisor.

Social Work

Social workers with master's degrees have completed a two-year program in social work and typically receive a Master's of Social Work (MSW) degree. It is also possible to work as a social worker with a bachelor's degree in arts (BA) or in science (BS).

Social workers are licensed in all fifty states. If a social worker is licensed to practice independently, he or she lists the credential as a licensed clinical social worker (LCSW). Each state sets the requirements for licensure. Those requirements are not the same from state to state. As an example, some states will license persons who received a bachelor's degree in social work, whereas other states will only license persons who have earned a master's degree.

Because social workers and counselors[7] both provide counseling, it is logical to wonder what the differences are between them. Generally, social workers and counselors both provide counseling and therapy. Social workers have training that also prepares them to advocate for changes in the environment around the client. For example, social workers might contact an employer for a client with special needs or might help the client tap into community resources to assist the client in his or her home.

The association is the National Association of Social Workers.[8] Social workers often have focused interests and may belong to specialty practice sections in the national association. Examples are aging, child welfare, social work and the courts, and health.

---

6. This is described later.
7. See the next section.
8. www.naswdc.org.

Mental Health Counseling

Mental health counselors have completed a graduate program in counseling and earned a Master's Degree in Arts (MA) or in Education (MEd). These programs are typically two years in length and involve curriculum on determining the nature of a client's concern (assessment, diagnosis); treatment (e.g., counseling, group therapy); and professional issues (e.g., ethics). Mental health counselors are licensed by the state in which they work. To be licensed, counselors need a master's degree, two years of supervision after the degree, and need to pass a state and/or national examination.

The national association is the American Counseling Association.[9] It is a large association with divisions[10] to which counselors who share a common focus choose to belong. In addition, if a counselor focuses on a specific area of practice such family therapy,[11] there may be specific national associations that are related to that area.

All fifty states license mental health counselors for *independent practice*, which means that their work with clients does not need supervision. Each state defines what activities can be offered by a counselor in that state. Insurance companies typically cover mental health treatment that is offered by counselors.

Psychologists

Psychologists are specialists in human health and behavior. Psychologists must complete a doctoral degree (a PhD or a PsyD). All states license psychologists. As with other providers, states have the authority to establish state-specific requirements. As an example, California requires all psychologists to have specific training in human sexuality, child abuse assessment and reporting, treatment of alcohol and other substance abuse dependency, elder abuse, and spouse/partner abuse in addition to the usual content of a doctoral degree in psychology.

9. www.counseling.org.

10. As examples, divisions include the American Mental Health Counselors Association (www.amhca.org); the Association for Adult Development and Aging (www.aadaweb.org); and the Association for Spiritual, Ethical and Religious Values in Counseling (www.aservic.org).

11. For family therapy, say, that association would be the American Association for Marriage and Family Therapy (www.aamft.org).

The education that is required to be a psychologist typically takes six to seven years to complete. Students complete curriculum in all the following areas:

- core areas of the discipline of psychology (i.e., social psychology, biological psychology);
- assessment and types of tests that are used for psychological assessment; treatments—both group and individual;
- supervision;
- ethics and professional practice; and
- research such as research design and the statistical analysis of data.

During their training, students complete about a thousand hours of supervised practice. After all their coursework and dissertation, students will also complete a one-year residency of full-time supervised clinical work before they graduate. An additional year or two years of supervised clinical work after graduation will need to be completed for licensure eligibility.

Because of this additional training, psychologists have a *scope of practice* that differs from people in counseling and social work. The term *scope of practice* means the activities that are defined by the state as those only the provider can perform. Psychology's scope of practice includes diagnosis and treatment of all psychological conditions for children and adults.

Because of their expertise in research, psychologists are involved in using research to evaluate the effects of treatments, in developing improved methods of assessment, in providing testimony in court settings, and in setting policy at state and national levels. Psychologists are also involved in primary-care teams alongside other healthcare providers. The reason is that many health conditions are initiated or resolved through behaviors. Using diabetes as an example, *unhealthy eating* and *noncompliance with medicine taking* are both behaviors which a psychologist can assist the client in changing; those changes should in turn improve the person's diabetic condition.

Psychologists have a national association—the American Psychological Association.[12] As with other providers, there are divisions within the larger organization that represent specialized interests. There are currently fifty-four divisions in psychology; many[13] pertain to certain groups of cli-

12. www.apa.org.

13. An example is the division on Adult Development and Aging.

ents. The Trauma Psychology[14] division—which is pertinent to this book—contains many resources about trauma and would be informative for the nonpsychologist reader.

Psychiatrists

Psychiatrists are physicians with specialized training in mental health. Thus, psychiatrists have an MD degree that they earned after completing medical school, which is generally four years. Psychiatrists will then have completed a residency of three years, which is usually in a psychiatric department of a hospital. Psychiatrists by virtue of their training as physicians can prescribe medications as treatments for mental health concerns. In contrast to psychologists, however, psychiatrists are not qualified to administer and interpret tests of personality and behavioral problems such as ADHD. However, psychologists—with the exception of four states[15]—are not qualified to prescribe medications.

Some psychiatrists are interested in the provision of counseling and therapy and will have received training in delivering these treatments. Other psychiatrists rely on medication and brief counseling[16] to treat mental health concerns. The national organization for psychiatrists is the American Psychiatric Association,[17] which has no divisions or sections.

Best Practices in Mental Health Treatment

Psychology and other mental health specialties counsel clients who present themselves for treatment with symptoms of anxiety, depression, panic attacks, and the like. Clients also need treatment for relational problems (e.g., divorce, relational violence), parenting problems, substance use and abuse problems, and physical problems (e.g., chronic pain).

For many years, the primary terminology that had been used regarding treatment was *diagnostic* in nature. Thus, clients were diagnosed with labels that characterized their symptom cluster such as *major depressive*

14. www.apatraumadivision.org.

15. Illinois, New Mexico, Iowa, and Louisiana have laws which allow psychologists who receive special training to prescribe medications that are commonly used for mental health concerns.

16. This is typically a fifteen-minute appointment every month to every two months.

17. www.psychiatry.org.

disorder, borderline personality disorder, paranoid schizophrenia, or *bipolar disorder.*

Only recently has *trauma-informed treatment* been a term of widespread use. This term recognizes that clients with a history of trauma have specific treatment needs that differ from clients without that history. So, for example, a person with depression and no trauma might be best helped by a brief course of cognitive therapy; whereas a person with depression *and* trauma might be better served by one of the trauma-focused treatments which recognize that treating the depression alone will not help the client with the many other problems of trauma.

A definition[18] of *trauma-informed care* is as follows:

> Trauma-informed approaches suggest clinicians, organizations and whole systems of care are in an active and reflective process of engaging consumers with histories of trauma. Trauma-informed treatment transcends the isolated, "in session," application of specific clinical interventions that are designed to "treat" the symptoms and sequelae [aftereffects] of trauma.

The isolated treatment of single symptoms such as depression or insomnia is then compared to treatment that creates an environment in which clients' needs in many domains are recognized and responded to with respect and hopefulness. For example, in trauma-informed treatment environments, clients are treated with respect and dignity in a healing and soothing physical environment, in which hope, opportunity for choice, and empowerment are achieved.[19]

The best parallel is to think of a patient who arrives at a hospital emergency room with a single symptom such as a broken leg, a heart attack, or a major infection. Caregivers will focus on the resolution of that symptom as well as any additional problems that result from it. So caring for a broken leg might require surgery, physical therapy for rehabilitation, and follow-up visits for monitoring recovery of functional abilities such as walking and climbing stairs. If a patient is taken to the emergency room after a major car accident, however, multiple types of caregivers are involved. The accident likely affected many bodily systems such as brain function and vision problems because of concussion, skin infection because of glass damage, ligament and bone sprains or breaks, cardiac complications due to oxygen shortage, and so on.

18. Acharya, "Care," para. 1.
19. Ibid., para. 2-3.

In a similar way, the best practice for trauma treatment is an approach that considers all the ways that the victim has been affected by the trauma. Treatment, however, is not a script; rather, it is a relationship between two people—the expert who is deeply invested in helping the client heal and the client who trusts the therapist and the counseling process. There are, however, specific types of trauma-informed treatment that are commonly used, and these are described as follows:

Psychodynamic Treatments

There are several versions of psychodynamic treatments, but they share a focus on emotional issues and use client emotions as signals for necessary change. For example, a client might be fearful or avoidant of certain types of people: the therapist and the client talk about what avoiding these people means for the client and how these people might be slowly approached within the helping context of treatment.

Psychodynamic treatments also focus on patterns of behavior, particularly within relationships. A female client might describe how she is overly anxious about pleasing her husband, and then without seeing a parallel, talk about trying hard but unsuccessfully to please her father during childhood. The therapist would help her see that parallel and then focus on how to change that long-standing pattern of behavior. Last, psychodynamic treatment focuses on the past and how past events influence the present with or without the person's knowledge or intention.

Psychodynamic treatments would likely involve meeting with the therapist each week for thirty or forty-five minutes; psychodynamic treatments can vary in their length, from a moderate length of fifteen to twenty sessions to much longer. Psychodynamic treatment is often used for adult survivors of child abuse, because it concentrates on the past and involves a focus on emotions. A common theme in psychodynamic treatment is considering the lack of an adequate attachment experience in childhood, an event that the first chapter explains is critical in development.

Cognitive Behavioral Treatments

Although there are several types, all cognitive behavioral treatments (CBT) share an emphasis on the client's understanding how thoughts and emotions are interrelated and learning how thoughts or thought patterns in each case affect their feelings and behaviors. Thoughts can be changed in two ways.

- One way is *direct*—learning not to use certain typical thoughts, such as "I am to blame for being raped. I am a failure," and to replace those thoughts with more realistic and helpful thoughts, such as "I am not to blame" and "I will grow stronger and change."

- A second way is *indirect*—learning to not let thoughts be in control of a person, but rather having a flexibility of mind that lets thoughts occur in a loose, nonjudgmental way so that the thoughts have less of a hold over the client.

Cognitive behavioral treatments are also based in conversation, but clients are often asked to do work between sessions and to keep track of that work and its outcomes. Cognitive behavioral treatments are also of moderate duration: a typical course of treatment would be fifteen or fewer weekly sessions. There is less focus on the past and more consideration given to learning specific adaptive strategies to deal with problems as they occur in the future.

Acceptance and Commitment Therapy

Acceptance and commitment therapy (ACT) is an approach to treatment that emphasizes client values—examining what has been "not working" in the client's life and developing new values-driven life directions. There are three major phases: acceptance of what has occurred in the past, choosing a value-based new direction, and taking action by building patterns of committed action toward the future.

Child sexual abuse always involves *shame*, which acceptance and commitment therapy directly targets. Therefore, clients benefit from realizing that they are more than what has happened to them in the past and that they can overcome the shame of the past.

As with cognitive behavioral treatments, acceptance and commitment therapy is conversation based but with work between sessions. Treatment is also of moderate duration, likely fifteen to twenty weekly sessions.

Eye Movement Desensitization and Reprocessing

Eye movement desensitization and reprocessing (EMDR) is a treatment that assists the client in momentarily attending to past experiences and memories while simultaneously focusing on a set of stimuli such as sounds, taps, or eye movements. This treatment allows a client to access trauma memories[20] that have been previously unavailable and experience either insight, changes in memories, or new associations. With EMDR, client work is typically not required outside sessions. Treatment is typically about twenty sessions, although longer work for more traumatic memories can occur.

It should be noted that all these treatments can incorporate clients' religious beliefs and practices as well as spirituality. Within acceptance and commitment therapy, for example, faith-related values can be articulated and built upon. However, an alternate point of view is expressed by Pargament.[21] His point is that all treatments ultimately are about change, which in his view means control. He notes, somewhat correctly, that treatments rarely use language such as *suffering, transcendence, forbearance,* and *surrender* as goals for clients. Yet for Christians, these may well be desired goals.

Every successful counseling experience needs agreement between the counselor and the client on the goals of treatment. If the client expresses a goal such as *surrendering* that the therapist does not believe that he or she endorses, then the resolution would be a referral to another counselor. The resolution may also be to seek treatment with an explicitly Christian therapist. Virtually all providers are willing to schedule an initial consultation session with clients, and most do not charge for this session. During the initial session, clients can decide whether or not to work with a particular therapist. If it is a good choice, clients can move ahead with treatment; otherwise, they can seek a referral to another provider.

Digital Resources

Many websites that have been mentioned in the book so far contain information that is helpful to survivors. Typically, a more general website will have a specific portal or link for survivors. There are also online groups that

20. Refer to the discussion in chapter 3.
21. See Pargament, *Spiritually*, 11–12.

are focused on survivors within a Christian context and others that are not faith based but provide excellent information and resources. The four listed here were chosen for their national and international presence; length of service to victims, and balanced presentation. Other support groups can be located through online searches.

Godly Response to Abuse in the Christian Environment

This Facebook group exists to "empower and train the Christian community to recognize and respond to the sin of child abuse." The group provides extensive resources for survivors and includes articles, videos, audios, books, blogs, and presentations. The group also uses Twitter and maintains an email list.

Joyful Heart Foundation (www.joyfulneartfoundation.org)

The Joyful Heart Foundation exists to serve survivors of violence, such as child abuse. The site contains extensive resources for survivors and is focused on healing and wellness, education and awareness, and policy and advocacy. Joyful Heart is active across all social media including Facebook, Twitter, Pinterest, YouTube, and Instagram. There is also a blog.

Rape, Abuse, and Incest National Network (www.rainn.org)

One of the largest organizations that exists, this network advocates for survivors of child abuse. The website has links to immediate help and to information and resources. Website content is directed to the survivor. The website addresses specific issues such as self-injury, flashbacks, revictimization, and the like with sympathy and care. The network is also active across social media including YouTube, Facebook, Twitter, Google+, and Pinterest.

Women for Sobriety (www.womenforsobriety.org)

Many survivors struggle with substance abuse. Women for Sobriety maintains an online presence with many subgroups; one subgroup is for women who are Christian survivors of childhood sexual abuse. Because it is an international organization, women will be online at all times; this is true for moderators and facilitators.

Text Resources

At the time this chapter was written, an Amazon search on books that refer to childhood sexual abuse within the category of Christian living produced 15,000 hits. Obviously, many of those books refer only briefly to the issue within a larger context. Other books target child abuse, but only physical and emotional abuse. Many books target adults who had been abused as adults. Other books are memoirs—stories by persons who have suffered abuse and who have achieved healing.[22]

It is impossible to list all relevant books, but this section of the chapter contains several books that were chosen for the quality of their writing and content and because the victim is approached with affirmation and dignity. Books are listed by the author, in alphabetical order.

Allender, Dan B. *The Wounded Heart: Hope for Adult Victims of Childhood Sexual Abuse*. Rev. ed. Colorado Springs: NavPress, 2008. (271 pages)

This book is a straightforward and compassionate conversation with the survivor reader. Allender confronts many confusing issues such as our wondering whether our experiences had really been abuse, how we learn to feel shame and contempt for ourselves, and how we deal with the destructive nature of our abuse memories. The context is explicitly Christian and outlines a path to healing that brings God into our difficult lives with honesty.

Bass, Ellen, and Laura Davis. *The Courage to Heal: A Guide for Women Survivors of Child Sexual Abuse, 20th Anniversary Edition*. 4th ed. New York: HarperCollins, 2008. (606 pages)

This book is not written from a Christian perspective. However, many Christians have found this classic book on survivor recovery to be a useful guide to understanding symptoms, treatment, and recovery.

---

22. Most survivors find reading those books to be very difficult, and so they are left out of this list. They can be easily located within Internet searches by entering the term *memoir*.

Bishop, John. *God Distorted: How Your Earthly Father Affects Your Perception of God and Why It Matters.* Colorado Springs: Multnomah, 2013. (221 pages)

In this thoughtful book, earthly fathers and their shortcomings—angry, absent, abusive, demanding, passive, and so on—are considered. When we experience our fathers' significant shortcomings, particularly abuse, we unconsciously incorporate the shortcomings into our relationship with God. Bishop clearly and cleanly confronts our distortions and helps revise them in light of Scripture about the nature of God. Both theological and practical, the text challenges the reader gently to make important changes in knowing God.

Blume, E. Sue. *Secret Survivors: Uncovering Incest and its Aftereffects in Women.* New York: Ballantine, 1997. (321 pages)

This book is not written from a Christian perspective. The author deals with incest and its aftereffects with explicit, thoughtful content that walks the reader through a journey of understanding, developing nondestructive responses, and beginning a new life.

Brown, Brené. *Daring Greatly: How the Courage to Be Vulnerable Transforms the Way We Live, Love, Parent, and Lead.* New York: Penguin, 2012. (320 pages)

This is the latest of several books by Dr. Brown that consider shame, imperfection, and vulnerability as critical to our becoming human. This book—not explicitly Christian but compatible with a Christian worldview—examines how we shrink back from our vulnerabilities and our shortcomings. Those actions then result in our failing to engage in our family, our organizations, and our worlds. Although Dr. Brown is a professor of social work at the University of Houston, her books are intentionally written to fully engage any reader.

Chapman, Gary. *Anger: Handling a Powerful Emotion in a Healthy Way.* Chicago: Northfield, 2007. (240 pages)

Readers may be familiar with Gary Chapman's conferences and books on the five love languages. He has also written an excellent book[23] about

---

23. Note that the previous edition of this book was published as *The Other Side of*

anger—a very difficult emotion for abuse survivors because they are frequently told that they should not be angry. Chapman covers issues that are very important. These include being angry for a good reason, forgiveness, and being angry at God.

Chester, Tim. *You Can Change: God's Transforming Power for Our Sinful Behavior and Negative Emotions.* Wheaton, IL: Crossway, 2010. (192 pages)

I would like to quote from a reviewer who said it so well: "There are few books that are shockingly honest, carefully theological, and gloriously hopeful all at the same time. Tim Chester's book is all of these and more." Much of the journey to healing involves change—sometimes change of habits that are especially hard to change because their childhood roots had been desperate fear. This book lays out ways to think about change that are hopeful and helpful.

Cloud, Henry. *Changes that Heal: How to Understand Your Past to Ensure a Healthier Future.* Grand Rapids, MI: Zondervan, 1992. (267 pages)

This classic text has been revised; it is available in several editions and includes a workbook. Dr. Cloud, a Christian psychiatrist, carefully and clearly explains the four tasks that we need to accomplish to become mature image bearers of God (e.g., bonding to others, sorting out good and bad in others). He explains how abuse problems in our lives interfere with our accomplishing these necessary tasks. Dr. Cloud has published several related books such as titles on boundaries, on finding people with whom to have safe relationships, and on spiritual wisdom.

Leehan, James. *Defiant Hope: Spirituality for Survivors of Family Abuse.* Louisville, KY: Westminster/John Knox, 1993. (179 pages.)

This book was an early examination of adult problems of survivors of family abuse—whether physical, sexual, emotional, or by neglect. The text offers a clear and compelling guide for a journey to recovery. Chapters cover such topics as recovering trust, understanding forgiveness, and ways in which our adult lives reveal our abuse and need alteration. Appendices offer a set

---

Love in 1999 (183 pages). The reprint edition from 2015 now has the title *Anger: Taming a Powerful Emotion* (224 pages).

of readings on Bible verses that are misinterpreted in support of abuse, a series of guided meditations for survivors, and psalms by a survivor.

Maltby, Tammy, with Anne Christian Buchanan. *Confessions of a Good Christian Girl: The Secrets Women Keep and the Grace that Saves Them.* Nashville: Nelson, 2007. (288 pages)

This book contains stories of brokenness and healing that are thoughtfully written and focused on "good Christian girls" who look at themselves and see their true selves—hidden from others—that contain only shame, rage, and despair. Although not focused on childhood sexual abuse, the content is very pertinent. Further, the writers speak clearly from the heart and with great wisdom.

Bibliography

Acharya, Bharati. "Trauma-Informed Care." *Areas of Consulting Expertise, Consulting and Best Practices*, para. 1–3. http://www.thenationalcouncil.org/areas-of-expertise/trauma-informed-behavioral-healthcare.

AG Financial Solutions. "What You Need to Know about Church Risk and Child Abuse Reporting." *AG Financial Solutions* (blog), October 1, 2013. http://blog.agfinancial.org/bid/102108/What-You-Need-to-Know-about-Church-Risk-and-Child-Abuse-Reporting.

Kolisetty, Akhila. "Why Words Matter: Victim v. Survivor." *Journeys towards Justice* (blog), March 13, 2012. http://akhilak.com/blog/2012/03/13/why-words-matter-victim-v-survivor.

Aldwin, Carolyn M. *Stress, Coping, and Development: An Integrative Approach*. 2nd ed. New York: Guilford, 2007.

Allender, Dan B. "Dealing with Past Sexual Abuse: Bringing Up the Memories is the First Step in Fighting the Battle." *FamilyLife*. http://www.familylife.com/articles/topics/life-issues/challenges/cultural-issues/dealing-with-past-sexual-abuse.

———. *The Wounded Heart: Hope for Adult Victims of Childhood Sexual Abuse*. Rev. ed. Colorado Springs: NavPress, 2008.

American Medical Association Council on Scientific Affairs. "Report on Memories of Childhood Abuse." *International Journal of Clinical and Experimental Hypnosis* 43 (1995) 114–17. http://www.tandfonline.com/doi/abs/10.1080/00207149508409955.

American Psychiatric Association. *DSM-III: Diagnostic and Statistical Manual of Mental Disorders*. 3rd ed. Washington, DC: American Psychiatric Association, 1980. http://dsm.psychiatryonline.org/doi/pdf/10.1176/appi.books.9780521315289.dsm-iii.

———. *History of the DSM*. http://www.psychiatry.org/psychiatrists/practice/dsm/history.

Applewhite, Monica, et al. "Model Policies for the Protection of Children and Youth from Abuse." New York: Church Pension Group in partnership with the Nathan Network, April 2004. http://www.episcopalchurch.org/files/model_policies.pdf.

Armstrong, Louise. *Kiss Daddy Goodnight: A Speak-Out on Incest*. New York: Hawthorn, 1978.

Balswick, Judith K., and Jack O. Balswick. *Authentic Human Sexuality: An Integrated Christian Approach*. 2nd ed. Downers Grove, IL: InterVarsity, 2008.

Barkin, Carol, et al., as told to Ellen Mitchell. *Beyond Tears: Living after Losing a Child*. Rev. ed. New York: St. Martin's, 2009.

Bibliography

Barskova, Tatjana, and Rainer Oesterreich. "Post-Traumatic Growth in People Living with a Serious Medical Condition and Its Relations to Physical and Mental Health: A Systematic Review." *Disability and Rehabilitation* 31 (2009) 1709–33. http://www.tandfonline.com/doi/abs/10.1080/09638280902738441.

Bayer, Alicia, "Another Couple Found Guilty of Murder for Parenting by 'To Train Up a Child.'" *Examiner,* November 15, 2013. http://www.examiner.com/article/another-couple-found-guilty-of-murder-for-parenting-by-to-train-up-a-child.

Beck, J. Gayle, et al. How Do Negative Emotions Relate to Dysfunctional Posttrauma Cognitions? An Examination of Interpersonal Trauma Survivors. *Psychological Trauma: Theory, Research, Practice, and Policy* 7 (2015) 3–10. http://dx.doi.org/10.1037/a0032716.

Bernstein, Rosemary E., et al. "Hypervigilance in College Students: Associations with Betrayal and Dissociation and Psychometric Properties in a Brief Hypervigilance Scale." *Psychological Trauma: Theory, Research, Practice, and Policy* 7 (2015) 448–55. http://dx.doi.org/10.1037/tra0000070.

Birrell, Pamela J., and Jennifer J. Freyd. "Betrayal Trauma: Relational Models of Harm and Healing." *Journal of Psychological Trauma* 5 (2005) 49–63.

Bishop, John. *God Distorted: How Your Earthly Father Affects Your Perception of God and Why It Matters.* Colorado Springs: Multnomah, 2013.

BishopAccountablilty.org. "Our Archives and the Circumstances of Their Release." *Introduction to the Archives.* http://bishopaccountability.org/Introduction_to_the_Archives.

Bosgraaf, Emke. "Breaking the Will: Relations between Mental Mortification in Monastic Life and the Psychological Abuse of Children in Catholic Institutions." *Mental Health, Religion and Culture* 16 (2013) 580–94. http://www.tandfonline.com/doi/abs/10.1080/13674676.2012.706271.

Boston Globe. "Archive of Coverage." *The Boston Globe Spotlight Investigation: Abuse in the Catholic Church, Boston Globe.* http://www.boston.com/globe/spotlight/abuse/chronological.htm.

Bowlby, John. *A Secure Base: Clinical Applications of Attachment Theory.* London: Routledge, 1988.

Brandon, Sidney, et al. "Recovered Memories of Childhood Sexual Abuse: Implications for Clinical Practice." *British Journal of Psychiatry* 172 (1998) 296–307.

Briere, John, and Diana M. Elliott. "Prevalence and Psychological Sequelae of Self-Reported Childhood Physical and Sexual Abuse in a General Population Sample of Men and Women." *Child Abuse and Neglect* 27 (2003) 1205–22. http://dx.doi.org/10.1016/j.chiabu.2003.09.008.

Brown, Brené. *Daring Greatly: How the Courage to Be Vulnerable Transforms the Way We Live, Love, Parent, and Lead.* New York: Penguin Random House, 2012.

Brown, Nicola R., et al. "Working the Double Edge: Unbraiding Pathology and Resiliency in the Narratives of Early-Recovery Trauma Survivors." *Psychological Trauma: Theory, Research, Practice, and Policy* 4 (2012) 102–11. http://dx.doi.org/10.1037/a0024969.

Brueggemann, Walter. *Hope within History.* Atlanta: John Knox, 1987.

Bryant-Davis, Thema, and Eunice C. Wong. "Faith to Move Mountains: Religious Coping, Spirituality, and Interpersonal Trauma Recovery." *American Psychologist* 68 (2013) 675–84. http://dx.doi.org/10.1037/a0034380.

Bibliography

Buckholtz, Alison. "Feeling the Heat: Some Parents Apply Hot Sauce to a Child's Tongue as Punishment. The Practice Has Some Experts Burning." *The Washington Post*, August 10, 2004. http://www.washingtonpost.com/wp-dyn/articles/A52899-2004Aug9.html.

Canadian Centre for Child Protection. *Child Sexual Abuse—It Is Your Business*. 3rd ed. Winnipeg, Manitoba: Canadian Centre for Child Protection, August 2014. https://www.protectchildren.ca/app/en/order?action=view&productid=117; https://www.protectchildren.ca/pdfs/C3P_ChildSexualAbuse_ItIsYourBusiness_en.pdf.

Caruth, Cathy. *Unclaimed Experience: Trauma, Narrative, and History*. Baltimore, MD: Johns Hopkins University Press, 1996. http://muse.jhu.edu/books/9780801896194.

Centers for Disease Control and Prevention, National Center for Injury Prevention and Control, Division of Violence Prevention. "The Adverse Childhood Experiences (ACE) Study." http://www.cdc.gov/violenceprevention/acestudy.

Chapman, Morris H. "Light for the Darkness." *SBC Life*, August 2008. http://www.sbclife.net/Articles/2008/08/sla1.

"Character Strengths and Virtues Descriptions." *Strength-Oriented Tools*. Los Angeles: Azusa Pacific University, Noel Academy for Strengths-Based Leadership and Education. http://www.apu.edu/strengthsacademy/tools.

Child Welfare Information Gateway. "Clergy as Mandatory Reporters of Child Abuse and Neglect." Washington, DC: US Department of Health and Human Services, Children's Bureau, 2014. https://www.childwelfare.gov/topics/systemwide/laws-policies/statutes/clergymandated.

Claussen, Dane S., ed. *Standing on the Promises: The Promise Keepers and the Revival of Manhood*. Cleveland, OH: Pilgrim, 1999.

Cloud, Henry. *Changes that Heal: How to Understand Your Past to Ensure a Healthier Future*. Grand Rapids: Zondervan, 1992.

Cloud, Henry, and John Townsend. *Boundaries: When to Say Yes, How to Say No to Take Control of Your Life*. Grand Rapids: Zondervan, 1992.

Cole, Brenda S., et al. "Assessing Spiritual Growth and Spiritual Decline Following a Diagnosis of Cancer: Reliability and Validity of the Spiritual Transformation Scale." *Psycho-Oncology* 17 (2008) 112–21. http://onlinelibrary.wiley.com/doi/10.1002/pon.1207/abstract.

Coleman, Linda, and Paul Kay. "Prototype Semantics: The English Word *Lie*." *Language* 57 (1981) 26–44. http://www.jstor.org/stable/414285.

Cook, Linda J. "The Ultimate Deception: Childhood Sexual Abuse in the Church." *Journal of Psychosocial Nursing and Mental Health Services* 43 (October 2005) 19–24.

Combs, G., and G. Freedman. "Narrative, Poststructuralism, and Social Justice: Current Practices in Narrative Therapy." Major Contribution: Emerging Theoretical Approaches. *The Counseling Psychologist* 40 (2012) 1033–60. http://tcp.sagepub.com/content/40/7/1033.

Courtois, Christine A. *Healing the Incest Wound: Adult Survivors in Therapy*. 2nd ed. Norton Professional. New York: Norton, 2010.

———. *Recollections of Sexual Abuse: Treatment Principles and Guidelines*. New York: Norton, 1999.

Cozzens, Donald. *Sacred Silence: Denial and the Crisis in the Church*. Collegeville, MN: Liturgical, 2002.

Davies, Jody Messler, and Mary Gail Frawley. *Treating the Adult Survivor of Childhood Sexual Abuse: A Psychoanalytic Perspective.* New York: Basic, 1994.

De Castella, Rosemary, and Janette Graetz Simmonds. "'There's a Deeper Meaning as to What Suffering's All About': Experiences of Religious and Spiritual Growth Following Trauma." *Mental Health, Religion and Culture* 16 (2013) 536–56.

DeMuth, Mary. *Not Marked: Finding Hope and Healing after Sexual Abuse.* Rockwall, TX: Uncaged, 2013.

Dickinson, Emily. "Hope is the Thing with Feathers (254)." *Academy of American Poets,* 1890. https://www.poets.org/poetsorg/poem/hope-thing-feathers-254.

Douglas, Emily M., and David Finkelhor. "Childhood Sexual Abuse Fact Sheet." *Fact Sheets, Crimes against Children Research Center.* Durham: University of New Hampshire, May 2005. http://www.unh.edu/ccrc/factsheet/pdf/childhoodSexualAbuseFactSheet.pdf.

Easley, Christopher. "How to Start an Accountability Group: Become Accountable to Grow in Your Christian Life." *Spiritual Formation, Featured Articles, Christian Bible Studies,* October 4, 2006. http://www.christianitytoday.com/biblestudies/articles/spiritualformation/061004.html.

Ellicott, Charles John, ed. *A Bible Commentary for English Readers by Various Writers.* London: Cassell, 1905. http://biblehub.com/commentaries/ellicott/genesis/3.htm.

———. *An Old Testament Commentary for English Readers by Various Writers.* Vol. 1. London: Cassell, Petter, Galpin, 1892. https://books.google.com/books?id=OKkGA AAAQAAJ&output=html.

Elliott, Diana M. "The Impact of Christian Faith on the Prevalence and Sequelae of Sexual Abuse." *Journal of Interpersonal Violence* 9 (1994) 95–108. http://jiv.sagepub.com/content/9/1/95.

Enright, Robert D. *Forgiveness is a Choice: A Step-by-Step Process for Resolving Anger and Restoring Hope.* Washington, DC: American Psychological Association, 2001.

Enright, Robert D., and Richard P. Fitzgibbons. "Empirical Validation of the Process Model of Forgiveness." In *Helping Clients Forgive: An Empirical Guide for Resolving Anger and Restoring Hope,* edited by R. D. Enright and R. P. Fitzgibbons, 89–109. Washington, DC: American Psychological Association, 2000. http://dx.doi.org/10.1037/10381-006.

Erikson, Erik H. *Childhood and Society.* New York: Norton, 1950.

———. *Identity: Youth and Crisis.* Austin Riggs Monograph No. 7. New York: Norton, 1968.

Ettinger, Hännah. "A Guide to the Sovereign Grace Ministries Scandal and the End of New Calvinism." *Friendly Atheist* (blog), *Patheos,* May 29, 2014. www.patheos.com/blogs/friendlyatheist/2014/05/29/a-guide-to-the-sovereign-grace-ministries-scandal-and-the-end-of-new-calvinism.

Exline, Julie Juola, et al. "Not So Innocent: Does Seeing One's Own Capability for Wrongdoing Predict Forgiveness?" *Journal of Personality and Social Psychology* 94 (2008) 495–515. http://dx.doi.org/10.1037/0022-3514.94.3.495.

Evans, Rachel Held. "The Abusive Theology of 'Deserved' Tragedy." *Rachel Held Evans* (blog), May 21, 2013. http://rachelheldevans.com/blog/abusive-theology-piper-mahaney.

Fee, Gordon D. *1 and 2 Timothy, Titus.* Understanding the Bible Commentary Series. Grand Rapids: Baker, 1989.

Fehr, Ryan, et al. "The Road to Forgiveness: A Meta-Analytic Synthesis of its Situational and Dispositional Correlates." *Psychological Bulletin* 136 (2010) 894–914. http://dx.doi.org/10.1037/a0019993.

Ferguson, Christopher J. "Spanking, Corporal Punishment and Negative Long-Term Outcomes: A Meta-Analytic Review of Longitudinal Studies." *Clinical Psychology Review* 33 (2013) 196–208. http://dx.doi.org/10.1016/j.cpr.2012.11.002.

Fergusson, David M., et al. "Childhood Sexual Abuse and Adult Developmental Outcomes: Findings from a 30-Year Longitudinal Study in New Zealand." *Child Abuse and Neglect* 37 (2013) 664–74. http://dx.doi.org/10.1016/j.chiabu.2013.03.013.

Finkelhor, David. *Child Sexual Abuse: New Theory and Research.* New York: Free, 1984.

———. "The Prevention of Childhood Sexual Abuse." *The Future of Children* 19 (2009) 169–94. http://muse.jhu.edu/journals/future_of_children/v019/19.2.finkelhor.pdf. (Preventing Child Maltreatment)

Finkelhor, David, et al. "First Report: Numbers and Characteristics." *National Incidence Studies of Missing, Abducted, Runaway, and Thrownaway Children in America.* NCJ 123668 Washington, DC: US Department of Justice, Office of Justice Programs, Office of Juvenile Justice and Delinquency Prevention, May 1990. https://www.ncjrs.gov/App/Publications/abstract.aspx?ID=123668; https://www.ncjrs.gov/pdffiles1/ojjdp/nismart90.pdf. (NISMART-1)

Finkelhor, David, et al. "Sexually Assaulted Children: National Estimates and Characteristics." OJJDP Bulletin NISMART Series. *National Incidence Studies of Missing, Abducted, Runaway, and Thrownaway Children in America.* NCJ 214383. Washington, DC: US Department of Justice, Office of Justice Programs, Office of Juvenile Justice and Delinquency Prevention, August 2008. https://www.ncjrs.gov/pdffiles1/ojjdp/214383.pdf. (NISMART-2.)

Fitzpatrick, Laura. "6. Southern Baptist Decide Against Pedophilia Database," *Top 10 Underreported News Stories, The Top 10 Everything of 2008, Time,* November 3, 2008. http://content.time.com/time/specials/packages/article/0,2880 4,1855948_1861760_1862212,00.html.

Fonagy, Peter, and Mary Target. "The Rooting of the Mind in the Body: New Links between Attachment Theory and Psychoanalytic Thought." *Journal of the American Psychoanalytical Association* 55 (2007) 411–56. http://apa.sagepub.com/content/55/2/411.

Fontaine, Ann. "Confronting Sexual Abuse in the Episcopal Church." *Episcopal Church, Daily Episcopalian, Episcopal Café,* April 14, 2010. http://www.episcopalcafe.com/confronting_sexual_abuse_in_the_episcopal_church.

Fortune, Marie Marshall. *Sexual Violence: The Sin Revisited.* New York: Pilgrim, 2005. (Revised with new title).

———. *Sexual Violence: The Unmentionable Sin.* New York: Pilgrim, 1983.

Foust, Michael. "Southern Baptist Convention Wrap Up." *SBC Life,* August 2008. http://www.sbclife.net/articles/2008/08/sla4.

Frankl, Viktor. *Man's Search for Meaning: An Introduction to Logotherapy.* Part 1 translated by Ilse Lasch. 4th ed. Boston: Beacon, 1992.

Franklin, Cynthia, and Rowena Fong, eds. *The Church Leader's Counseling Resource Book: A Guide to Mental Health and Social Problems.* New York: Oxford University Press, 2011.

Fredrickson, Barbara L. "Positive Emotions." In *Handbook of Positive Psychology*, edited by C. R. Snyder and Shane J. Lopez, 120–34. New York: Oxford University Press, 2002. ProQuest ebrary, Google Books.

———. "The Role of Positive Emotions in Positive Psychology: The Broaden-and-Build Theory of Positive Emotions." *American Psychologist* 56, (2002) 218–26. http://dx.doi.org/10.1037/0003-066X.56.3.218.

———. "What Good Are Positive Emotions?" *Review of General Psychology* 2 (1998). 300–319. http://dx.doi.org/10.1037/1089-2680.2.3.300.

Freyd, Jennifer J. *Betrayal Trauma: The Logic of Forgetting Childhood Abuse.* Cambridge, MA: Harvard University Press, 1996.

Freyd, Jennifer J., and Pamela J. Birrell. *Blind to Betrayal: Why We Fool Ourselves We Aren't Being Fooled.* Hoboken, NJ: Wiley, 2013.

Ganje-Fling, Marilyn A., and Patricia McCarthy. "Impact of Childhood Sexual Abuse on Client Spiritual Development: Counseling Implications." *Journal of Counseling and Development* 74 (1996) 253–58. http://onlinelibrary.wiley.com/doi/10.1002/j.1556-6676.1996.tb01861.x/abstract.

Gershoff, Elizabeth T. "More Harm Than Good: A Summary of Scientific Research on the Intended and Unintended Effects of Corporal Punishment on Children." *Law and Contemporary Problems* 73, no. 2 (2010) 31–56. http://scholarship.law.duke.edu/lcp/vol73/iss2/3.

Gil, Vincent E. "In Thy Father's House: Self-Report Findings of Sexually Abused Daughters from Conservative Christian Homes." *Journal of Psychology and Theology* 16 (1998) 144–52. http://journals.biola.edu/jpt/volumes/16/issues/2/articles/144; EBSCOhost (ATLA0000804987).

Gilkerson, Luke. "Ten Steps to Finding a Great Accountability Partner." *Help Others Restore Integrity* (blog), *CovenantEyes*, March 8, 2013. http://www.covenanteyes.com/2013/03/08/accountability-partner-script.

Goldberg, Alan B., et al. "Compassion or Cover-Up? Teen Victim Claims Rape; Forced Confession in Church." *ABC News*, April 8, 2011. http://abcnews.go.com/2020/teen-rape-victim-forced-confess-church/story?id=13299135.

Goodman, Gail S. "The Child Witness: An Introduction." *Journal of Social Issues* 40, no. 2 (Summer 1984) 1–7. http://onlinelibrary.wiley.com/doi/10.1111/j.1540-4560.1984.tb01090.x/abstract.

Hall, Terese A. "Spiritual Effects of Childhood Sexual Abuse in Adult Christian Women." *Journal of Psychology and Theology* 23 (1995) 129–34. http://journals.biola.edu/jpt/volumes/23/issues/2/articles/129. EBSCOhost (ATLA0000898287).

Hammond, Carl B., et al. *Law Enforcement Response to Child Abuse.* Portable Guides to Investigating Child Abuse Series. NCJ 162425. Washington, DC: US Department of Justice, Office of Justice Programs, Office of Juvenile Justice and Delinquency Prevention, May 1997 (Second printing March 2001). http://www.ncjrs.gov/pdffiles/162425.pdf.

Harvey, Bob. "Cleaning Up Our Churches from Sexual Abuse: The Exposure of Sexual Abuse in Many Faith Communities Is Making Churches More Cautious." Church Life. *Church* (room), *christianity.ca: Canada's Christian Library Online*, May 23, 2013. http://www.christianity.ca/page.aspx?pid=11553.

Heggen, Carolyn Holderread. *Sexual Abuse in Christian Homes and Churches.* Eugene, OR: Wipf & Stock, 1993.

Heintzelman, Samantha J., and Laura A. King. "Life is Pretty Meaningful." *American Psychologist* 69 (2014) 561–74. http://dx.doi.org/10.1037/a0035049.

Heller, Laurence, and Aline LaPierre. *Healing Developmental Trauma: How Early Trauma Affects Self-Regulation, Self-Image, and the Capacity for Relationship.* Berkeley, CA: North Atlantic, 2012.

Herman, Judith. *Trauma and Recovery: The Aftermath of Violence—From Domestic to Political Terror.* New York: Basic, 1992.

Herman, Judith Lewis. "Complex PTSD: A Syndrome in Survivors of Prolonged and Repeated Trauma." *Journal of Traumatic Stress* 3 (1992) 377–91. http://onlinelibrary.wiley.com/doi/10.1002/jts.2490050305/abstract; http://link.springer.com/journal/10960/5/3/page/1.

Hill, Patrick L., and Matthias Allemand. "Forgivingness and Adult Patterns of Individual Differences in Environmental Mastery and Personal Growth." *Journal of Research in Personality* 44 (2010) 245–50. http://dx.doi.org/10.1016/j.jrp.2010.01.006.

"Hope-Lit Database." *Hope Studies Central,* December 15, 2015. Edmonton, AB, Canada: University of Alberta Faculty of Education. http://www.hope-lit.ualberta.ca/Hope-LitDatabase.html.

Howell, A. J., et al. "Enhanced Psychological Health among Chronic Pain Clients Engaged in Hope-Focused Group Counseling." *The Counseling Psychologist* 43 (2015) 586–613. http://tcp.sagepub.com/content/43/4/586.

Howerton, Kristen. "How Churches Should Address Abuse." *The Washington Post,* April 10, 2013. https://www.washingtonpost.com/national/on-faith/how-churches-should-address-abuse/2013/04/10/ea39fdb8-9fb5-11e2-9c03-6952ff305f35_story.html.

Howes, Paul W., et al. "Affective, Structural, and Relational Characteristics of Maltreating Families: A Systems Perspective." *Journal of Family Psychology* 14 (2000) 95–110. http://dx.doi.org/10.1037/0893-3200.14.1.95.

Irish, Leah, et al. "Long-Term Physical Health Consequences of Childhood Sexual Abuse: A Meta-Analytic Review." *Journal of Pediatric Psychology* 35 (2010) 450–61. http://jpepsy.oxfordjournals.org/content/35/5/450.full; http://www.ncbi.nlm.nih.gov/pmc/articles/PMC2910944.

Jackson, David. "Huckabee Defends Duggar over Molestation Accusations." *USA Today,* May 22, 2015. http://onpolitics.usatoday.com/2015/05/22/huckabee-defends-duggar-over-molestation-accusations.

Jacobson, Matthew L. "Who is Your Real Accountability Partner?" *mlj Matthew L Jacobson* (blog), November 5, 2013. http://matthewljacobson.com/2013/11/05/who-is-your-real-accountability-partner.

Janoff-Bulman, Ronnie. *Shattered Assumptions: Towards a New Psychology of Trauma.* New York: Simon and Schuster, 1992.

John Jay College of Criminal Justice Research Team. *The Nature and Scope of Sexual Abuse of Minors by Catholic Priests and Deacons in the United States 1950–2002: A Research Study Conducted by the John Jay College of Criminal Justice, The City University of New York, February 2004, for the United States Conference of Catholic Bishops.* Washington, DC: United States Conference on Catholic Bishops, June 2004. http://www.usccb.org/issues-and-action/child-and-youth-protection/upload/The-Nature-and-Scope-of-Sexual-Abuse-of-Minors-by-Catholic-Priests-and-Deacons-in-the-United-States-1950-2002.pdf.

Jonah, Hieromonk. "Forgiveness and Reconciliation: How to Forgive Others and Receive Forgiveness." *Discover Orthodox Christianity*. http://www.antiochian.org/content/forgiveness-and-reconciliation-how-forgive-others-and-receive-forgiveness.

Kamins, Melissa L., and Carol S. Dweck. "Person versus Process Praise and Criticism: Implications for Contingent Self-Worth and Coping." *Developmental Psychology* 35 (1999) 835–47. http://dx.doi.org/10.1037/0012-1649.35.3.835.

Kane, Donna, et al. "Perceptions of God by Survivors of Childhood Sexual Abuse: An Exploratory Study in an Underresearched Area." *Journal of Psychology and Theology* 21 (1993) 228–37. http://journals.biola.edu/jpt/volumes/21/issues/3; EBSCOhost (ATLA0000870010).

Kendall-Tackett, Kathleen A., et al. "Impact of Sexual Abuse on Children: A Review and Synthesis of Recent Empirical Studies." *Psychological Bulletin* 113 (1993) 164–80. http://dx.doi.org/10.1037/0033-2909.113.1.164.

Klenck, Robert. "What's Wrong with the 21st Century Church?" Part 2. *News, Kjos Ministries*, August 8, 2000. http://www.crossroad.to/News/Church/Klenck2.html.

Klerman, Gerald L. "The Psychiatric Patient's Right to Effective Treatment: Implications of Osheroff v. Chestnut Lodge." Debate. *American Journal of Psychiatry* 147 (1990) 409–418. http://dx.doi.org/10.1176/ajp.147.4.409.

Kylie. "Body Shame 101: Lies the Church Told Me about My Own Sexuality." *Godless in Dixie* (blog), *Patheos,* August 4, 2015. http://www.patheos.com/blogs/godlessindixie/2015/08/04/body-shame-101.

Lawler, Kathleen A., et al. "A Change of Heart: Cardiovascular Correlates of Forgiveness in Response to Interpersonal Conflict." *Journal of Behavioral Medicine* 26 (2003) 373–93. http://link.springer.com/article/10.1023%2FA%3A1025771716686.

Lawson, Louanne, and Mark Chaffin. "False Negatives in Sexual Abuse Disclosure Interviews: Incidence and Influence of Caretaker's Belief in Abuse in Cases of Accidental Abuse Discovery by Diagnosis of STD." *Journal of Interpersonal Violence* 7 (1992) 532–42. http://jiv.sagepub.com/content/7/4/532.abstract.

Lawson, Ronald, et al. "The Long-Term Impact of Child Abuse on Religious Behavior and Spirituality in Men." *Child Abuse and Neglect* 22 (1998) 369–80. http://dx.doi.org/10.1016/S0145-2134(98)00003-9.

Leehan, James. *Defiant Hope: Spirituality for Survivors of Family Abuse.* Louisville: Westminster/John Knox, 1993.

Lukowski, Angela F., and Patricia J. Bauer. "Long-Term Memory in Infancy and Early Childhood." In *The Wiley Handbook on the Development of Children's Memory*, edited by Patricia J. Bauer and Robyn Fivush, 230–54. Malden, MA: Wiley-Blackwell, 2013. http://onlinelibrary.wiley.com/book/10.1002/9781118597705.

Lutz, Susan M. "Promise Keepers." Revised. *World Religions and Spirituality Project, Virginia Commonwealth University,* July 23, 2001. http://www.wrs.vcu.edu/profiles/PromiseKeepers.htm.

Lynch, Michael P. *Truth as One and Many.* New York: Oxford University Press, 2009.

Mabry, Richard L. *The Tender Scar: Life after the Death of a Spouse.* Grand Rapids: Kregel, 2006.

Malloy, Lindsay C., et al. "Filial Dependency and Recantation of Child Sexual Abuse Allegations." *Journal of the American Academy of Child and Adolescent Psychiatry* 46 (2007) 162–70. http://www.jaacap.com/article/S0890-8567(09)61823-2/abstract; Elsevier ClinicalKey journals database.

Markus, Hazel, and Paula Nurius. "Possible Selves." *American Psychologist* 41 (1986) 954–69. http://dx.doi.org/10.1037/0003-066X.41.9.954.

Masten, Ann S. "Resilience in Developing Systems: Progress and Promise as the Fourth Wave Rises." *Development and Psychopathology* 13 (2007) 1021–38. http://dx.doi.org/10.1017/S0954579407000442.

McCrory, Cathal, et al. "The Lasting Legacy of Childhood Adversity for Disease Risk in Later Life." *Health Psychology* 34 (2015) 687–96. http://dx.doi.org/10.1037/hea0000147.

McCullough, Michael E., et al. "Interpersonal Forgiveness in Close Relationships." *Journal of Personality and Social Psychology* 73 (1997) 321–36. http://dx.doi.org/10.1037/0022-3514.73.2.321.

McCullough, Michael E., et al. "Writing about the Benefits of an Interpersonal Transgression Facilitates Forgiveness." *Journal of Consulting and Clinical Psychology* 74 (2006) 887–97. http://dx.doi.org/10.1037/0022-006X.74.5.887.

McCullough, Michael E., and Everett L. Worthington Jr. "Models of Interpersonal Forgiveness and Their Applications to Counseling: Review and Critique." *Counseling and Values* 39 (1994) 2–15. http://onlinelibrary.wiley.com/doi/10.1002/j.2161-007X.1994.tb01003.x/abstract.

McGee, J. Vernon. "Blind Faith vs. Testing God." *Thru the Bible with Dr. J. Vernon McGee.* http://www.oneplace.com/ministries/thru-the-bible-with-j-vernon-mcgee/read/articles/blind-faith-vs-testing-god-9265.html

Merz, Michael R. "A History of the National Review Board." Washington, DC: United States Conference of Catholic Bishops, National Review Board, 2011. http://www.usccb.org/issues-and-action/child-and-youth-protection/upload/NRB-History-5-17-2011.pdf.

Michaelson, Jay. "Church Sex Scandals Are Rooted in Theology: A Unique Report on the Ultra-Conservative Bob Jones University Points to the Theological Roots of Sexual Abuse and Scandals." *Daily Beast,* December 15, 2014. http://www.thedailybeast.com/articles/2014/12/15/church-sex-scandals-are-rooted-in-theology.html.

Morton, Dawn Renee. "The Correlation between Church Leaders' Understanding of the Issue of Child Sexual Abuse and Preventive Steps Taken within Their Churches." PhD diss., The Southern Baptist Theological Seminary, 2005.

Name Withheld. "My Easy Trip from Youth Minister to Felon: My Spiral of Sin Destroyed My Life and Ministry." *Leadership Journal* (online only), June 9, 2014. https://web.archive.org/web/20140613190102/http://christianitytoday.com/le/2014/june-online-only/my-easy-trip-from-youth-minister-to-felon.html. (Removed from *Christianity Today*; second version of the article is available at the website *Internet Archive.*)

National Association of Evangelicals. "Code of Ethics for Pastors." Letter/Statement. *NAE National Association of Evangelicals,* June 2012. http://nae.net/code-of-ethics-for-pastors.

———. "NAE Releases Code of Ethics for Pastors." Press Release. *NAE National Association of Evangelicals,* June 12, 2012, http://nae.net/nae-releases-code-of-ethics-for-pastors.

Nouwen, Henri J. M. "The Path of Peace." In *Finding My Way Home: Pathways to Life and the Spirit,* 51–86. New York: Crossroad, 2001.

Oates, R. Kim, et al. "Erroneous Concerns about Child Sexual Abuse." *Child Abuse and Neglect* 24 (2000) 149–57. http://dx.doi.org/10.1016/S0145-2134(99)00108-8.

Ohlheiser, Abby. "Jill, Jessa Say the Release of Josh Duggar's Police Report Is A 'Re-victimization.'" *Washington Post*, June 5, 2015. https://www.washingtonpost.com/news/acts-of-faith/wp/2015/06/04/josh-duggars-sister-comes-to-his-defense-following-molestation-reports.

Oppenheimer, Mark. "An Argument to Turn to Jesus before the Bar." *The New York Times*, February 28, 2014, http://www.nytimes.com/2014/03/01/us/before-turning-to-a-judge-an-argument-for-turning-first-to-jesus.html.

Ornstein, Peter A., et al. "Adult Recollections of Childhood Abuse: Cognitive and Developmental Perspectives." In *Working Group on Investigation of Memories of Childhood Abuse*, edited by Judith L. Alpert et al., 150–97. Washington, DC: American Psychological Association, 1996.

———. "Adult Recollections of Childhood Abuse: Cognitive and Developmental Perspectives." *Psychology, Public Policy, and Law* 4 (1998) 1025–51. http://dx.doi.org/10.1037/1076-8971.4.4.1025.

Orrison, David. *Grace for my Heart* (blog). https://graceformyheart.wordpress.com.

Osheroff v. Chestnut Lodge, 63 Md. App. 519, 490 A.2d 720 (Md. Ct. App.), *cert. denied*. http://www.leagle.com/decision/198558162MdApp519_1539/OSHEROFF%20v.%20CHESTNUT%20LODGE,%20INC.

Pargament, Kenneth I. *Spiritually Integrated Psychotherapy: Understanding and Addressing the Sacred*. New York: Guilford, 2007.

Pearl, Michael, and Debi Pearl. *To Train Up a Child*. Pleasantville, TN: No Greater Joy Ministries, 1994. (Previous online version from ca. 1990 is available from web archive, http://web.archive.org/web/20101103070349/http://www.achristianhome.com/to_train_up_a_child.htm)

———. "Who is No Greater Joy?" *No Greater Joy*. http://nogreaterjoy.org/about-us.

Perriman, Wendy. K. *A Wounded Deer: The Effects of Incest on the Life and Poetry of Emily Dickinson*. Newcastle, UK: Cambridge Scholars Press, 2006.

Petersen, Jason, and Brad Hoefs. "Overcoming Internal-Stigma." *Fresh Hope for Mental Health* (podcast), June 12, 2015. http://freshhopeformentalhealth.com/overcoming-internal-stigma.

Plante, Thomas G. *Spiritual Practices in Psychotherapy: Thirteen Tools for Enhancing Psychological Health*. Washington, DC: American Psychological Association, 2009.

Plantinga, Cornelius, Jr. *Not the Way It's Supposed to Be: A Breviary of Sin*. Grand Rapids: Eerdmans, 1995.

Prichard, Robert. "A Leaner, More Nimble Church (1990–)." In *A History of the Episcopal Church: Complete Through the 78th General Convention*, 3rd rev. ed, 375–433. New York: Morehouse/Church, 2014.

Pritt, Ann F. "Spiritual Correlates of Reported Sexual Abuse among Mormon Women." *Journal for the Scientific Study of Religion* 37 (1998) 273–85. http://www.jstor.org/stable/1387527.

Prochaska, James O., et al. "In Search of How People Change: Applications to Addictive Behaviors." *American Psychologist* 47 (1992) 1102–14. http://dx.doi.org/10.1037/0003-066X.47.9.1102.

Puente, Maria. "Duggars Reeling from Josh's Sex Abuse Scandal." *USA Today*, May 22, 2015. http://www.usatoday.com/story/life/tv/2015/05/21/duggars-reeling-from-joshs-sex-abuse-scandal/27741883.

Rand, Kevin L., and Jennifer S. Cheavens. "Hope Theory." In *The Oxford Handbook of Positive Psychology*, edited by Shane L. Lopez and C. R. Snyder, 2nd ed., 323–34.

Oxford Library of Psychology. New York: Oxford University Press, 2009. http://dx.doi.org/10.1093/oxfordhb/9780195187243.013.0030; Oxford Handbooks Online.

Rizzuto, Ana-Maria. *The Birth of the Living God: A Psychoanalytic Study*. Chicago: University of Chicago Press, 1979.

Roosevelt, Theodore. "The Man in the Arena." *Citizenship in a Republic*, April 23, 1910. www.theodore-roosevelt.com/trsorbonnespeech.htmlo.

Royal Australian and New Zealand College of Psychiatrists. "Guidelines for Psychiatrists Dealing with Repressed Traumatic Memories." Clinical Memorandum 17. Melbourne: Royal Australian and New Zealand College of Psychiatrists, 1996, 2005. https://www.ranzcp.org/Files/Resources/College_Statements/Clinical_Memoranda/cm17-pdf.aspx; https://www.ranzcp.org/News-policy/Policy-and-advocacy/Therapeutics-and-interventions.aspx.

Russell, Diana E. H. *The Secret Trauma: Incest in the Lives of Girls and Women*. Rev. ed. New York: Basic, 1999.

Samples, Kenneth Richard. *A World of Difference: Putting Christian Truth-Claims to the Worldview Test*. Reasons to Believe Series. Grand Rapids: Baker, 2007.

Samples, Tara C. "Ten Myths of Abuse in the Church." *Sexual Violence and the Church* (blog), *Sojourners*, May 21, 2013. http://sojo.net/blogs/2013/05/21/10-myths-abuse-church.

Saul, Janet, and Natalie C. Audage. *Preventing Child Sexual Abuse within Youth-Serving Organizations: Getting Started on Policies and Procedures*. Atlanta: US Department of Health and Human Services, Centers for Disease Control and Prevention, National Center for Injury Prevention and Control, Division of Violence Prevention, 2007. http://www.cdc.gov/violenceprevention/pdf/PreventingChildSexualAbuse-a.pdf.

Scazzero, Peter. *Emotionally Healthy Spirituality: Unleash a Revolution in Your Life in Christ*. Nashville: Nelson, 2006.

Schaeffer, Frank. "The Truth about Christian 'Sexual Purity'—A Former Evangelical Speaks Out." *Why I Still Talk to Jesus—In Spite of Everything* (blog), *Patheos*, July 6, 2015. http://www.patheos.com/blogs/frankschaeffer/2015/07/the-truth-about-christian-sexual-purity-a-former-evangelical-speaks-out.

Schultz, Jessica M., et al. "Pathways to Posttraumatic Growth: The Contributions of Forgiveness and Importance of Religion and Spirituality." *Psychology of Religion and Spirituality* 2 (2010) 104–14. http://dx.doi.org/10.1037/a0018454.

Schultz, Jessica M., et al. "A Study of Posttraumatic Spiritual Transformation and Forgiveness among Victims of Significant Interpersonal Offenses." *Mental Health, Religion and Culture* 17 (2014) 122–35.

Schwab, Joseph R. "Religious Meaning Making: Positioning Identities through Stories." *Psychology of Religion and Spirituality* 5 (2013) 219–26. http://dx.doi.org/10.1037/a0031557.

Seligman, Martin E. P. *Flourish: A Visionary New Understanding of Happiness and Well-being*. New York: Simon & Schuster, 2011.

"Shattered Faith." ABC News video, 3:00, from a *20/20* report with Elizabeth Vargas, April 8, 2011. http://abcnews.go.com/2020/video/scarred-childhood-13334532.

Shelley, Marshall, and Harold B. Smith. "From Youth Minister to Felon: An Article We Never Should Have Published." *Leadership Journal* (online only), June 2014. http://

www.christianitytoday.com/le/2014/june-online-only/my-easy-trip-from-youth-minister-to-felon.html.

Shonkoff, Jack P., et al. "Neuroscience, Molecular Biology, and the Childhood Roots of Health Disparities: Building a New Framework for Health Promotion and Disease Prevention." Special Communication. *JAMA* 301 (2005) 2252–59. http://jama.jamanetwork.com/article.aspx?articleid=184019.

Silver, Roxanne L., et al. "Search for Meaning in Misfortune: Making Sense of Incest." *Journal of Social Issues* 39 (1983) 81–101. http://onlinelibrary.wiley.com/doi/10.1111/j.1540-4560.1983.tb00142.x/abstract.

Singer, Jefferson A. "Narrative Identity and Meaning Making across the Adult Lifespan: An Introduction." *Journal of Personality* 72 (2004) 437–59. http://onlinelibrary.wiley.com/doi/10.1111/j.0022-3506.2004.00268.x/abstract; http://dx.doi.org/10.1111/j.0022-3506.2004.00268.x.

Sjöberg, Rikard L., and Frank Lindblad. "Limited Disclosure of Sexual Abuse in Children Whose Experiences were Documented by Videotape." Brief Report. *American Journal of Psychiatry* 159 (2002) 312–14. http://dx.doi.org/10.1176/appi.ajp.159.2.312.

Slattery, Julie. "Five Lies That Make Sexual Purity More Difficult." *Boundless*, May 26, 2014. http://www.boundless.org/relationships/2014/5-lies-that-make-sexual-purity-more-difficult.

Smedes, Lewis B. *Shame and Grace: Healing the Shame We Don't Deserve.* San Francisco, CA: HarperCollins, 1993.

Smith, Carly Parnitzke, and Jennifer J. Freyd. "Dangerous Safe Havens: Institutional Betrayal Exacerbates Sexual Trauma." *Journal of Traumatic Stress* 26 (2013) 119–24. http://onlinelibrary.wiley.com/doi/10.1002/jts.21778/abstract.

———. "Institutional Betrayal." *American Psychologist* 69 (2014) 575–87. http://dx.doi.org/10.1037/a0037564.

Smith, Colin. "God Can Restore Your Lost Years." *Christian Living, The Gospel Coalition*, July 18, 2014. http://www.thegospelcoalition.org/article/god-can-restor-your-lost-years.

Snyder, C. R., et al. "Hope Theory: A Member of the Positive Psychology Family." In *Handbook of Positive Psychology*, edited by C. R. Snyder and Shane L. Lopez, 257–76. New York: Oxford University Press, 2002. ProQuest ebrary.

Snyder, Howard N. "Sexual Assault of Young Children as Reported to Law Enforcement: Victim, Incident, and Offender Characteristics." Bureau of Justice Statistics. NCJ 182990. Washington DC, US Department of Justice, July 2000. (A NIBRS Statistical Report) http://www.bjs.gov/index.cfm?ty=pbdetail&iid=1147; http://www.bjs.gov/content/pub/pdf/saycrle.pdf.

Solas, Marc. "The Top 10 Reasons Our Kids Leave Church." *Marc5Solas: Soli Deo gloria* (blog), February 8, 2013. http://marc5solas.com/2013/02/08/top-10-reasons-our-kids-leave-church.

Southern Baptist Convention. "On Protecting Children from Abuse." Resolution. Meeting, San Antonio, Texas, June 12–13, 2007. http://www.sbc.net/resolutions/search/resolution.asp?ID=1173.

———. "On Sexual Abuse of Children." Resolution. Meeting, Houston, Texas, June 11–12, 2013. http://www.sbc.net/resolutions/search/resolution.asp?ID=1230.

Bibliography

———. "On the Sexual Integrity of Ministers." Resolution. Meeting, Saint Louis, Missouri, June 11–12, 2002. http://www.sbc.net/resolutions/search/resolution. asp?ID=1117.

———. "Resources for Sexual Abuse Prevention." *Church Resources*. http://www.sbc.net/ churchresources/sexabuseprevention.asp.

Southern Baptist Convention, Executive Committee. "Responding to the Evil of Sexual Abuse." Report. Meeting, June 2008. http://www.sbc.net/pdf/2008ReportSBC.pdf.

Spurgeon, Charles Haddon. "God's Law in Man's Heart." *Spurgeon's Sermons*, No. 2506, 1897. http://www.ccel.org/ccel/spurgeon/sermons43.ix.html; http://www.spurgeon. org/sermons/2506.htm.

Stackaruck, Christian. "Three Ways Christian Use Theology to Misuse the Bible." *Nomad* (blog), *Patheos,* July 15, 2014. www.patheos.com/blogs/revangelical/2014/07/15/3-ways-christians-use-theology-to-misuse-the-bible.

Starks, Glenn L. *Sexual Misconduct and the Future of Mega-Churches: How Large Religious Organizations Go Astray*. Santa Barbara, CA: Praeger, 2013.

Stoop, David. *Forgiving the Unforgiveable*. Reprint. Grand Rapids: Revell, 2014.

Storms, Sam. "From Forgiven to Forgiving." *Bridgeway Church Sermon* (podcast), October 4, 2009. http://www.bridgewaychurch.com/sermons#month_10-2009.

Stout-Miller, Ruth, et al. "Religiosity and Child Sexual Abuse: A Risk Factor Assessment." *Journal of Child Sexual Abuse* 6 (1998) 15–34. http://www. tandfonline.com/doi/abs/10.1300/J070v06n04_02.

Strichartz, Abigail F., and Roger V. Burton. "Lies and Truth: A Study of the Development of the Concept. *Child Development* 61 (1990) 211–20. http://www.jstor.org/ stable/1131060.

Tanquerey, Adolphe. *The Spiritual Life: A Treatise on Ascetical and Mystical Theology*. Translated by Herman Branderis. 2nd ed. Tournai, Belgium: Society of St. John the Evangelist, Desclée, 1930. https://openlibrary.org/books/OL14025430M/ The_spiritual_life.

Tedeschi, Richard G., and Lawrence G. Calhoun. "The Clinician as Expert Companion." Decade of Behavior Series. In *Medical Illness and Positive Life Change: Can Crisis Lead to Personal Transformation?*, edited by Crystal L. Park et al., 215–35. Washington, DC: American Psychological Association, 2009.

———. "The Posttraumatic Growth Inventory: Measuring the Positive Legacy of Trauma." *Journal of Traumatic Stress* 9 (1996) 455–71. http://onlinelibrary.wiley. com/doi/10.1002/jts.2490090305/abstract.

Tedeschi, Richard G., et al., eds. *Posttraumatic Growth: Positive Changes in the Aftermath of Crisis*. Personality and Clinical Psychology. Mahwah, NJ: Erlbaum, 1998.

ten Boom, Corrie. "Guideposts Classics: Corrie ten Boom on Forgiveness." *Guideposts,* November 1972. https://www.guideposts.org/inspiration/stories-of-hope/ guideposts-classics-corrie-ten-boom-on-forgiveness.

"Ten Keys to Happier Living" *Action for Happiness.* http://www.actionforhappiness. org/10-keys-to-happier-living.

Thumma, Scott, and Dave Travis. *Beyond Megachurch Myths: What We Can Learn from America's Largest Churches*. A Leadership Network Publication. San Francisco: Jossey-Bass/Wiley, 2007.

Toussaint, Loren L., et al. "Forgive to Live: Forgiveness, Health, and Longevity." *Journal of Behavioral Medicine* 35 (2012) 375–86. http://link.springer.com/article/10.1007% 2Fs10865-011-9362-4.

Tracy, Steven R. *Mending the Soul: Understanding and Healing Abuse.* Grand Rapids: Zondervan, 2005.

Trepper, Terry S., and Mary Jo Barrett. *Systemic Treatment of Incest: A Therapeutic Handbook.* Brunner/Mazel Psychosocial Stress Series No. 15. New York: Taylor & Francis, 1989.

Trepper, Terry S., et al. "Family Characteristics of Intact Sexually Abusing Families: An Exploratory Study." Clinical Research. *Journal of Child Sexual Abuse* 5, no. 4 (1996) 1–18.

Triplett, Kelli N., et al. "Posttraumatic Growth, Meaning in Life, and Life Satisfaction in Response to Trauma." *Psychological Trauma: Theory, Research, Practice, and Policy* 4 (2012) 400–410. http://psycnet.apa.org/journals/tra/4/4/400.pdf.

United States Conference of Catholic Bishops. "Charter for the Protection of Children and Young People." *Child and Youth Protection, Issues and Action.* http://www.usccb.org/issues-and-action/child-and-youth-protection/charter.cfm.

———. *Charter for the Protection of Children and Young People; Essential Norms; Statement of Episcopal Commitment.* Rev. June 2011. Publication No. 7-232. Washington, DC: USCCB Communications, September 2011. http://www.usccb.org/issues-and-action/child-and-youth-protection/upload/2011-Charter-booklet.pdf.

———. "Child and Youth Protection," *Issues and Action.* http://www.usccb.org/issues-and-action/child-and-youth-protection.

———. "The National Review Board." *Child and Youth Protection, USCCB Offices, About USCCB.* http://www.usccb.org/about/child-and-youth-protection/the-national-review-board.cfm.

———. "Reports and Research." *Child and Youth Protection, Issues and Action.* http://www.usccb.org/issues-and-action/child-and-youth-protection/reports-and-research.cfm.

———. "What has the Catholic Church Done to Effectively Respond to Sexual Abuse by Church Personnel?" April 17, 2013. *Child and Youth Protection, Issues and Action.* http://www.usccb.org/issues-and-action/child-and-youth-protection/upload/What-has-the-Catholic-Church-done-to-effectively-respond-to-sexual-abuse-by-church-personnel.pdf.

University of Pennsylvania. "Authentic Happiness." https://www.authentichappiness.sas.upenn.edu.

US Department of Health and Human Services, Administration for Children and Families, Children's Bureau. "Child Abuse and Neglect Statistics." Child Welfare Information Gateway. https://www.childwelfare.gov/topics/systemwide/statistics/can.

US Department of Justice, Center for Sex Offender Management. "Section 3: Common Characteristics of Sex Offenders." *Understanding Sex Offenders: An Introductory Curriculum, Training Curricula.* http://www.csom.org/train/etiology/3/3_1.htm.

US Department of Justice; Office of Offender Sentencing, Monitoring, Apprehending, Registering, and Tracking. "Facts and Statistics." *Raising Awareness about Sexual Abuse.* The Dru Sjodin National Sex Offender Public Website. https://www.nsopw.gov/en-US/Education/FactsStatistics.

van der Kolk, Bessel A. "Traumatic Memories." In *Trauma and Memory: Clinical and Legal Controversies,* edited by Paul S. Appelbaum et al., 243–60. New York: Oxford University Press, 1997.

Bibliography

Van Leeuwen, Mary Stewart. *Gender and Grace: Love, Work and Parenting in a Changing World*. Downers Grove, IL: InterVarsity, 1990.

Van Loon, Michelle. "Voice of the Victims: Sex Abuse Survivors and the Church." Hermeneutics. *Christianity Today*, April 30, 2012. http://www.christianitytoday.com/women/2012/april/voice-of-victims-sex-abuse-survivors-and-church.html.

Vieth, Victor. I., and Basyle Tchividjian. "When the Child Abuser Has a Bible: Investigating Child Maltreatment Sanctioned or Condoned by a Religious Leader." *Center Piece* 2, no. 12 (2010) 1–7. http://www.gundersenhealth.org/ncptc/publications-resources/centerpiece.

Viola, Frank. "Reimagining a Woman's Role in the Church: An Open Letter," 2008. http://frankviola.org/role.pdf. (Intended as chapter for *Reimagining Church*)

————. "Rethinking Women in Ministry." *Beyond Evangelical* (blog), *Reimagining Church*, April 17, 2012. frankviola.org/2012/04/17/womansroleinchurch.

Wade, Nathaniel G., and Everett L. Worthington Jr. "Overcoming Interpersonal Offenses: Is Forgiveness the Only Way to Deal with Unforgiveness?" *Journal of Counseling and Development* 81 (2003) 343–53. http://onlinelibrary.wiley.com/doi/10.1002/j.1556-6678.2003.tb00261.x/abstract.

Whelchel, Lisa. *Creative Correction: Extraordinary Ideas for Everyday Discipline*. Focus on the Family Books. Carol Stream, IL: Tyndale House, 2005.

Wilson, Michael Todd. *Unburdened: The Christian Leader's Path to Sexual Integrity*. Downers Grove, IL: InterVarsity, 2015.

Witvliet, Charlotte vanOyen, et al. "Granting Forgiveness or Harboring Grudges: Implications for Emotion, Physiology, and Health." Research Article. *Psychological Sciences* 12 (2001) 117–23. http://pss.sagepub.com/content/12/2/117.long.

Wolf, Ernest S. *Treating the Self: Elements of Clinical Self Psychology*. New York: Guilford, 1988.

Wolfelt, Alan D. *Companioning the Bereaved: A Soulful Guide for Counselors and Caregivers*. Fort Collins, CO: Companion, 2006.

————. "Dr. Wolfelt's Eleven Tenets of Caring for the Bereaved." *Companioning Philosophy*. http://www.centerforloss.com/companioning-philosophy.

————. *The Handbook for Companioning the Mourner: Eleven Essential Principles*. Fort Collins, CO: Companion, 2009.

Wong, Y. Joel. "The Psychology of Encouragement: Theory, Research, and Applications." Major Contribution. *The Counseling Psychologist* 43 (2015) 178–216. http://tcp.sagepub.com/content/43/2/178.

Worthington, Everett L., Jr., and Steven J. Sandage. *Forgiveness and Spirituality in Psychotherapy: A Relational Approach*. Washington, DC: American Psychological Association, 2015.

Worthington, Everett L., Jr., et al. "Forgiveness, Health, and Well-Being: A Review of Evidence for Emotional versus Decisional Forgiveness, Dispositional Forgivingness, and Reduced Unforgiveness." *Journal of Behavioral Medicine* 30 (2007) 291–302. http://link.springer.com/article/10.1007%2Fs10865-007-9105-8.

Zach, Jeremy. "The One Danger of Relational Youth Ministry." Student Ministry Skills, Adult Volunteers. *Re Youth Pastor* (blog), March 7, 2012, http://www.reyouthpastor.com/student-ministry-skills/leadership/counseling-teens.

Glossary

Active listening

Active listening is a type of listening that involves focusing on and validating the speaker. Active listening shows the speaker that the listener is present and attentive and has accurate empathy for the speaker.

Agents

Agents are people who act with purpose on their environment.

Alexithymia

Alexithymia is a psychological trait that is marked by three core features: emotional unawareness (inability to identify one's own emotions), lack of social attachment, and difficulty relating interpersonally.

Alliance

An *alliance* is a companioning relationship in which the companion is willing to come alongside the trauma survivor on a journey. An alliance can be developed by providing hope to and focusing on the survivor. This allows the survivor to discover his or her own insights and solution.

Amygdala

The *amygdala* is a part of the brain that is central to our experience of emotions.

Anxiety

See *anxiety disorders.*

Anxiety disorders

Anxiety disorders are a cluster of psychological disorders that are characterized by persistent and overwhelming feelings of fearfulness and anxiety that interfere with daily activities. There are several types of anxiety disorders, each with its own set of symptoms. Some examples are generalized anxiety disorder, post-traumatic stress disorder, panic disorder, and phobias. Anxiety disorders are the most common emotional disorder among American children and adults.

Attachment

Attachment is an emotional bond between people. Attachment between children and their caregivers is especially important and will have lasting effects on a child's life.

Betrayal trauma

Betrayal trauma is abuse that violates the victim as well as the culture in which it occurs. These cultures include families, churches, communities, and organizations, among other interconnected networks of people.

Boundaries

Physical, emotional, mental, and spiritual *boundaries* define what is ours and the things for which we alone are responsible. Boundaries define our own wants, needs, desires, and beliefs as well as plans and goals.

Boundary violation

A *boundary violation* is a crossing of a boundary by another person. For example, when parents with reasons of their own (such as prestige, status, or family tradition) demand that a college student choose a major in a subject in which the student has little or no interest or ability, a boundary crossing with regards to goals has occurred.

Childhood abuse

Childhood abuse may be physical, emotional, or sexual. (See *childhood sexual abuse.*)
Childhood physical abuse is an intentional act of violence toward a child by a parent or caregiver. Childhood emotional abuse—also called psychological abuse—is repetitive behaviors and verbal assaults toward a child by a parent or caregiver that may cause the child psychological harm. These behaviors include but are not limited to ignoring, rejecting, isolating, ridiculing, or terrorizing the child.

Childhood neglect

Childhood neglect is the failure by a parent or caregiver to provide necessary care to a child when financially able to do so or offered other means to do so. Childhood neglect includes (1) physical neglect, which is the failure or refusal to provide a child with basic necessities, such as food, clothing, and shelter, or child abandonment or inadequate supervision; (2) educational neglect, which is the failure or refusal to provide appropriate education to children of mandatory school age; and (3) medical neglect, which is the failure or refusal to provide a child necessary healthcare at the risk of dying, serious disability, or disfigurement.

Childhood sexual abuse

Childhood sexual abuse is contact between a child and an adult in which the child is used for the sexual stimulation of another. The child is involved in sexual activity that he or she does not comprehend and to which the child is not developmentally prepared to consent. This contact may include but is not limited to asking or coercing a child to engage in sexual activities, indecent exposure, or the use of a child in prostitution or pornography.

Compulsions

Compulsions are repetitive, yet seemingly uncontrollable behaviors such as washing, counting, checking, hoarding, or eating that are often an attempt to counteract an *obsession*—a frequently occurring unwanted thought or image. Many people with compulsions would rather not engage in the behavior and find the compulsions to be time consuming and unpleasant.

Corporal punishment

Corporal punishment is a physical means of punishment. Whereas *spanking* refers to the mild physical punishment of using an open hand on a child's bottom, *corporal punishment* refers to hitting a child with an object that results in bruises or welts, slapping the child on the face, or forcing the child to drink vinegar or receive hot pepper sauce in the mouth.

Deontology

A *deontology* is an ethical philosophy that asserts our most moral actions occur when we fulfill our duties and responsibilities.

Depression

See *major depressive disorder.*

Diagnosis

A *diagnosis* is the identification of a disease or other problem by examining whether a person has the symptoms that are usually associated with the disease. Professional healthcare providers rely on diagnostic systems that were developed over many years by professionals. Examples are the *Diagnostic and Statistical Manual of Mental Disorders* (DSM) and the *International Statistical Classification of Diseases and Related Health Problems* (ICD).

Dissociation

Dissociation is detachment from reality and may occur as a way of coping with unpleasant or traumatic experiences. Dissociation ranges from mild— a normal occurrence of losing track of the present during a repetitive activity such as driving—to extreme, which is loss of conscious awareness.

Eating disorders

Eating disorders are food-related problems that cause serious health damage. Examples are *anorexia nervosa* (self-starvation), *bulimia nervosa* (binge eating followed by purging, fasting, or excessive exercise), and *binge-eating disorder* (binge eating not followed by purging, fasting, or excessive exercise).

Emotional recognition

Emotional recognition is awareness of one's own feelings. Being present, slowing down emotional reactions, and noticing physical sensations and thoughts can help develop emotional recognition.

Enmeshment

Enmeshment is the characteristic of a family system in which family members have unclear or permeable boundaries. *Permeable* boundaries allow frequent boundary crossings.

False memories

False memories involve memory of an event that did not occur.

Family systems theory

Family systems theory is an approach to viewing individuals that holds that they cannot be understood in isolation, but rather must be understood within the complex interactions of their family.

Flashbacks

Flashbacks involve memory of a traumatic event that feels as if it were occurring in the present. Flashbacks are one of the symptoms of post-traumatic stress disorder.

Forgiveness

Forgiveness is releasing one set of feelings, beliefs, and behaviors and adopting another set. In particular, releasing anger, intent to revenge, avoidance of the offender, bitterness, rumination, and fear of future harm by the offender and adopting empathy, good will, benevolence, and resolution. Forgiveness is not condoning or justification.

Healthy shame

Healthy shame is guilt over an action that we recognize as wrong such as actions that hurt ourselves or someone else. This shame is healthy because it teaches us how to change our behaviors for the better.

Hippocampus

The *hippocampus* is the part of the brain that is involved in memory storage and retrieval.

Homeostatic coping

Homeostatic coping involves coping activities—such as seeking social support or engaging in problem solving—that lead to a return to pre-trauma levels of functioning after experience of trauma.

Hypervigilance

Hypervigilance is a heightened state of awareness in order to detect threats in the environment. Hypervigilance is associated with increased and extended arousal of the fight-or-flight response. This extended experience of fight or flight will usually lead to exhaustion. Hypervigilance is also associated with changes in behavior, such as visual scanning of the environment and increased responsiveness to environmental stimuli. Hypervigilance can be a symptom of post-traumatic stress disorder and other anxiety disorders.

Identity building

Identity building is taking ownership of oneself, one's actions and choices, one's feelings and desires, one's past, and one's future.

Incidence data

Incidence data is the number of new cases of a given disorder or disease in a given period of time.

Insomnia

Insomnia is the sleep disorder that is characterized by difficulty falling asleep, staying asleep, or both. Insomnia may occur in the absence of other health concerns or may be a symptom of something else such as medication, arthritis, or depression.

Intrusive thoughts

Intrusive thoughts are involuntary, unpleasant thoughts that are difficult to control. Intrusive thoughts are associated with a number of psychological disorders that include post-traumatic stress disorder, obsessive-compulsive disorder, and other anxiety disorders.

Major depressive disorder

Major depressive disorder is a cluster of symptoms that are present every day for at least two weeks and that interfere with daily activities. Symptoms include feelings of intense sadness; loss of energy and interest in pleasurable activities; sleep and eating disturbances; thoughts of suicide, worthlessness, and guilt; and impaired concentration and decisiveness.

Mandatory reporting

Mandatory reporting is the duty of certain professionals under state law to report suspected or actual abuse of a child.

Meta-analysis

Meta-analysis is the use of particular statistical methods to transform data from studies that originally are independent to data that can be compared across studies.

Mortification

Mortification is the physical or mental process of reducing the sinful self to promote self-sanctification or to become more holy.

Narrative identity

Narrative identity is defined as people's stories about themselves.

Negative coping

Negative coping involves ways of coping that typically prevent a person from returning to pre-trauma levels of functioning following a trauma. Examples include avoiding the problem or even discussion of it, substance abuse, and self-harm.

Neural pathways

Neural pathways are the pathways along which information travels through the brain. These pathways are made up of neurons (hence neural). Neural pathways serve as maps of how we tend to think, feel, and behave.

Neuroendocrine system

The *neuroendocrine system* involves interactions between the nervous (*neuro-*) system and hormonal or endocrine system that keep the body functioning normally. The neuroendocrine system influences body functions such as metabolism, growth, reproduction, and the stress response.

Neurons

Neurons are cells that transmit messages throughout the body.

Night terrors

Night terrors (also sleep terrors) are episodes of extreme fear or dread during sleep that may last seconds to a few minutes. A person who is experiencing a night terror may also exhibit screaming, crying, or flailing and may be difficult to rouse from sleep. Whereas nightmares occur during the rapid eye movement (REM) stage of sleep, night terrors occur during non-REM sleep. Night terrors are more common in children but may also affect adults.

Pedophilia

Pedophilia is a psychiatric disorder in which an adult or an older adolescent is sexually attracted by prepubescent children (younger than the age of puberty). A person with this disorder is called a pedophile.

Obsessions

Obsessions are frequently occurring unwanted thoughts or images that tend to cause anxiety. People sometimes develop compulsions as a way to cope with obsessions. Examples of obsessions are *contamination* (such as fear of diseases or household chemicals), *loss of control* (such as fear of blurting out obscenities or insults), *harm* (such as fearing harming oneself or others by not being careful), and *perfectionism* (such as a concern over exactness or evenness).

Panic episodes

Panic episodes or panic attacks are periods of intense anxiety that begin suddenly and may be accompanied by shortness of breath, sweating, chest pain, dizziness, increased heart rate, and a fear that one is dying or going insane.

Para-suicidal behaviors

Para-suicidal behaviors are deliberate, nonfatal, injurious acts toward the self. Para-suicidal behaviors may occur with or without intent to die as a result of the behavior. Examples are cutting oneself with a razor but not deep enough to cause significant blood loss and taking a nonlethal overdose of drugs. The occurrence of para-suicidal behaviors is linked to subsequent completed suicides.

Patriarchy

A *patriarchy* is a social organization with a set of beliefs in which men have the right to power and control over women and children as well as the right to enforce that control.

Posttraumatic growth

Posttraumatic growth involves growth that is above and beyond pre-trauma levels of functioning as a result of engaging in activities that transform the consequences of trauma.

Post-traumatic stress disorder

Post-traumatic stress disorder is a disorder that developed in response to a traumatic event (see *trauma*) that interferes with a person's functioning in important areas such as work and social interactions. People with post-traumatic stress disorder (PTSD) experience four categories of symptoms: *re-experiencing* (e.g., flashbacks, nightmares); *avoidance* (e.g., avoiding reminders of the trauma); *negative cognitions and mood* (e.g., inability to remember aspects of the trauma); and *arousal* (e.g., hypervigilance). If symptoms last for three months or less, PTSD is considered *acute* and if symptoms last for more than three months, *chronic*. Post-traumatic stress disorder may also occur at a *delay*—six months or more after the traumatic event.

Prevalence data

Prevalence data is the total number of cases of a particular disease or disorder within a population.

Principle-based ethics

Principle-based ethics is an ethical philosophy in which certain principles are seen as central to ethical choices. These principles may include *nonmaleficence* (i.e., doing no intentional harm); *autonomy*; *beneficence* (i.e., promoting others' welfare); *justice*; and *fidelity* (i.e., faithfulness and loyalty).

Resilience

Resilience is the ability to effectively adapt to life's stressors.

Rumination

Rumination or ruminative thinking involves a person thinking about something over and over without resolution.

Schema

A *schema* is a pattern of thought that helps organize and interpret information. Schemata influence what we attend to in our environments, how we learn new information, how we retrieve information, and how we understand the future. Examples of schemata are stereotypes and prejudices; other terms that are similar in content are frame, scene, and script.

Self-mutilation

Self-mutilation—also self-harm or self-injury—involves deliberate, injurious acts toward the self without intent to die. Forms of self-mutilation include cutting, burning, scratching, and *trichotillomania* (hair-pulling).

Self-mutilation is often used as an unhealthy way to cope with emotional pain.

Suicidal attempt

A *suicidal attempt* is a deliberate injurious act toward the self with some intent to die as a result of the action. Suicide attempts are nonfatal and may or may not result in actual injury.

Suicidal ideation

Suicidal ideation is thinking about or planning suicide. Most people who experience suicidal ideation do not attempt suicide, but suicidal ideation is a risk factor for suicide.

Sympathetic nervous system

The *sympathetic nervous system* involves the body's way of activating the fight-or-flight response. Increased heart rate, blood pressure, muscle tension, and breathing rate are associated with activation of the sympathetic nervous system.

Substance abuse

Substance abuse involves addiction to a substance such as prescription or street drugs, alcohol, or other mind-altering medication.

Teleological meaning

Teleological meaning is meaning that is defined by final causes and purposes.

Transformational coping

Transformational coping is coping that leads to improvement over pre-trauma levels of functioning following trauma. Areas in which transformation occur are interpersonal relationships, one's sense of self-worth, one's goals and future plans, and one's religious and spiritual life.

Trauma

Trauma is defined as experiences that are deeply emotionally distressing or disturbing. These experiences may be onetime incidents or chronic and repetitive. Examples of trauma include experiencing or witnessing violence, sexual assault, natural disasters, accidents, life-threatening illness, poverty, and oppression. Long-term reactions to trauma may include flashbacks, nightmares, relationship difficulties, unpredictable emotions, and physical symptoms such as headaches and nausea. (See also *post-traumatic stress disorder.*)

Trigger

A *trigger* is an experience that causes the recall of a previous trauma. The trigger may not itself be of a frightening nature, but rather it may be closely associated with the trauma. Examples are certain words, visual cues, sounds and smells, and environments.

Unhealthy shame

Unhealthy shame involves shameful feelings about aspects of the self over which we have no control. Unhealthy shame acts as an inner critic—causing us to feel worthless or flawed. This shame is unhealthy because it blocks healthy responses.

Utilitarianism

Utilitarianism is an ethical philosophy that bases the moral judgment of an action on the action's consequences. The collective benefit is emphasized over individual benefit—the greatest good for the greatest number of people.

Index

Index

Index

82889719R00151

Made in the USA
San Bernardino, CA
20 July 2018